THE PEP TALK

HOW TO ANALYZE
POLITICAL LANGUAGE

HUGH RANK

THE COUNTER-PROPAGANDA PRESS
PARK FOREST, ILLINOIS 60466

1984

Published by
The Counter-Propaganda Press
Box 365, Park Forest, Illinois 60466

Library of Congress Cataloging in Publication Data

Rank, Hugh D., 1932–
  The Pep Talk

  Bibliography: p.
  Includes index.
  1. English language—Rhetoric.   2. Persuasion (Rhetoric)   I. Title
II. Title: Political language.
PE1431.R36   1984   808.042   83-15318
ISBN 0-943468-01-9 (soft)

An earlier version of Chapter 11 appeared in *English Journal* (December, 1980) as "Analyzing Political Rhetoric"; portions of Chapters 4 & 5 appeared in *The Pitch* (1982) also published by the Counter-Propaganda Press. In the Appendix, the simplified teaching aids, designed to be photocopied by teachers *(who need not request permission)* were published:

The Intensify/Downplay Schema	(1976)
The 30-Second-Spot Quiz	(1982)
Not-So-Great Expectations	(1984)
Images & Issues	(1984)

  The author wishes especially to acknowledge the help of his students at Governors State University whose aid and encouragement, insight and efforts are greatly appreciated.

"I know of no safe depository of the ultimate powers of the society but the people themselves; and if we think them not enlightened enough to exercise their control with a wholesome discretion, the remedy is not to take it from them, but to inform their discretion by education."

—Thomas Jefferson

CONTENTS

This book will show you **how** to analyze political language. This chapter will tell you **why** it's important and useful for you.

THIS BOOK IS ABOUT
THE LANGUAGE OF POLITICS:
name-calling and mudslinging;
pussyfooting and side-stepping;
weasel-words and doublespeak;
b.s., bunk, and baloney;
circumlocution and beating around the bush;
red herrings and red tape;
hidden meanings and double-messages;
flag-waving and sabre-rattling;
smoke-screening and obfuscation;
Pentagonese and bureaucratese;
guilt by association;
lies and deceptions;
half-truths and quoting out of context;
broken promises and dozens of things people do with words.

1

THE NEED FOR PERSUASION ANALYSIS

Although political language is very important to our lives, we very seldom think about it in any systematic way. In our society, because we grow up with many negative images about politicians, many people simply have a cynical knee-jerk reaction. If people are asked about "the language of politics," most frequently they respond with a cluster of clichés about deception, broken promises, and high-faluting rhetoric: "They're all liars. . . . Why don't they ever *keep* their promises? . . . It's all a bunch of baloney."

Certainly there's a kernel of truth in these negative stereotypes about politicians and their language. And there's also good reason for people to have a healthy skepticism. But, it can be harmful to us, as individuals and as a society, if we don't make an effort to have a more realistic and responsible way of looking at political language.

Today, especially, as professional persuaders become more sophisticated (using computers, television, demographic research, and other modern tools), we need to increase our own skills in *persuasion analysis*. More and more persuaders are asking us to *believe* in something, or to *do* something: asking us to give them our time, our money, our support, and—sometimes—our lives.

Self-defense is the most important reason for us to learn more about the ways persuaders compose their messages to tie in with our own needs. Persuaders will continue to use these techniques, whether or not *we* know anything about them. Such knowledge helps us to defend ourselves against being deceived, duped, or exploited by others. Knowing these techniques helps to equalize the situation, to counterbalance, to offset the great advantage that the professional persuaders now have because of their money and media access, their skill and expertise. We must prepare ourselves. To be informed is better than to be ignorant. *"Praemonitas, praemunias"* is the traditional advice: "Forewarned is forearmed."

Persuasion needs careful analysis, especially that persuasion which is designed to bond people together and incite them to action. But, during a crisis, when emotions are high and tempers are short, we often don't have the detachment, the calmness, or the time needed to examine things carefully and objectively. Furthermore, in such situations, persuaders are pressing us for *response,* not analysis. Thus, the more we know beforehand, before we are involved in an emotionally-charged situation, the better able we are to act appropriately: to choose to respond, or to withhold response.

Free choice can be made only if it is an *informed* choice. Most people agree with this idea, but usually think only about the *content:* the adequacy and accuracy of information within a message. For us to make a "good" choice we want to know all the facts, and we want them to be accurate. However, knowing the *form* of messages—the common patterns, the probable sequences, and the available options—is also a part of an informed choice. If we know the mechanics, if we can identify and specify the parts of a process, then we are more able to deal with any kind of persuasive message.

The *most common* kind of persuasive message that we see in our society is commercial advertising, selling consumer products and services. The *easiest* way to start analyzing any kind of persuasion is to focus first on analyzing ads (e.g., my earlier book, *The Pitch*). But, ultimately, we have to analyze the more important issues involving social, religious, and political persuasion.

Advertising is fairly easy to analyze. Ads are usually found in carefully crafted packages (30-second-spots, full-page ads, etc.) with coherent messages, and involving very simple transactions: "buy this."

Political persuasion, in contrast, is much harder to analyze because it's often *fragmented, intrinsicially complex,* and *emotionally upsetting.* Furthermore, most people, in their formal schooling, have not been well prepared to analyze political language.

Fragmented. We usually see only bits and fragments of political messages: often in headlines or on the TV news *(edited by others),* or in informal discussions at home, at work, or at bars. Such discussions are usually random, fragmentary, chaotic, often generating more heat than light. We seldom listen to a whole political speech or read a whole book or even an essay of political argument or exposition. Even during the conventions and election year, TV coverage will not stay fixed on one coherent sequence, but instead offers a montage, a kaleidoscopic picture of "highlights" *(edited, chosen by others)*. TV execs argue that it's more *exciting,* more *interesting,* more *viewer engaging,* more *entertaining* if they do such editing and packaging of the political messages being transmitted by the speakers.

Furthermore, the media, functioning as "gatekeepers" have a great impact on both the *kind* and the *degree* of political messages we see and hear: on *what* we see, and on *how much* attention is given to various concerns. Some critics, for example, have complained in the past that the TV network newscasts are biased in favor of one party or one ideology. Other critics have pointed out that even if the networks were to give equally balanced *bi-partisan* coverage, the major problem would still be the *omission* of viewpoints (minority, extremist, atypical, etc.) outside of the "mainstream." In discussing political rhetoric today, analysts have to consider such problems as fragments and omissions.

Complex. Political persuasion is intrinsically more complex, more complicated, more abstract, and, often, more remote than persuasion limited to *individual* benefits. Politics is concerned with *social* benefits, with the *common* good: a difficult task in even the smallest of groups, a very complicated one in a nation of millions.

Emotional. Usually, we're more emotionally involved in political, social, and religious issues than we are in the simple sales transactions in most commercial ads. Although ads for products may appeal strongly to some of our emotional needs (esteem, desire, etc.), political and social persuasion often involves our basic *beliefs,* our fundamental *world views,* about the *meaning* of life, and our own *roles*. For example, if a person were to see one's own *role* as a "crusader in the army of God," this is a very powerful belief which can influence a wide scope of that person's actions. Political persuasion aimed at encouraging this belief, and counter-arguments which might threaten this worldview, are very emotionally intense.

Such emotional sensitivity makes it much harder for us to have a calm, rational, dispassionate analysis of those particular issues which may touch on *our own* basic beliefs. In this book, for example, readers may calmly assent to seeing certain patterns being demonstrated in a variety of issues; then, suddenly object to seeing *their own* favorite issue being analyzed in the same way. Many people feel threatened when they see things from a different perspective.

Schools do little or nothing about teaching students to analyze political persuasion. Generally speaking, persuasion analysis doesn't fit into the system anywhere, doesn't have a "home," a place in the curriculum. In some colleges, "Political Rhetoric" courses are offered as upper-level courses for *the few;* but there's very little training for *the many* in high schools and colleges.

In the Social Sciences, most of the "basics" taught concentrate either on political *history* or on process and structures. In the Language Arts, most instruction focuses on the *composition* of expository prose and on the *analysis* of narratives and poetry. Almost nothing is taught about the *analysis* of *persuasion* despite the growing sophistication of commercial and political persuaders.

Analyzing current political issues isn't easy. Some schools and teachers simply avoid it because it's a "hot potato," a sensitive issue with great risk of causing controversy, complaints from parents and students, and charges of partisanship. Many people fear teachers will use the podium as a pulpit, or a soapbox, for their own political beliefs. The "safest" thing for schools to do is to avoid these problems, to leave such risky topics out of the planned curriculum.

At present, despite some lip service about preparing students to be more informed citizens of a democracy, our school systems are not doing very much. Thus far, the League of Women Voters, a volunteer group, has done the best job in developing a more sophisticated public awareness of political affairs. The League, best known for its non-partisan sponsorship of political debates, has a variety of educational materials; it has played an honorable, yet rather limited role, in American political education. In the future, changes are possible within the schools if they heed the advice of two major studies which called for increased attention to critical reading skills.

Texts do little, and do that badly. For example, George Orwell's piece on "Politics and the English Language" is the most frequently reprinted essay in college freshman readers. Although it focuses attention on the language of politics, this essay encourages paranoia. ("All issues," Orwell writes, "are political issues, and politics itself is a mass of lies, evasions, folly, hatred, and schizophrenia.") It is a poorly written essay by a good man who has written better things *(1984, Animal Farm)*. Historically, it's important because it alerted a whole generation to the manipulation of language as a tool of political repression; specifically, it called attention to the use of euphemisms and obscuring jargon to conceal the atrocities of war. But it's a rambling diatribe, raving and ranting at times, and certainly not a systematic study. Yet, this is the standard "token" essay-about-political-language offered at the college level.

Verbal conflict is essential in a democracy. In a free society, people must have arguments, disagreements, and attempts to persuade others with *words,* rather than to coerce them with force or violence. But a "fair fight" in such verbal conflict depends on everyone "knowing the rules" and being prepared. If there is mutuality and equality among competing interests, society benefits as a whole.

Obviously some persuaders will be better than others, will be more talented or better prepared; this has always been true. But the modern concentration of power (in television, media access, computer technology, demographic research, etc.) is creating a more serious imbalance than ever before in history. To counterbalance this, we need to increase the political language skills of the greatest number of people, the *"re-*

ceivers." Most people will read more than they write, will be public listeners more than they will be public speakers. Society's problem today is not in training the few how to be good political speakers and writers, but in training the many how to be good political listeners and readers.

Overview: New Ways to Categorize & Analyze

This chapter opened with a hodge-podge listing of familiar political phrases (name-calling and mudslinging, etc.); in the rest of the book a sorting out process will re-shuffle these terms and others so that these specific items fit into broader contexts and more coherent relationships.

To better understand political language, this book introduces some new ways to _categorize_ (to place in broader categories, wider perspectives) and to _analyze_ (to examine the parts and the process). By analogy, if this were a book of _literary_ studies, it might begin by discussing a novel in some broader categories (e.g., _Moby Dick_ as _sea_ novel, as _psychological_ novel, etc.), then shift focus to an analysis of _techniques_ (characterization, plotting, etc.) and, finally, to _content_ (ideas, themes, motifs, etc.).

The opening chapters give a broader context to political language by discussing persuasion as a _transaction_ between our own behaviors as _benefit-seekers_ (Chap. 2) and persuaders' behaviors as _benefit-promisers_ (Chap. 3). Using this basic concept of benefit-seeking, it's easier to understand certain behaviors in terms of the Haves and Have-Nots (those who possess benefits, and those who do not) and to see some basic kinds of political persuasion as Conservative and Progressive.

This next chapter (Chap. 4) then begins _to analyze_ the parts and process by showing the most common ways we use to _intensify_ some elements of communication (by means of repetition, association, and composition) and to _downplay_ other elements (by means of omission, diversion, and confusion).

The mid-section of the book follows up on the earlier discussion of "composition" by focusing on two very common strategies used by persuaders: these larger structures are here called "the pitch" and "the pep talk." These are the two _most common_ overall strategies of persuasion today; unlike the pattern of the classical oration which emphasized a _rational_ appeal, these two strategies stress _emotional_ appeals and _image-building_. Modern political campaigns are likely to use both "the pitch" and "the pep talk." In this book, "the pitch" is briefly summarized, but most of the emphasis is on "the pep talk," a strategy which seeks to bond people together for a "good cause." Thus, this strategy is also frequently seen in fund-raising efforts, charity appeals, recruiting efforts, and in much "junk mail."

The final section of the book focuses on the _content_ (not the _form_) of political messages in the typical election campaign. The basic _claims_ and _charges_ made by _any_ politician are summarized here in one key sentence

("I am competent and trustworthy; from me, you'll get more 'good' and less 'bad.' ") and the rest of the chapter explains and qualifies this statement. Lying and deception are discussed in the concluding chapter by sorting out many controversial topics *not* necessarily deceptive, including: opinions, illusions, errors, fictions, imitations, suggestions, evasions, and promises.

To counteract the real problems of the inherent complexity of political language and fragmented bits that we receive, this book suggests some predictable patterns in *form* and *content* so that we know what to expect. Our awareness of these patterns helps us anticipate the parts of a complex process, see their relationship and overall coherence, and even notice the omissions.

Furthermore, the book contains some useful teaching aids, ranging from pages designed to be photocopied (e.g., the 30-Second-Spot Quiz; Not-So-Great Expectations) to memory devices (the 1-2-3-4-5 fingertip formula of "the pitch"; the epitome sentence, "I am competent and trustworthy . . ."). Thus, with intent of giving some useful, common sense, non-partisan guidelines, this book will show some new ways to view political language and perhaps will give some new insights into understanding our own behavior and that of the persuaders.

Perhaps, most important, are certain attitudes expressed in the book: that political language is important because democracy depends on *verbal conflict,* on free speech, on arguments and disagreements worked out with *words;* that we accept our own responsibility as benefit-seekers and that we don't blame or scapegoat other people—"the politicians"—as being "the bad guys, out there"; that we can do some fair and rigorous analysis without being partisan or paranoid; finally, that we learn to recognize our own roles, and our own patterns of persuasion, as well as to understand and to tolerate similar ones in those who disagree with us.

To recap: Although we have many negative attitudes toward political language, there's little systematic analysis of it. Because "professional persuaders" are becoming more sophisticated, the average citizen—for self-defense—needs to learn more skills in persuasion analysis. In contrast to commercial advertising, political persuasion is more difficult to analyze: often the messages are fragmented, intrinsically more complex, emotionally upsetting, and most people have had very little training in the schools and from texts. Free speech and verbal conflict are vital to a democracy; but to make it a "fair fight" we need to increase the political language skills (esp. critical analysis) of the greatest number of people. An introductory overview of the book notes a variety of new ways to categorize and to analyze the form and content of political language.

2

BENEFIT-SEEKING BEHAVIORS: THE HAVE & THE HAVE-NOTS

All people are benefit-seekers. The rest of the book is based on this premise: an assumption so simple, a truism so self-evident that we seldom state it so bluntly or consider it very carefully. Yet, this is an important starting point because once we accept this premise there are certain implied *relationships* which can be explicitly stated.

For example, for every benefit, for every "good," there's an *opposite* "bad" which is either the *contradictory* or the *absence* of that "good." So also, every "good" and "bad" can be described in terms of *degree: very* "good," *very* "bad," etc. Or, consider that every "good" we seek is an *end*, related to our *behaviors* (what we do), our *beliefs* (what we think), and our *emotions* (how we feel). Or, consider that every "good" and "bad" has a whole *cluster* of such relationships associated with it, and that the whole cluster can be triggered in our mind by any of the related parts.

People are benefit-seekers: for survival and growth, we seek after the "good"—as we perceive it. But there's a great deal of argument about different *kinds* of "goods," about *degree* and *priorities* (most people say that certain "goods" are more important, better than others), about *relativity* (what's "good" for one person may be "bad" for another), and about the *definitions* of the terms. Ambiguities exist. In this book, we'll call attention to these problems by using *quotes* and *parentheses* when using the words "good" and "bad" to suggest that *any* "good" or "bad" —*however conceived or defined by a person*—can be inserted, because the focus here is on *relationships* among ideas.

One common relationship, for example, is to make a *generalization* (e.g., "all people are benefit-seekers") and then to illustrate this directly with a *specific* example or an itemized *list* of examples (e.g., people seek money, new cars, love, happiness, clothing, TV sets, etc.) Such a listing could continue indefinitely, often producing a chaotic jumble as we specify the millions of possible items, products, or experiences people seek. However, another common way to link ideas is to follow up a broad generalization with other not-so-broad generalizations, a set of sub-divisions. For example, some people may be interested in sub-dividing "benefits" by *time* (instant gratification/delayed gratification) by *tangibility* (material "goods"/spiritual "goods"), by *scope* (individual/social benefits); all of these suggesting interesting ways to think about benefits.

In this book, however, the most useful sub-sorting to describe our *basic behaviors as benefit-seekers* will be to focus on two key factors: (1) our **perception** of a "good" or a "bad"; and (2) our **possession**—that is, whether we have it or do not have it. With these concepts, we are able to sub-sort the generalization ("all people are benefit-seekers") into four related aspects. This can be illustrated with a diagram: a simple grid which relates *perception* and *possession*. Thus, the dynamics of our benefit-seeking can be more specifically described in terms of four common behaviors: protection, relief, acquisition, and prevention.

Perception of the:

		"good"	"bad"
have		*protection* **KEEP THE "GOOD"**	*relief* **CHANGE THE "BAD"**
have not		*acquisition* **GET THE "GOOD"**	*prevention* **AVOID THE "BAD"**

Possession

Basic Benefit-Seeking Behaviors.
(E.g., upper left quadrant represents those who *have* a "good ")

—**Protection:** If people have a "good," they want to keep it.
—**Relief:** If people have a "bad," they want to get rid of it.
—**Acquisition:** If people don't have a "good," they want to get it.
—**Prevention:** If people don't have a "bad," they want to avoid it.
All persuasion—including advertising and political persuasion—can be analyzed in terms of these four common benefit-seeking behaviors. This four-part grid is useful to visualize multiple aspects of our benefit-seeking which occur simultaneously even though our attention is usually focused on only one. All aspects exist at the same time, but often only one is *explicitly* stated and the others implicitly suggested. These patterns are easiest to see in advertising; simply watch the TV ads and note how they fall into these basic categories.

Protection	*Relief*
KEEP THE "GOOD"	**CHANGE THE "BAD"**
Maintenance products and services to protect things we already have:soaps and cleansers, car-care items, savings and investments, etc.	Pain relief products, medicines, remedies; a relatively small, but very sensitive area (e.g., fraud, cancer cures, etc.)
Acquisition	*Prevention*
GET THE "GOOD"	**AVOID THE "BAD"**
Most ads, perhaps 80-90% simply stress acquisition of items to consume or collect: food, drinks, entertainments, clothing, cosmetics, records, etc.	Health and safety items for advance preparation against potential problems (e.g., tires, smoke alarms, insurance); any ad which emphasizes fear or anxiety can be called a "scare-and-sell" ad.

Advertising Examples of our 4 Basic Benefit-Seeking Behaviors (For details, see: *The Pitch,* p. 43ff.)

Most ads, for example, call for simple acquisition, *(get a "good"),* but this can simultaneously *imply* prevention *(avoid a "bad")* or relief *(get rid of a "bad").* For example, most food products are advertised in such positive terms, emphasizing only the delightful benefits. But, many variations can occur: ads for de-caffeinated and diet drinks, for example, often divide their emphasis between praising the product's good taste and indirectly suggesting the problems avoided. Ads for health and safety products often emphasize the "bad" (the problems, the danger) before they offer relief or prevention.

Sometimes ads explicitly use a double-barreled approach, a seeming paradox which urges us to save money by spending it: *"buy* this and *save* money." Yet this tandem coupling of these two aspects is very common and is explainable by the unspoken qualifications *implied:* e.g., "you'll save money *in the long run* by buying this now." Another common coupling is the linking (diagonal, in this grid) of protection/prevention (If you have a "good," you want to keep it and avoid the "bad") and of relief/acquisition (If you have a "bad," you want to get rid of it, and get the "good").

Observers need not try to pigeonhole an ad into one category, or use this grid as an inflexible straightjacket in analyzing persuasion. It's best to grasp the *dominant impression,* to recognize the gist of the message. The most important thing for us, as observers and analysts, is to recognize our own involvement as benefit-seekers and to get an overall sense of what to expect from persuaders. Awareness of our own benefit-seeking keeps us from self-righteousness and paranoia, blaming all the problems on the persuaders: many people, for example, complain about the constant benefit-promising by advertisers and politicians, yet do not recognize our own constant benefit-seeking. Although it may be easier (and more emotionally comforting) to see ourselves as victims, being acted upon by others, it's more realistic to see persuasion as a *transaction:* both sides are involved and responsible; mutual benefits are sought, and are possible.

This same kind of four-part chart (first introduced in *The Pitch,* analyzing advertising) could be used to analyze social and political persuasion, identifying four major kinds of our benefit-seeking behaviors. But, there are some traditional two-part divisions already in common use: the Haves and the Have-Nots; conservatives and progressives.

Reality is complex, dynamic, fluid, obviously hard to describe in simple charts or two-part classifications. But people do make generalizations and create labels (such as Haves and Have-Nots, conservatives and progressives). If we remember that such labels change in time, and change with the observer, then we can stipulate some useful working definitions:

> Conservative rhetoric, as used here, is the rhetoric of the Haves who seek to keep the "good" (protection) and to avoid the "bad" (prevention).
> Progressive rhetoric, as used here, is the rhetoric of the Have-Nots who seek to change the "bad" (relief) and to get the "good" (acquisition).

Conservative rhetoric is the rhetoric of the Establishment, defending the *status quo,* justifying the way things are. Generally, this is the rhetoric of the current administrative (*whoever* is in the White House, the State House, and City Hall); of corporations, organizations, and government bureaucracies; of those people who have control and power. Conservative rhetoric stresses satisfaction, contentment, appreciation, and enjoyment of the existing "goods"; pride in the group, its past history, traditions and heroes; and in its present accomplishments and leaders. Conservative rhetoric encourages the self-image of being a defender of the society (the nation, the culture, the faith); warnings, precautions and anxieties are focused on the main threat, the *fear of loss* —either suddenly (by seizure, by being overwhelmed or conquered) or slowly (by decay, attrition, or infiltration). It is reasonable to expect that people who have a "good" will want to keep it, and to avoid the "bad" of losing it, or having it taken away.

Progressive rhetoric is the rhetoric of dissatisfaction, discontent, and anger for not having the "good"; and it is also the rhetoric of hopes, dreams, change, progress, and improvement; it attacks the existing evils, and stresses hope for a better future. Generally, this is the rhetoric of the opposition, the Outs, the protesters and the picketers, the people *not* in power; progressive rhetoric ranges from reformers, who want to fix up parts of the existing system, to revolutionaries, who want to destroy it and replace it with a better one. Progressive rhetoric stresses the problems of the existing order and criticizes the caretakers, especially for corruption (intentional) or incompetence (unintentional). Progressive rhetoric encourages the self-image of being a defender of the poor (the unfortunate, the underprivileged, the victims); in addition to the specific problem involved, progressive rhetoric often suggests fears of *stasis:* being stalled, thwarted, stopped, either suddenly (banned, controlled) or slowly (exhausted, burned out). It is reasonable to expect that people who have a "bad" will want to get rid of it, and to get the "good."

Conservative rhetoric		Progressive rhetoric
The HAVES		**The HAVE-NOTS**
To keep the "good" (protection) & To avoid the "bad" (prevention)		To change the "bad" (relief) & To get the "good" (acquisition)
Stability, order "staying in" power	**Ideals, goals**	Progress, improvement, change "Getting in" power
Satisfaction (with "good") Fear, anxiety (of "bad")	**Related emotions, feelings**	Desire, hope (of "good") Anger, frustration (at "bad")
Loss of the "good" possessed (suddenly, by seizure) (slowly, by decay)	**Key threat**	Deprivation: continued absence of the "good" desired
In the past: "the good old days"	**"Golden age"**	In the future: "the promised land
Save, keep, defend, maintain, protect, support, prevent, avoid	**Key verbs**	Reform, change, improve get better, get more, reduce, stop, get rid of.
"You've never had it so good," "Keep America strong" "Stay the course"	**Typical slogans**	"It's time for a change," "Throw the rascals out" "Leaders, for a change"
Defenders of "country," culture, decency, standards law & order	**Self-image**	Defenders of "the people," the poor, the weak, victims, underpriviledged, unfortunate.
Ruthless exploiters, greedy, selfish, smug, uncaring, etc.	**As seen by foes**	Impractical dreamers, naive, irresponsible, lazy, hotheads, malcontents, etc.
Rituals, ceremonials, memorials honoring the past, accomplishments, etc.	**Situations of strength (specific)**	Planned change: scheduled elections; votes of confidence, Unplanned change: crisis, riots.
"Good times" —peace and prosperity	**(general)**	'Bad times" —depression, food shortages, hardships

Such a two-part dichotomy between conservatives and progressives can be useful to do some general sorting. But problems can occur if people try to affix these labels rigidly, ignoring the various meanings assigned by different observers. For example, it's very common for people to use these two terms very loosely, as *praise* or *attack* words, and, by using a certain tone of voice, to load them with emotional connotations. But, in this book, the intent is to try to use these two terms as *neutral describers* of certain *specific behaviors* in *specific situations*.

President Ronald Reagan, for example, is generally considered a "conservative." Yet, in several specific situations (such as arguments over school prayer and tuition tax credits), Reagan favored *changing* existing laws while his opponents (generally considered "progressive") defended the existing policies of no sectarian prayer in schools and no tax credits. Although Reagan favored change, he argued that he was *really* going back to the *older* tradition, the *fundamental* freedoms, the *basic* protections. He saw his change as *restoring* the "good," *recovering* the lost tradition.

Propaganda, if defined as "organized persuasion," is always conservative, *in relation to the sender,* because it is designed to defend or promote the growth of the sponsoring organization. *In relation to the receiver,* some propaganda may be progressive: that is, it may call for the *outside* target audience to reform or to change. Soviet propaganda, for example, may stimulate discontent *abroad,* but *not* at home.

Advertising, for example, has often been described as "revolutionary" because it stimulates people to be discontented, dissatisfied with their lack of "goods" and to change, to want more. Yet, *in relation to the sender,* advertising is always conservative, like other organized persuasion, seeking to promote the welfare of the sponsor.

In reality, there are very few revolutions, and very few major reforms. Usually, there's constant flux and gradual change, continuous conflicts and compromises. Instead of two-party, sharply-defined conflicts, we're more likely to see temporary coalitions of smaller special-interest groups get together for a while, negotiate, compromise, and bargain for lesser reforms.

"Reform" is a commonly used purr word, meaning different things to different people. In city politics, for example, some people see reforms in terms of cost-cutting, *decreasing* spending for social services; others see reform in terms of serving the people, *increasing* spending for social services. In many cases, reformers are merely rivals for power, eager to put their policies or their people to work.

If such words can be used by different people in different ways, and with different meanings, is there any merit at all trying to use them as neutral describers? Perhaps it helps us to remember that our opponents are usually acting in good faith, trying to protect the "good" or change the "bad." It also helps us to identify the issues better and to focus attention on the basic disagreements about what differing factions perceive as "good" and "bad." Finally, it helps us to anticipate certain

Back to Basics: Conservatives using "reform" language.
Extracts from Ronald Reagan's 1980 GOP Acceptance speech.

"to renew the American spirit and sense of purpose . . ."

"to renew our compact of freedom . . ."

"We need a *rebirth* of the American tradition of leadership . . ."

"Together, let us make a *new beginning* . . ."

"to restore, in our time, the American spirit . . ."

"to restore to the federal government the capacity . . ."

"to bring our government *back* under control . . ."

"We are to *reestablish* that truth . . ."

"Restore sanity to our economic system . . ."

"put our nation *back* on the road to being competitive . . ."

"It is time to *put* America *back* to work . . ."

"We'll *restore* hope . . ."

"This nation will *once again* be strong enough . . ."

"Tonight let us dedicate ourselves *to renewing* the American compact . . ."

"The time is now . . . *to recapture* our destiny.

Conservatives such as Reagan, favoring change and reform of a specific existing situation, usually emphasize that they are *really* going back to basics, to fundamentals, to an older tradition. Key words: re-, as in: renew, revive, restore, refresh, rededicate, etc.

statements from certain roles: if people see themselves as reformers, we know what kind of rhetoric to expect.

In popular usage, the terms Haves and Have-Nots are most commonly used simply in terms of economic goods, as synonyms for "rich" and "poor." But here these terms are used in a broader sense, relating to the possession of *any* "good." Economic issues are very important, but people are also concerned with other "goods."

Nobody has everything, nor lacks everything; we'll always be concerned with the mixture of elements within the individual and within society. Seldom (if ever) will there be an absolutely polarized situation of Haves and Have-Nots; in a democratic society, we're likely to have different segments arguing *degree* (which group should get more or less benefits; pay more or less taxes) and *priority* (which problem gets attention first).

Everyone has such benefit-seeking behaviors, but the mix varies with the person and the focus changes with the situation. Our desires can be endless. The benefits we seek are *unlimited*, but we have to "pay" for them in some way because we have limits on our money, our time, and our ability. This leads to tension and conflict. In a situation of *abundance* ("good times"), when we have plenty of time, money, and possessions, we don't recognize any conflict: people seem to get all they want. But, in *scarcity* situations ("hard times") we are forced to make choices (greater-of-two-goods; lesser-of-two-evils), to set priorities, and to make trade-offs.

Everyone is involved in benefit-seeking and in such constant decision making. We're always having such inner arguments: the cautious conservative part of us emphasizing what we have, or fear losing ("maybe I shouldn't risk it . . . things aren't *that* bad") is in conflict with the risk-taking, progressive part ("things are *really* bad . . . if I don't do it now, I'll never do it").

We inherit certain conservative and progressive attitudes from our family, our community, our social and economic position, and our religious beliefs. Thus, as *receivers,* we too have a bias: often we filter out things we don't want to hear; we ignore or refuse to listen to opposing views. Reform rhetoric, for example, can be very disturbing, emotionally upsetting, to people who hear their long-standing attitudes and cherished beliefs being criticized.

People want to get the good and to avoid the bad. In consumer transactions, for example, people want to get the product, but don't want to pay the price. If things were "free," everyone would get a new car, new clothes, a vacation trip, whatever. In governmental relations, everyone wants increased services (better roads, schools), but no one wants to pay the price (higher taxes). In actual practice, people learn to compromise, to make trade-offs.

In real life, there are very few simple choices. For example, a person buying a car would have a *relatively* simple choice of trade-offs if this were the *only* debt or obligation a person had. But, for most people, that $200 debt exists in the *context* of other economic facts and variables: "Is my job secure? Will I continue to receive enough money to cover this, and other, debts? Or, will I lose all? Will my other expenses increase, taking a larger share of my fixed income? Will I need more, or have less, income 2 or 3 years from now when these debts are still due? Instead of a car, would I rather spend the money on a trip (on clothes, furniture, hospital bills, children, etc.)?" Thus, the prudent person is concerned with *priorities,* an *uncertain future,* and the *effects of change.* The prudent person seeks to *keep the "good"* and *avoid the "bad" in the future* as well as the present: a sustained gratification.

People vary with age, experience, awareness, and temperament. Conveniently society has a wealth of folk-sayings supporting both positions ("haste makes waste" . . . "strike while the iron is hot") which either side can use to get outside support for any decision made.

Young people are apt to be more progressive than older people. Related to consumer products, for example, young people are usually more interested in *acquisition* (in getting goods, in buying new things) than in *maintenance* (in conserving the goods they already have). Teenagers are caught between ads saying one thing ("Buy this") and their parents saying another ("Pick up your clothes. . . . Take care of your room."). Furthermore, it's not only that young people want to get the "good," but also that they usually respond very quickly and very genuinely to change the "bad." If they see or hear about the "bad," they usually make a progressive response ("Why don't they *do something* about that . . . they *ought* to . . . they *should* . . .") seeking to change the "bad." Young people are such good hearted idealists. But, in most cases, problems do not yield to simple solutions. Often, when we change one "bad," it causes another to occur, or we find out that other people don't agree with us as to the degree or severity, or even that it's "bad."

Just as we must learn to cope with the massive advertising blitz always stimulating our desires for the goodies and pleasant dreams, so also we must learn to cope with the various political and "cause" groups stimulating our anxieties and angers about the problems and nightmares of the world. Just as we learn, as we grow up, that we don't have the potency (the money, the time, or the ability) to get every "good," so also we learn we don't have the potency to change every "bad." Yet, we can get *some* "goods" and change *some* "bads."

Maturity may be the process of reconciling these various aspects of our benefit-seeking behaviors, of defining which "goods" are to be conserved, which "bads" are to be changed, and which have to be endured, tolerated, avoided, or ignored. The AA's famous "serenity" prayer suggests an attitude here: "God grant me the serenity to accept the things I cannot change, courage to change the things I can, and wisdom to know the difference."

Generally speaking, in good times most people are conservative: they want to keep the good; in bad times, some people become radicalized and want change. Yet, even people who are in "bad" situations (from an outsider's opinion) may remain there, clinging to what goods they have: "things could get worse," they think. Unemployed people may live in abject poverty, yet be afraid to change themselves (move to another area) or change society (revolution) because they are afraid of losing what little benefits they have (food stamps, shelter, nonconfinement). Certainly one motive (other than the advertised, humanitarian motives) for social welfare programs is to de-fuse a potentially revolutionary situation: if poor people have no benefits, and no hope, they have nothing to lose.

"Workers of the world, unite; you have nothing to lose, but your chains" may have been an inspiring revolutionary slogan earlier in this century; but, today, in Europe and America, most workers do have something to lose. However, in many Third World countries, as the sufferings of the Have-Nots increase, often the Haves protect themselves by repressive laws, armies and strong police forces, and the *threats* of worse suffering. The world is in a volatile and dangerous condition: at the same time that many people in rich countries are getting more benefits, many others in poor countries are becoming aware of the gap. Conflict between Haves and Have-Nots seems unavoidable; people speculate as to the kind (violent or nonviolent) and the degree.

Most people are in a middle-of-the-road situation: they *have* some benefits and *lack* others. People may not be totally happy with what they have, but often they tend to be conservative (to protect what they have) because *change* most frequently involves *uncertainty* and *risk*. Change constantly occurs. The most common change is that from Have-Not to Have: as people get more things, they tend to be more conservative, to be more protective of them. Employers know, for example, that a married person, with children and a house mortgage, is likely to be more conservative, stable, and responsible than a single person with no ties.

Other changes can also occur. People who suddenly lose everything because of a catastrophe often undergo a major change in attitude. Survivor stories, after floods, fires, and wars, often emphasize their changing values as they see things from a new perspective. Workers who are suddenly unemployed, sometimes become radicalized; as they change from Haves to Have-Nots, they see things in a new way.

Such changes affect political parties too. The Democratic party, for example, during FDR's time created a coalition of various Have-Nots including the white ethnics in the Northern cities. For years after, the Republicans simply assumed they couldn't get the Irish, Italian, and Polish votes away from the Democrats. But, as these once-poor immigrant groups became prosperous and middle class, they lost their sense of being deprived and victimized. In fact, they noted it was their tax money, "their hard-earned dollars" as they put it, which was now being "given away" to the new poor. So, as they became the Haves, the white ethnics became more conservative. In 1976, the GOP systematically (using computerized name-lists, etc.) campaigned for this ethnic vote and destroyed the old Democratic coalition. Democrats since then have tried to put a new coalition of Have-Nots together, but it's a very complicated task to do this in a fluid, changing society.

The Role of the Writer

The writer as conservative:

The writer as advocate, defender, apologist, publicist, press agent of the system or its parts (its heroes, traditions, leaders, values, customs).

Large organizations (including all governments and corporations) often employ large staffs of "public relations" writers to present their side of an issue, release favorable information, defend the group, and attack foes.

Establishment writers are often *concealed* advocates: one-sided, without appearing to be so. Due to their placid assumptions and benign omissions, they do not explicitly plead a cause; they are often amusing, comfortable entertainers, bland, "neutral," or targeted on (what reformers think) are lesser evils, thus diverting attention away from the "real" problems.

Foes see them as: hacks, flacks, toadies, pimps, hired hands, tools.

The writer as progressive:

The writer as critic, gadfly, reformer of the existing order, investigator and exposer of the hidden "bad"; satirist contrasting ideals with real practices.

Most critics are self-appointed, unpaid, free-lancers. Reformers usually get poet's wages. At best, inspiring ideals; at worst, incoherent rage.

Reform writers are often *noticeable* advocates, overtly one-sided, pleading a cause, often heavy-handed, blunt polarities and melodramas; often emotionally charged language, scenes, strident tone, discomforting, disturbing, upsetting standards and conventions.

Foes see them as: crazies, cranks, crackpots, zealots, dupes.

Awareness of our benefits being threatened varies. Some people (ACLU types) are sensitive to distant or abstract violations of principle, alert to precedent-setting court decisions, test cases, and symbolic gestures, worrying about possible future implications. Other people recognize a problem only if there is a nearby, concrete violation of something they hold dear: "You can do anything you want, but stay off my blue suede shoes." Most people are selective and self-centered in their awareness; as the folk adage notes: "it all depends on whose ox is being gored."

Most people don't think about these things very often, nor very systematically. However, the professional persuader's job is to be very conscious and systematic when trying to persuade an audience. Conservative persuaders have two functions: to emphasize the existing "goods" so that we appreciate what we have; and to emphasize the potential threats so that we fear losing what we have. Progressive persuaders have two functions: not only to *make* vivid and desirable the "goods" to be sought, but also to intensify the existing evils needing to be changed.

Persuaders often "make problems." That is, they consciously stir up fears and hatreds: to an audience of Haves, conservative persuaders stir up fears and anxieties of loss; to an audience of Have-Nots, progressive persuaders stir up anger and resentment, discontent and dissatisfaction toward an existing "bad."

After stirring up these fears and hatreds, persuaders often try to bond a group together, focus, direct, and trigger their energies toward a specific action: a process described in later chapters as the "pep talk."

QUESTIONS YOU CAN ASK ABOUT MESSAGES DIRECTED AT OUR BENEFIT-SEEKING BEHAVIORS

1. Is the message primarily *conservative* (stressing protection to keep a "good" or prevention to avoid a "bad")? Is it designed to stimulate fear or anxiety? Pride or satisfaction?
2. Is the message primarily *progressive* (stressing relief, change, or getting rid of a "bad" or acquisition to get a "good")? Is it designed to stimulate anger or resentment? Hope or desire?
3. What is the "good" desired? What is the "bad" feared?
4. Who is the target audience? In terms of Haves and Have-Nots, do the sender and receiver (target audience) share the same status: Have-to-Have, or Have-Not to Have-Not?
5. Is the *sender* of the message generally considered conservative? Progressive? If "unknown," what inferences can be made?
6. Is the *receiver* of the message, the target audience, generally considered conservative? Progressive?

To recap: We are all benefit-seekers: our basic benefit-seeking behaviors can be described in terms of protection, prevention, relief, and
acquisition. However, a commonly-used two-part division—the Haves
and Have-Nots—is useful to analyze social and political persuasion: (1)
the "conservative" rhetoric of the Haves who seek to keep the "good"
(protection) and to avoid the "bad" (prevention); and (2) the "progressive" rhetoric of the Have-Nots who seek to get rid of the "bad" (relief)
and to get the "good" (acquisition). We all have such benefit-seeking
behaviors, but the *mix varies* with the person and the *focus changes* with
the situation. For both the individual and society, every decision is an
intricate process complicated by complex trade-offs, inherited tendencies,
and constant change. Our own awareness of our benefit-seeking behaviors is often unconscious and random, but the professional persuaders'
awareness is conscious and systematic. Persuaders often make problems
and then offer solutions: to an audience of Haves, conservative persuaders stir up fears, anxieties of loss, that a "good" possessed may be
taken away; to an audience of Have-Nots, progressive persuaders stir up
discontent with the existing "bad." After stirring up these fears, persuaders often try to bond a group together, focus, direct, and trigger their
energies toward a specific action.

"Remember I am sending you out like sheep among wolves;
so be as cunning as serpents and yet as harmless as doves."
—Matthew 10:16

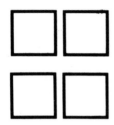

3

BENEFIT-PROMISING BEHAVIORS: INTENSIFYING & DOWNPLAYING

In the previous chapter, our *benefit-seeking* behaviors were more clearly specified by sub-dividing that generalization into four smaller categories: our desire for protection and acquisition of the "good," and relief and prevention of the "bad."

In this chapter, our *benefit-promising* behaviors will be more clearly specified by sub-dividing this generalization into four smaller categories. Again, the words "good" and "bad" will always be set in quotation marks to suggest the many qualifications needed. Next, we add two concepts: a social relationship between the self ("own") and others, and a description of the general behaviors involved in the transaction. To avoid jargon (of using four uncommon nouns: glorification, vilification, exculpation, denigration), these four sub-divisions will be labeled with verbal phrases which more clearly convey their meanings. Thus, the diagram below represents the concepts that it can be observed that people intensify their own "good" and downplay their own "bad"; and, in many situations, they intensify others' "bad" and downplay others' "good."

INTENSIFY OWN "GOOD"   INTENSIFY OTHERS' "BAD"

DOWNPLAY OWN "BAD"   DOWNPLAY OTHERS' "GOOD"

[The next chapter will discuss more specifically the most common *ways:* to intensify (both one's own "good" and the others' "bad") by means of repetition, association, and composition; and to downplay (both one's own "bad" and others' "good") by means of omission, diversion, and confusion.]

Just as we are all benefit-seekers, so also we are all benefit-promisers when we are trying to persuade others. Persuaders are response-seekers and benefit-promisers. Persuasion is a social behavior in which one person tries to get another to do something which will benefit the persuader. One way to get that response from others is to promise a benefit, something the other person wants. Thus, the following ideas about the patterns and techniques of benefit-promising apply to everyone. But, in this book, the primary focus will be on the professional persuaders: these people are more conscious, deliberate, and articulate in the use of these techniques.

Own and Others. The self or "own"—as used in these diagrams—can refer to an individual person, but it also an refer to a larger group (the family, a team, an ethnic group, a nation) or to a product, policy, or idea with which the person is closely identified. The idea of "other" need not be restricted to "enemies," "foes," "strangers," "outsiders," "rivals," "competitors," or "opponents." Although all of these are included in the concept, "others" can mean any person or policy, however mildly or temporarily, not in agreement with the "self."

Non-aggressive relations can be diagrammed simply by using the left side of this four-part diagram. For example, in a non-aggressive parent-child relationship, the "own" of the parent is extended to include the child: the parent intensifies the "good," praising the child, sees all sorts of good behaviors, while at the same time, downplays the "bad," excuses or ignores other behaviors: "Boys will be boys." So also with lovers: "Love is blind."

Such non-aggressive relationships are seldom permanent or full-time: lovers quarrel, parents and children "get mad" at each other. When this happens, the full four-part aggressive pattern can be applied to domestic and personal communication, too. Non-aggressive situations do exist in much of our daily life with family and friends, but the emphasis in this book is going to be on aggressive situations, especially those in which there is a great inequality among the participants: in commercial advertising, for example, or political propaganda.

This diagram helps us to identify and sort out the many things going on at the same time. Any static chart has limited usefulness in trying to describe a dynamic and fluid process. But it has some value as an aid to understanding complex situations. Focus first on the four individual parts of this diagram. After this, examine how these parts work together.

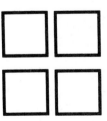

INTENSIFY OWN "GOOD"
(Glorification)

In other words: To praise, brag, boast, exalt, stress, extol, emphasize, glorify, accentuate, magnify, show off the "good" aspects.

"Glittering generalities," "purr words," "God words," "cleans," "praise words"—are terms which have been used in the past to describe words which intensify one's own "good." In advertising, "puffery" refers to vague favorable generalities, superlatives, exaggeration, hyperbole. To idealize, romanticize, glamorize, make heroic, or larger-than-life; all refer to the process of intensifying the "good."

Assertions and claims may be true or false. If intentionally false, they are lies.

Compliments are expression of esteem, approval, respect, affection, admiration, which intensifies the "good" of those whom we have absorbed into our "own" or our "self." If exaggerated, untrue or seeming to be untrue, such praise is called "flattery" (about other individuals), pretentious "boasting" or "immodesty" about self.

Promises and exhortations are related to praise language, intensifying future good (If . . . then; Do this . . . and) or urging to intensify beneficial actions: endurance, effort, devotion, etc. (Don't give up the ship; Hit 'em again, harder; Never say die).

Ceremonial speech, ritual language, is often elevated, formal, literary or high style: vocabulary, sentence structure, tone are dignified for religious ceremonies, certain important political and social events.

Nonverbal praise includes smiles, patting, stroking, any positive reinforcement cues.

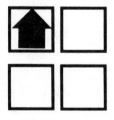

INTENSIFY OTHERS' "BAD"
(Vilification)

In other words: To blame, criticize, denounce, defame, malign, vilify, scold, find fault with others' "bad."

"Name-calling," "snarl words," "devil words," "dirties," "attack words"—are terms which have been used in the past to describe words which intensify others' "bad." In politics, related to: "mudslinging," "smear campaigns," "confrontation tactics."

Libel and slander laws make many distinctions as to intent, malice, public or private figures, true or false charges; generally, any public statement which defames others or exposes them to hatred, contempt, ridicule, or injury, is libelous. (You insult people at your own risk.)

Insults, invectives, and epithets, often use vulgarity or slang words ("creep," "turkey") of general disapproval, or words focused on more specific traits: ignorance ("stupid"), ineptitude ("clumsy"), physical features ("fatty").

Threats and warnings are often used as part of aggressive language; such commands about the future, or prohibitions are usually phrased as ultimatums: "If . . . then, Don't . . . or."

Harangue, tirade, philippic: terms used to describe "attack" speeches filled with condemnations, vituperations, and censorious language against others.

Nonverbal attacks range from silence and the "hate stare" to physical violence.

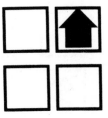

DOWNPLAY OWN "BAD"
(Exculpation)

In other words: To suppress, hide, conceal, omit, mask, disguise, excuse, exculpate, divert attention from, minimize one's own "bad."

Extreme examples: political censorship, government control of the press, re-writing of history to exclude, gloss over, any "errors" made by those in power.

Common expressions relating to downplaying by omission, diversion, confusion:

whitewash	stonewalling
sweep under the rug	File 13, Circular File
behind closed doors	snarled in red tape
skeletons in the closet	passing the buck
sub rosa	getting the run around
under the table	on a wild goose chase

Excuses, alibis to avoid guilt or responsibility by downplaying importance ("it's only . . .") or shifting blame to circumstances, others, or, lesser faults. Excuses divert attention from the main issue (e.g., not getting something done) by intensifying side-issues. For example, common excuses heard in an office: overworked ("only human . . . only have two arms"), understaffed ("we need . . ."), newness ("still a few bugs in the system"), or shifting blame and denying responsibility: "Not my job . . . factory-error . . . the computer's fault . . ."); pleas for sympathy or acceptance: ("I'm not perfect . . . at least I tried . . . I meant well").

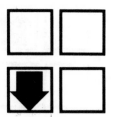

DOWNPLAY OTHERS' "GOOD"
(Denigration)

In other words: To denigrate, belittle, put down, slight, neglect, ignore, deny, undervalue, disconfirm, depreciate, disregard, minimize, or forget the value, merit or importance of the other.

Extreme examples: political censorship, book burning, re-writing of history to eliminate favorable references to the opponents of those in power.

A "put down" is the most common expression relating to downplaying others' "good." A "put down" is a lack of due response, due respect, an omission of due praise, a deflation, degradation, a disparaging comment, a squelch (a retort intended to silence the other) as being unworthy of esteem, low in value. Commonly sarcastic or mocking: "So what?"; "Big deal!"; "Who cares?"; "What difference does that make?"

Snide remarks, catty remarks, are often related to envy and invidious comparison with others; frequently one can "put down" by comparing unfavorably to another.

Neglect, total deprivation can be an extreme form of downplaying others' "good." Child neglect, for example, is the passive counterpart of child abuse. In other social situations, people can be snubbed, given the "silent treatment" or isolated: e.g., at West Point, "the Silence"; in England, "sent to Coventry."

Attributing others' "good" to something other than their merit: luck ("He got a lucky break . . . stumbled into it . . . dumb luck"), external circumstances ("She was born with a silver spoon in her mouth . . . handed to her on a silver platter").

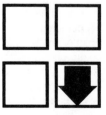

Multiple and Simultaneous. In communication, many things go on at the same time. Such multiple and simultaneous action can only be suggested by a printed diagram of this four-part pattern. In practice, usually one aspect is explicitly stated, the other three implied. The dominant aspect may seem very obvious, but the others can usually be inferred if we apply this pattern to analyze persuasion.

Most advertising, for example, is "puffery": praise language which intensifies the "good" of the product. Yet, *at the same time,* we can infer that the "bad" of the product is being downplayed by omission. Furthermore, the "good" of other products is downplayed by omission; occasionally, in some comparative advertising, the "bad" of other products is intensified.

War propaganda commonly *intensifies the "bad"* about the enemy. Yet, *at the same time,* it downplays the "good": war propaganda will not depict enemy soldiers as being humans, as being someone else's fathers, brothers, and sons. War propaganda dehumanizes, depersonalizes through stereotypes (subhuman monsters, brutes) and through jargon ("We wasted some gooks") which downplays the human qualities. At the same time, war propaganda idealizes, romanticizes, glorifies one's own side: intensifies one's own "good."

Political campaigns are often dominated by aggressive rhetoric *intensifying the "bad"* of the opponents. Although the actual campaign funds may be primarily spent on repetition devices (posters, buttons, signs, TV commercials) and the political "image-makers" may be concerned with establishing favorable "associations," there's still a great deal of attack language involved. Often the name-calling and personal attacks are done by subordinates ("hatchet men") and followers rather than by the principal political candidates.

Difficult to Detect. Any downplaying is difficult to detect or to analyze. It's very difficult to find out when something has been *omitted;* it's often hard to understand a *confusing* situation if there is a great deal of technical jargon, complicated statistics, obscure procedures, missing parts, and so on.

The Watergate affair is the classic example of *downplaying one's own "bad":* a secret conspiracy to conceal a crime. This cover-up ultimately led to President Nixon's resignation and the imprisonment of many of his co-conspirators. There are probably many, many cover-ups, in government and in corporations, going on right now which will never be detected, or if detected, never be understood by more than a few people. Watergate will remain as one of the very few fully-investigated, documented, significant, and available (to future readers) cases of a cover-up. Yet even with all the attention given to Watergate, there are still "loose-ends," unexplained details, and controversies which will never be resolved.

The *dominant* features (the omissions, concealment, cover-up, evasions, etc.) of the Watergate affair would best be represented in the lower left box in the diagram. Yet, Watergate illustrates how *all* aspects occur together simultaneously. By recognizing this, we can avoid the trivial hair-splitting arguments trying to pigeonhole things into single categories, attempting to force a complex reality into simplistic packages. While Watergate was primarily downplaying one's own "bad" by the Nixon conspirators, they were simultaneously intensifying other things (Nixon's successful foreign relations with China and Russia) and were launching attacks on the press and others for being biased or partisan.

The Watergate Affair

This pattern applied to a specific situation, such as the Watergate affair, can be a useful way of seeing and of sorting out the complex processes going on simultaneously.

Intensify Own "Good"

Stress successful foreign policy:

– Detente with Russia and China;
– Peace, end of Vietnam war;
– Return of POWs.

Image Building: "too busy" with important affairs to know about "minor problems"; protestations of innocence: "I am not a crook." "Operation Candor"

Intensify Others' "Bad"

Attacks on *Democrats* as being partisan, biased

Attacks on *press;* on "leaks" as dangerous to "national security"; on any factual press errors

Attacks on some *witnesses* (Dean) as disloyal "squealers" or liars

Downplay Own "Bad"

Generally: a cover-up conspiracy

Some specifics:
– 1,800 deletions in the tapes
– 18 minute "gap" in key tape
– documents witheld, destroyed
– evasive answers by witnesses
– perjury

Downplay Others' "Good"

Denying, ignoring, not responding to opponents' true *claims.*

Denying valid *motives* or good intentions of others.

Denying *competency* of opponents: of the judge, of the jury, of the House Committee, the tape-experts.

Try Applying This Pattern. Simply "quarter" a page, by drawing two lines, and use it as a guide for making notes. Pick any *controversial topic,* one which you know some of the arguments. (The following alphabetical listing is artificial, but it serves as a starter suggesting others.) Now, make an assertion: "Something *should* (or) *should not* be done because . . ."

Pick A Topic . . . Any Topic

A   Abortion, Advertising, Apartheid

B   Birth Control, Busing

C   Child Abuse, CIA, Cities, Crime

D   Death Penalties, Divorce, Drinking Age, Drugs

E   Education, Energy Crisis, Environment Protection, ERA

F   FBI, FDA, Free Enterprise, Freedom of Press

G   Gays, Gun Control

H   Handicapped, Health Insurance, Hunting

I   Income Tax, Inequality, Integration

J   Junk Food, Junk Mail, Justice

K   Ku Klux Klan

L   Labor Unions, Land, Lobbyists

M Marijuana, Marriage, Medical Fraud, Medicare

N   Neighborhoods, Nukes, Nuclear Power Plants

O   Offshore Drilling, Oil, Old Age, OPEC

P   Pollution, Population, Pornography, Poverty, Privacy

Q   Quota Systems

R   Racism, Resources, Riots

S   Smoking, Senior Citizens, Sexism, Suburbs

T   Taxes, Teacher Strikes, Teenagers, Transportation

U   Unemployment, Urban Development, Urban Renewal

V   Veterans, Vietnam, Violence on TV

W War, Welfare, White House, Women's Lib, Work

X   X-rated Movies, Xenophobia

Y   Yuletide Commercialization

Z   Zero Population Growth, Zoning Laws

CONTROVERSIAL TOPICS

**INTENSIFY
OWN "GOOD"**

**WHAT ARE THE "GOOD THINGS"
YOU'D SAY, THE ARGUMENTS IN
FAVOR OF YOUR POSITION?**

**INTENSIFY
OTHERS' "BAD"**

**WHAT ARE THE "BAD THINGS"
ABOUT THE OPPOSING
ARGUMENTS?**

(In many controversies, attacks on the
issues often are accompanied by attacks on
the *persons* holding the opposing views.)

**DOWNPLAY
OWN "BAD"**

**WHAT ARE YOUR OWN
WEAK POINTS?**

"Who, me? I've got nothing to hide!
Everything's up front. My cards are all on
the table."

(It's much harder to see the demerits or the
disadvantages of our own position, or of
ourselves. *Listen* to the opposition's analysis of your "bad.")

**DOWNPLAY
OTHERS' "GOOD"**

**WHAT ARE THE MERITS
IN THE OPPOSING POSITION?**

"I can't see any. I don't understand why
anyone would act that way . . . would believe in that . . . would seriously hold that
position."

(Again, the denial of merit to another is a
very difficult thing to see. We tend not to
credit our opponents with "good faith" in
holding their position.)

History. This pattern can be applied not only to current controversies, but also to those of the past: history. At its best, the study of history will give us insight, balance, and perspective into the activities of mankind; at its worst, the study of history can be a passing on of the errors and prejudices of a previous generation.

About a century ago, German historians (Ranke, and others) advocated the writing of *"neutral"* or *"objective"* history as the ideal for which historians should strive. Although this is an impossible, unrealistic goal (because of the basic selection/omission process), it had a great impact on historical studies for nearly a century as writers and scholars sought to pass on the "Truth" about the past. This misunderstanding spread to other social sciences, and to journalism. Even today, some journalists and television commentators believe that *their* writings are "objective," although they seldom believe the same about *their colleagues.* However, most scholars today recognize the reality of their own *bias,* of their own process of selecting some things, omitting others, of giving more, or less, attention to different things. Even when scholars attempt to have a certain balance, or seek a diversity of viewpoints, they recognize that they function as a "filter" through which the past is seen.

School Texts. Some of the major problems in teaching history today originate with the writers who produce school texts for children. As they reduce complex issues into a few paragraphs, textbook writers are under the subtle (but real) pressures of catering to political pressure groups which insist that school texts intensify only the "good" about American history. Textbooks which even mention the "bad"—the unpleasant aspects of our history—are not likely to be adopted by school boards in many parts of the country. Many well-intentioned citizens feel that any mention of the "bad" is unpatriotic, disloyal, subversive, or potentially harmful to their children.

Yet, to teach children only about the "good" encourages unrealistic *illusions*. Such illusions may be as harmful to the individual and to the society as any harm which might come from an exposure to some of the unpleasant aspects of our history. In recent years, for example, there's been much comment about a "crisis of confidence" in the American people who have lost faith in their government because of the exposures of corruption in the White House and duplicity by the Pentagon. David Wise, in *The Politics of Lying* (1973) documents many of the political lies beginning with the U-2 affair and presents a strong case for the reduction of lying and secrecy in a democratic government.

However, such lying and secrecy may be more difficult to uproot than it would first appear. Another way of approaching this situation is to make the receivers of such information *less susceptible* to being gulled. This can start in the schools with a realistic approach to the study of human behavior, of human history, of the ways humans communicate. One of the functions of schools can be to *dis*illusion young people: to take away their illusions and replace them with realistic information, practical attitudes, and ways to cope with things such as language ma-

1984

Apply this four-part pattern to George Orwell's famous "anti-utopian" novel *Nineteen Eighty-Four*. Originally published in 1949, Orwell's novel was a nightmare vision of what the world of the future might be under a totalitarian dictatorship. Orwell envisioned a total propaganda blitz, with existing tendencies pushed to a greater degree. In that society, the constant repetition of posters and pictures ("Big Brother is Watching You"), slogans ("War is Peace, Freedom is Slavery, Ignorance is Strength"), and hypnotic chanting (B-B!) intensifying the "good" of the state is matched by intensification of the "bad" of the Enemies of the state, especially during the daily Two Minute Hate frenzy and the yearly Hate Week. The novel's main character is Winston Smith, a clerk in the Ministry of Truth, whose job it is to "rectify" history. Orwell spends several pages detailing Winston's work of readjusting figures, rewriting predictions and forecasts, promises and pledges, which had appeared in earlier writings: "in this way every prediction made by the Party could be shown by documentary evidence to have been correct; nor was any item of news or any expression of opinion, which conflicted with the needs of the moment, ever allowed to remain on record." In this process of rewriting history, the Party could downplay its own "bad" and the "good" of others: "if all others accepted the lie which the Party imposed—if all records told the same tale—then the lie passed into history and became truth. 'Who controls the past,' ran the Party slogan, 'controls the future: who controls the present controls the past.'" Orwell was specifically satirizing the Soviet Union which has had several major "rectifications" of history, obliterating unpleasant chapters of history and rewriting it to suit the present Party line. Even today, the Soviet leaders downplay the Gulag Archipelago, while they intensify the glories of their industrial and technological progress.

nipulation by the powerful persuaders in our society. If we encourage (or at least tolerate) in our history texts presentations which reveal both the "good" and "bad" of the history of our nation (or ethnic group, or church), we are less likely to fall into the trap of seeing ourselves as the "good guys," the Truth Possessors, an attitude so easily manipulated by demagogues. Not to trust the people, and our children, with *both* the "good news and the bad news" is insulting to them and to our democratic ideals.

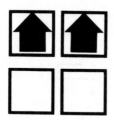

It's *easiest* for us to recognize when words are intensified, as "praise words" for one's own "good," or "attack words" for the "bad" of the opposition.

Consider, for example, the cartoon below which illustrates the top part of the diagram with words which might be spoken by a speaker defending an oil company:

In this case, note that an oil company executive might attack *any or all* of many different interests opposed: foreign competitors, federal regulators, "naive" reformers, etc. (If a four-part pattern were used here, *omissions* might include the omission of profits, using up natural resources, oil influence and lobbying, most oil companies are multi-national, etc.) Lest one assume that language manipulation is confined to capitalists, note below the same patterns applied to socialist rhetoric:

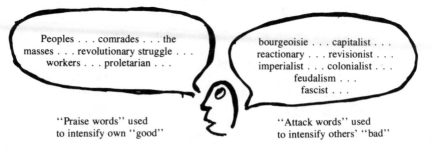

Here, too, the socialist speaker's opponents will vary, depending on whether it is an inter-mural conflict or an argument against non-socialists, depending on situation and context, and so forth.

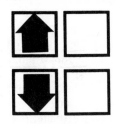

Concurrence. The most common process of things working together at the same time is the concurrent process of *intensifying one's own "good"* and *downplaying one's own "bad."* These two work in tandem, in conjunction with each other. In sports, the cliché is: "the best defense is a good offense." Or is it vice versa?

Bureaucrats, for example, are often accused of using language to make themselves or their jobs seem more important, to inflate their image, to extend their boundaries, to extend their empire: *to intensify their own "good."*

Yet, at the same time, the most common explanation given by them for their language is *defensive;* they use language *to downplay their own "bad,"* to "protect themselves," to be "covered." Much of the wordiness in bureaucracies is caused by people trying to "cover" every possible circumstance in writing regulations. Sincere efforts to do a good job sometimes result in exhaustive, complete and complicated writing. Writers not only "cover" every conceivable circumstance, but they too are "covered" by their prose.

Although *jargon* might start out in an effort to intensify, to make one's occupation sound more important by using polysyllabic words and acronyms, jargon frequently ends up by *producing confusion* in an uninitiated audience.

The Dangers of Dichotomies. Avoid a *"good guys/bad guys"* mentality, the kind of polarized thinking or "two-value orientation" or "either/or" thinking which divides everything neatly into two mutually exclusive contradictory categories.

This is a real problem. There *are* some polarized extremes; there *are* some things in contradiction. And it's easy to recognize some basic two-part patterns and to give them (as others have) some simple names, keeping them together in pairs or sets:

Glittering Generalities	&	Name Calling
Purr Words	&	Snarl Words
Praise Words	&	Attack Words
God Words	&	Devil Words
Cleans	&	Dirties

Or, it's easy to recognize some common two-part relationships involved:

Seller	Buyer
Defense	Prosecution
Proponent	Opponent
Conservative	Progressive
Have	Have-Not

Yet, within this book, based on a basic two-part division, the emphasis throughout has been on the need to also recognize *multiplicity, simultaneity, degree, change, context,* and *situation*.

The dilemma is that there is a human need to generalize, to categorize, *to intensify the similarities* of things within a category, and to downplay the differences. But, at the same time, the need also exists to define, distinguish, make qualifications, *to intensify the differences* within a category.

Because we do recognize that *some* words are obviously "attack" words (intensifying the others' "bad") and that *some* words are obviously "praise" words (intensifying one's own "good"), some people would prefer that *all* words could be so easily dealt with. These people are uncomfortable that we cannot make *all* words fit into pre-determined categories. But, it's impossible to "place" most words. It's easy to recognize the extremes. There will be a *few* words which practically everyone will agree have connotations which are *intensely positive* or *intensely negative*. However, connotations of words, or their suggested meanings, are relative to the era, the locale, and the audience. "Bloody," "bum," and "fanny" might be very vulgar and intensely negative in British usage, but these words are inoffensive or quaint in American usage. Our language *does* have pairs of polar opposites, but it is also rich in *qualifiers* (perhaps, possibly, probably, may, if, some, sometimes, usually, commonly, occasionally, partly, seemed to be, appeared to be, could have been, might have been, etc.) which we frequently use to back off from the extremes, from claiming certitude or totality.

Most words cannot be easily placed into the extremes. There is an intricate process going on within the brain as we are thinking about the possible circumstances, conditions, situations (specific speakers, tone of voice, etc.), and all of the possible qualifications which prevent us from saying *absolutely* that some words are always "praise" words and others always "attack" words. Such complex mental activity on our part is a good thing, although it's the very opposite of the simple, easy answer. Tolerate, *appreciate this lack of certitude* as being a genuine recognition of the complexity of things.

Self-aggression. In addition to the four-part pattern of our aggressive behaviors, we can also observe "self-aggressive" pattern in the language of depressed *individuals:* we intensify our own "bad" and others' "good"; we downplay our own "good" and others' "bad." Such depression is a mirror-image of the aggressive pattern: aggression is turned back on one's self, a very common behavior in the language of depressed persons. However, this self-aggressive, self-hating language is *not* normally found in commercial advertising or political propaganda. Granted, an individual neurotic writer could produce such material, but considering the group effort involved in public persuasion, the various committees and hierarchies which review production, it is not likely that a team of professional persuaders would produce genuinely self-aggressive material deprecating the product.

Concessive Arguments. However, one of the oldest persuasion techniques known is also one of the most sophisticated uses of language: the concessive argument. Often the speaker confesses some weaknesses (intensifies own "bad") or praises some of the oppositions' strengths (intensifies others' "good"); but this manuever is only temporary, only a lead-in to the major argument. In this deliberate tactic, the speaker *concedes,* or gives up or allows, some minor points, but later follows up with the main point. The *turning point* of the concessive argument is usually recognizable, commonly using the words—*but, however, yet, on the other hand,* etc. A major value of using the concessive argument is that it often gives the speaker the *appearance* of being fair, reasonable, humble, modest, and willing to compromise. Naive audiences can often be impressed and persuaded by this tactic, but eventually most people learn to recognize this *"but"* —pattern: Yes, I agree with you . . . *but";* "you're very correct in that . . . *however";* "I admit that . . . *but."*

Nonverbal Communication. This book emphasizes how *words* are used to intensify or downplay. But these same patterns can also be applied to analyze many elements of nonverbal communication: expressions and gestures, clothing and ornamentation, spacing and distancing. Those who are interested in "visual literacy," in the analysis of photography and of the cinema, will recognize the many applications of the intensify/ downplay patterns involved in lighting, background setting, in camera angles, pacing and timing, audio techniques, and so on.

The Numbers Game. The most complicated kinds of intensifying and downplaying, for the average person to understand, are those humanly-devised symbol systems for communicating, such as mathematics and computer languages. It takes special training and special aptitude to communicate in these languages, but most of us can sense the basic ways that figures and statistics can be used to intensify some items (inflating certain statistics to give favorable illusions—to sell stock, seek votes, etc.) and downplay other items (concealing profits, or losses). "Juggling the books" is not a new human activity, but now, with computers, it's going to be an increasingly more complicated one—with the odds favoring the rich, the powerful, the sophisticated, the huge corporations, and the governments.

The Patterns of Persuasion. Pattern recognition is important. Using these simple patterns will help us recognize and sort out some complex and complicated situations. The more we know about these patterns, and the more frequently we apply them, the easier it becomes, and the easier it is to analyze commercial advertising, political propaganda, contemporary and historical arguments.

When doing such analysis, seek first the *general tendencies* or *dominant impressions*. It's better to have a general overall sense of the whole than to be confused or diverted by focusing too closely on minor points and losing an overall sense of perspective.

It is good to know more about ourselves, our strengths and weaknesses, to know more about other people, about human behavior. Informally, we learn these things through our perception and experience; formally, the schools today teach these things under the labels of "psychology" and "sociology." Yet, in classical Greece, these studies first developed as part of *rhetoric*—the art of persuasion. So also, the Greek *rhetors* studied the other sides of arguments, the variety of opposing viewpoints, in order that they might prepare a stronger case in order *to win*. Today, lawyers—and debate teams—continue this tradition of learning the arguments of the opposition, again with the intention of winning. In contrast to this, the modern psychologist Carl Rogers urges us to learn the viewpoints of our opponents, not in order *to win* but in order *to understand:* to open ourselves to other viewpoints, to have empathy with others.

Without denying the usefulness of either of those motives—winning or understanding—as the reason for learning more about the patterns of persuasion, the major emphasis in this book tends to be on *defense:* to learn these patterns as a defense measure, as a "survival skill" simply because of the gross inequality today between the professional persuaders and the average *persuadee*. Here, such a "defensive rhetoric" will be called *counter-propaganda*.

Counter-Propaganda Axioms

"Propaganda" is used here to mean *organized persuasion;* for example, commercial advertising and public relations, political and governmental efforts to persuade. Propaganda seeks some kind of *response* from the people who are the target audience. Two general categories are: (1) *command propaganda* which seeks a specific, immediate response: "Buy this . . . Do that . . . Vote for"; (2) *conditioning propaganda* which seeks to mold public opinions, assumptions, and attitudes on a long-term widespread basis, often as a prelude for later command propaganda.

Counter-propaganda, as used here, is an attempt to inoculate or to immunize *individuals* in advance of any particular propaganda blitz or campaign by any organized persuaders *(whether from various advertisers, from politicians Left or Right, from governments domestic or foreign)* by teaching the common patterns and techniques of persuasion. Assume that, in the future, the professional persuaders will be *more* organized and *more* sophisticated than they are now. Assume also that reforms (through legislation or education) are difficult and slow. Here are some helpful axioms for individuals to cope with a propaganda blitz:

WHEN THEY INTENSIFY, DOWNPLAY.
WHEN THEY DOWNPLAY, INTENSIFY.

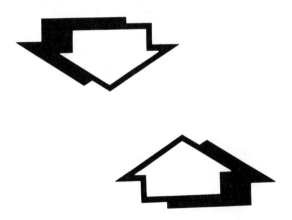

When they intensify, downplay

This axiom suggests caution, skepticism, and passive resistance as appropriate responses in some situations. Persuaders often want to rush, rush, rush people into a response. Creating a sense of urgency (''last chance,'' ''now or never''), triggering a response, and channeling it into specific actions (''buy this . . . do this . . . join us'') are common predictable parts of the persuasion process—unrelated as to whether the product or ''cause'' is ''good'' or ''bad.'' Be skeptical then of any intense urgency plea seeking a quick response; be especially careful in political situations (racial, religious, etc.) whenever anyone is intensifying the alleged threats or dangers of the opposition. Persuaders want us to *do something,* to *respond* in some way. As individuals, one counter-weapon we have is to do nothing.

Non-response, silence, passivity is often a very effective tactic. We know it by folklore (''Silence is golden'') and by scripture (''A soft answer turneth away wrath''), but we sometimes think of such silence as being weak or cowardly. Yet, if we see such downplaying as part of a strategy, we may better appreciate it. Passive resistance is an extremely interesting response available to individuals: witness Thoreau, Gandhi, Martin Luther King, Jr.

Most of us have been long conditioned to social authorities (parents, teachers, bosses, governments, advertisers, etc.) demanding our attention and confidence. Such group leaders (including teachers) place high value on enthusiastic response from their audience. Because of this common conditioning, some people need sanctions, ''permission to say *no.*'' Some people feel guilty about saying ''no'' even to an aggressive salesperson, or feel obligated to listen to a sales pitch (''didn't want to hurt their feelings''). Because we have been trained to be polite, sellers often exploit this to their own advantage, hooking in on our guilt-feelings. So too, the political demagogue (or racial fanatic) will hook in on our feelings of duty or obligation to our country (or racial group) in order to rush us into action. When we hear the phrase ''a breakdown of communication,'' it usually implies an unwanted failure has taken place. Yet, a breakdown can be a good thing: if we are being blitzed, pressured, overwhelmed, it's time to downplay.

Some *unwanted responses,* which may be appropriate defenses for individuals in some situations, include:

Silence	Not listening
Withholding applause	Distracting from the issue
Hanging up the phone	Sidetracking
Leaving the room	Asking trivial questions
Closing your eyes	Boycotting
''Just browsing''	Slowing down, delaying
Not buying the product	Confusing the issue
Not volunteering	Doing the wrong thing

When they downplay, intensify

This axiom suggests alertness, inquisitiveness, and active engagement as appropriate responses in some situations. Persuaders often omit the disadvantages, problems, and bad effects related to their proposals. People in power in corporations and governments often seek to conceal any of their mistakes, inefficiencies, incompetencies, crimes and abuses. Motives for omission are difficult to judge. Even without any evil motives involved, everyone is going to "put their best foot forward," "Put on their Sunday best": i.e., *intensify their own "good"* and *downplay their own "bad."* The basic selection/omission process is involved. Instead of worrying about what others' motives are, assume that their bad points are not going to be advertised or prominently displayed. Be more concerned with *consequences:* their "good" may not be *your* "good."

In buying products, investigation is sometimes simple: reading a label, comparing prices, asking a former owner, using a consumer guidebook, sampling, and so on. Different *degrees* of investigation are appropriate: buying a car deserves more care than buying a trinket. Some situations are not simple. Fraud, deception, misrepresentation and errors do exist and tend to thrive in the darkness. Here, *repeated* complaints are usually more effective than individual instances; attention-getting public displays are often more effective responses than private complaints. The squeaking wheel usually does get the oil!

Investigating downplaying in political life is usually much more difficult. Most individuals don't have the time, the talent, or opportunity to investigate complex cover-ups. But, as citizens, aware of these problems, we can support investigative reporters, disclosure laws, and the basic rights of reformers and critics. Any establishment seeks to label reformers as crackpots, spiteful cranks, disloyal malcontents, naive fanatics, opportunist rivals, and so on. Some individuals may well be in any of these dour categories. But, the *role* of the reformer, the function of the progressive critic, is to attack the "bad," often that which the Establishment would prefer to keep hidden.

Some *unwanted responses,* which may be appropriate defenses for individuals in some situations, include:

Questioning	Litigating, suing
Sorting out, clarifying	Joining reform groups
Comparison-shopping	Supporting investigators
Complaining	Voting
Demonstrating, picketing	Whistle-blowing
Budget analyzing	Writing letters

Equality. These counter propaganda axioms are *means* to an end. The goal is to equalize the situation between the professional persuaders and their audiences, to counter-balance, to seek a better equilibrium, to bring about a situation of mutuality in which the audience is *more nearly* on par with the speakers.

Realistic assumptions must be made: power exists, weakness exists. The strong do not voluntarily give up power. Total equality will never exist. Yet, despite this, a movement *toward* equality is better than a movement away. The American government was so founded on the realistic attitude of the check-and-balance system among the various forces in conflict. The result is a kind of shaky equilibrium, a moderating balancing act, usually denounced by all participants as favoring the others. When some segments of society grow too powerful, others seek a re-balancing. As organized persuasion becomes more powerful and sophisticated, *more* needs to be done to counter its effects: *more* people need to be well-informed themselves, and *more* supportive of education and laws which favor equity, balance, fairness.

Something Ought to be Done. Something is being done. Many laws have been passed, many agencies established to help equalize the situation, for example, concerning advertising in the United States.

Confusion exists, however, because of the fragmented approach, a history of haphazard and random efforts. The public is confused (perhaps the reformers and regulators are too) with the number of federal agencies involved in consumer reforms. Some agencies, for example, are empowered to focus on the *media:* the Federal Communications Commission (FCC) has jurisdiction over the airwaves—radio and television; the U.S. Postal Service is concerned with fraud and deception using the mails. Some agencies are concerned with *products:* the Food and Drug Administration (FDA) has jurisdiction over the *labeling* of drugs and cosmetics (the FTC, over the *advertising* of these same products); the Treasury Department over the labeling *and* advertising of alcohol. The U.S. Department of Agriculture is in charge of the grading and labeling of foods and agricultural products; the Civil Aeronautics Board, the Interstate Commerce commission, the Federal Power Commission, and other agencies all have their special areas to supervise.

None of these were originally set up as "consumer protectors," but as "business referees" because the constitution (I,8) gives Congress the right to "regulate Commerce." Thus, the Federal Trade Commission (FTC) started in 1914 to protect *established* businesses from unfair competition and "deceptive advertising" by fly-by-night competitors; it wasn't until 1938 that the consumer public received any protection. The Securities and Exchange Commission (SEC) "disclosure laws" were created to protect Wall Street investors from being fleeced by white-collar con men.

More confusion yet occurs when the varying consumer laws of each of the fifty states are looked at, covering hundreds of products, services, and industries. Add to this the scores of voluntary codes: more than 40 major industries have self-regulatory codes, and the FTC has issued "guidelines" for over 160 industries.

Citizen consumer groups have had the same problems of incoherence and randomness. Many young people, for example, are attracted by the idealism of the consumerist movement, but get totally confused when confronted with the chaos of the various reform groups. There are many "good causes": well-intentioned groups, often short-lived, poorly-funded, ill-organized volunteer efforts, sometimes led by a charismatic leader, sometimes focused on a popular issue.

Veteran consumerists recognize the problem and have attempted to form umbrella organizations to unify their efforts, to organize, and seek coherence. But this leads to other problems: internal disagreements about the varying degrees of emphasis, time, money, to be spent on different issues. In addition, there are very powerful special-interest groups who do *not* want to see an organized, coherent consumer movement. Every year since 1970, corporation lobbyists have defeated the bill to create a single Agency for Consumer Protection (ACP) which would consolidate 26 different federal agencies. While consumerists and reformers need to organize more coherently, to gain some specific legislation, we also need a wide audience of citizens aware of the general patterns and the overall directions.

Counter-Propaganda Axioms Applied to Laws

One way of making sense of the various laws, reforms, and consumer concerns is to apply these counter-propaganda axioms as a simple conceptual framework. Most civil laws can be divided into two main categories: *"Protection laws"* and *"Disclosure laws."* Here, these are not used as legal definitions or technical categories, but as common sense ways, or informal useful tools, to make the situation more easily understood:

1. Protection laws:

limit, restrict, restrain, regulate the *actions* of the more powerful in order to equalize, counter-balance conflicting interests. Such laws restrain the possible aggression of the powerful (government, corporation, or individual) to protect the rights of the less powerful, the individual, and the common good. In other words, the axiom *"When they intensify, downplay"* is applied: powerful forces are checked by laws which downplay, slow down, moderate, retard, hold back, lessen, restrain, decrease the potential situation of inequality.

2. Disclosure laws:

disclose, uncover, reveal, divulge, make public the *omissions* of the more powerful in order to equalize, counter-balance conflict interests. Such laws are directed to the "passive aggression" of the powerful (government, corporation, or individual) to protect the rights of the less powerful, the individual, and the common good. In other words, the axiom *"When they downplay, intensify"* is applied: powerful forces are required by laws not to conceal or hide things which would create an unfair advantage, or a situation of inequality.

Protection Laws   **"When they intensify, downplay"**

* Examples of laws designed to limit, restrict, or regulate the powerful
   in order to equalize situations:

"Privacy" laws	To restrict government (and others) from intruding into the privacy of individuals by unlawful search or seizure, including wiretapping, mail opening, use of computer records.
"Abuse of power" laws	To restrict powerful governmental agencies or individuals from abusing power: e.g. military officers may not be involved in politics; anti-patronage laws; U.S. foreign intelligence (CIA) and propaganda (USIA) agencies prohibited from domestic operations.
"Conflict of interest" laws	To restrict public officials from making personal profit by their decisions in spending public money: "influence peddling," "revolving door" laws.
"Airwaves" laws	To regulate the use of public airwaves for common good: e.g. number of radio and TV stations, number of commercials allowed, percentage of "public service" programming.
"Fair Campaign" laws	To limit the amount of money spent in elections.
"Zoning" laws	To limit the locations where commerce and industry may transact business; city ordinances and local laws restricting signs, advertisements, stores.
"License" laws	To regulate who may transact certain occupations, including the training requirements, backgrounds, state and local laws.
"Commerce" laws	To regulate industry practices which may affect the common good; e.g. environmental restrictions (EPA), safety restrictions (OSHA), specific "consumer laws" such as FTC "cooling-off period" laws.

---

* In the USA, most safeguards regarding the rights of individuals stem
   from the 1st, 4th, 5th, and 6th amendments to the Constitution.

Disclosure Laws   **"When they downplay, intensify"**

* Examples of kinds of laws designed to disclose what has been concealed, to clarify what is confusing:

"Access" laws	To open public records and files, e.g. federal "Freedom of Information" act de-classifying many documents, letting individuals see their own files kept about them; laws which give people access to inspect their own credit ratings.
"Sunshine" laws	To open public meetings to citizens, "open meeting" laws; to allow citizens—including reporters—to hear discussions of public policy and administration.
"Source" laws	To identify people and interests involved in public affairs: e.g. statement of ownership required of newspapers, TV, radio; to identify "paid political commercials"; to identify major contributors to political campaigns; to register lobbyists.
"Audit" laws	To audit, to investigate and account for funds involved in public agencies or corporations; annual reports, audits by CPAs; to account for other people's money, justify time, procedures.
"Label" laws	To identify contents, ingredients, to disclose what is in a product. Many varieties: ingredients, kind, grade, percentage, origin, amount, size, parts included, extras; warning labels for poison, potential danger (saccharin, cholesterol, cigarettes), expiration dates, manufacturer, clothing care instructions.
"Standardization" laws	To clarify by requiring standard sizes, weights, measurements; "unit pricing" laws.
"Simplification" laws	To clarify by requiring simple language and easy procedures: e.g. "Truth-in-Lending" (specifies key terms in contracts—APR); laws designed to simplify legal jargon in insurance policies, guarantees, warranties.
"Shield" laws	To protect journalists who report about corruption; "whistle-blowing" laws—to protect employees who reveal concealed harms being done by corporations or government agencies.

* Not all such examples are in effect, or adequately enforced; "whistle-blowing" laws are much discussed by reformers, but not very available.

Law is a process, an ever-changing development. Laws are written in response to problems, as needs become felt, as situations of inequality develop. Our system of *criminal* law was developed from centuries of court cases and precedents, but our *civil* laws mostly stem from the past century, developed by legislative bodies in response to the needs of an urban industrial society. Certain basic principles, such as equality and justice, remain constant; but there are new applications in each era. A few years ago, for example, there was no need for laws regarding chemical additives in food, electronic eavesdropping, computer storage of private records, and so on. These are very important needs today and we see many different law-making bodies (city, state, national, international) involved in these problems. Some laws we never notice unless they're broken. If there were *not* city ordinances on noise, we'd hear soundtrucks blaring commercials all day and night; if there were not ordinances against posters and billboards, there wouldn't be a building or tree still visible today in the country. The blitz could be worse! More laws are needed. In the future, persuaders will not be *less* sophisticated, *less* powerful. Nor will human nature change: old frauds will continue, often using new technology.

Law-making is not easy. In disclosure laws, for example, there are some legitimate needs for concealment: individuals need privacy, corporations need to protect trade secrets, certain professions need confidentiality, as well as certain functions of government—diplomacy and military secrets. Yet, for every legitimate need, there are also abuses possible. Government claims for secrecy in the 1950s produced a massive classification system (''Secret'' documents) that was so abused by the military and the politicians, that it prompted the various reforms in the 1970s which opened up some of the files, put some restrictions on the activities of our secret police. However, these reforms are already being protested by the CIA and the military who claim that ''too much'' is open now, ''too many'' restrictions have been made. It's quite likely that any future crisis will swing the pendulum the other way, creating more government secrecy and censorship. As one critic put it, the Bill of Rights functions well—during peacetime.

Special attention should be given to ''disclosure'' laws. Concealment and subterfuge may be as old as human history: *''caveat emptor''* — ''buyer beware''—suggests caution not only about false claims, but also about concealed defects and hidden problems. Laws about weights and measures are the oldest ''disclosure laws''; ancient civilizations devoted much of their rule-making trying to ensure an honest weight and an accurate count. Yet, despite old laws, established agencies to enforce and check, and modern electronic devices, some sellers *still* cheat on short weights, tampering with the scales (with a thumb or an ''electronic thumb''), adding ''filler,'' overcharging. If fraud can occur with something so simple as an accurate count of physical items, consider the possibilities of fraud in complex paper-shuffling or electronic number-grinding. Sometimes today we have a false sense of security, as if the law magically enforced itself; but it is still wise, as the miner's old song goes: "Keep your hand upon the dollar and your eye upon the scale."

Law-enforcement is not easy. Regulatory agencies will never be fully funded or fully staffed, nor ever receive enough money and people to do everything they're supposed to do. Which items will get the first priority? The most attention? (Tough, major issues? Or "soft" problems, easy to solve?) The best people? Will the people involved *come from,* or later *go to,* the very corporations they're supposed to regulate? (The "revolving door" problem.) If loopholes or weak spots aren't deliberately written into the laws, they often can be amended later when public interest lapses. Even when laws can be clearly made, and vigorously enforced, it's hard to catch the law-breakers: whether it's a simple mail fraud, a complex computer fraud, or a complicated corporate violation, the law-breakers usually tend to be clever, crafty, and secret.

Without public understanding, citizens can be hostile to reforms which benefit them. For example, the Food and Drug Administration (FDA) gets a great deal of hostile criticism ("meddling . . . interfering bureaucrats") because they administer the law prohibiting harmful substances in foods. But, during the past decade, over 5000 new chemicals have been added to our various foods by the major food companies. Instead of recognizing the difficulties that the FDA has in such a fast-paced changing situation with high-profit pressures, and recognizing the probable need for bans and prohibitions to avoid major catastrophes, public sentiment is often swayed by stereotyped visions of these regulators as "prudes," "nags," or "scolds." Such negative stereotypes, of course, create a political climate favorable to those special interest groups who want the regulations removed. More citizens will support such law-making and law-enforcing if they are aware of the underlying goal of fairness and equality involved in protection laws and disclosure laws. If more citizens have a historical perspective and sense of these relationships, it's easier to gain public tolerance for the real problems, difficulties, and complexities in developing and administering these laws.

To recap: A pattern, its parts, examples. The benefit-promising behaviors in the persuasion transaction can be described in terms of intensifying one's own "good" and downplaying one's own "bad"; and, in some cases, of intensifying others' "bad" and downplaying others' "good." A four-part diagram is useful to identify and sort out such multiple and simultaneous behaviors in a dynamic process. Previous writers described such intensifying in paired terms (purr/snarl words; glittering generalities/name-calling, etc.), but very little attention was paid to techniques of downplaying, which are much more difficult to detect or analyze. Most advertising and political propaganda can be described as predominantly intensifying one's own "good" or the others' "bad." But all aspects often co-exist, as in the Watergate affair, a well-documented example of a cover-up, downplaying one's own "bad." This four-part pattern can be usefully applied to current controversies and past history, verbal and non-verbal communication, obversely in self-aggressive patterns and obliquely in "concessive arguments." Because the reader is likely to be a Have-Not (in relation to powerful public persuaders), two counter-propaganda axioms are suggested, illustrated, and related to existing laws: "When they intensify, downplay"; "When they downplay, intensify."

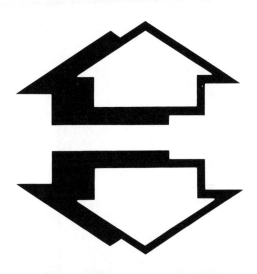

4

BENEFIT-PROMISING BEHAVIORS: WAYS TO INTENSIFY & DOWNPLAY

The **Intensify/Downplay schema** (see next page) focuses attention on a simple pattern useful to analyze communication, persuasion, and propaganda techniques. Binary computers, working on a very simple two-part positive/negative (±) basis, can generate very complex combinations. So also, one way of looking at human communication is to see that we can produce an almost infinite number of variations and combinations by intensifying or downplaying the various parts, or bits of information, communicated. Sometimes this pattern is very easy to recognize: people intensify by raising their voice, shouting, making certain gestures, using certain words or patterns of words. Downplaying is often harder to recognize and some very sophisticated techniques (e.g., satire, irony, concessive arguments) are often very difficult to analyze. But, people do *not* need to be "experts" to recognize the most common ways in which we all intensify or downplay. Using these Intensify/Downplay patterns, one can analyze: *an individual message* (e.g., a close analysis of a sentence, a picture, a TV commercial) or *the message in a wider context,* as part of an era, a movement, a sequence, or within a wider frame of reference.

INTENSIFY

Repetition

Intensifying by repetition is an easy, simple, and effective way to persuade. People are comfortable with the *known*, the *familiar*. As children, we love to hear the same stories repeated; later, we have "favorite" songs, TV programs, etc. All cultures have chants, prayers, rituals, dances based on repetition. Advertising slogans, brand names, logos, and signs are common. Much education, training, indoctrination is based on repetition to imprint on *memory* of the receiver to identify, recognize, and *respond.*

Association

Intensifying by linking (1) the idea or product with (2) something *already loved/desired by - or hated/feared by* (3) the intended audience. Thus, the need for **audience analysis:** surveys, polls, "market research," "consumer behavior," psychological and sociological studies. Associate by *direct* assertions or *indirect* ways; (metaphoric language, allusions, backgrounds, contexts, etc.) Some "good things" often linked with products are those common human needs/wants/desires for "basics," "certitude," "intimacy," "space," and "growth."

Composition

Intensifying by pattern and arrangement uses *design, variations in sequence* and *in proportion* to add to the force of words, images, movements, etc. How we put together, or compose, is important: e.g. in **verbal** communication: the choice of words, their level of abstraction, their patterns within sentences, the strategy of longer messages. Logic, inductive and deductive, puts ideas together systematically. **Non-verbal compositions** involve *visuals* (color, shape, size); *aural* (music); *mathematics* (quantities, relationships), *time* and *space* patterns.

The INTENSIFY/DOWNPLAY schema is a pattern useful to analyze communication, persuasion and propaganda. All people *intensify* (commonly by *repetition, association, composition*) and *downplay* (commonly by *omission, diversion, confusion*) as they communicate in words, gestures, numbers, etc. But, "professional persuaders" have more training, technology, money and media access than the average citizen. Individuals can better cope with organized persuasion by recognizing the common ways *how* communication is intensified or downplayed, and by considering *who is saying what to whom, when and where, with what intent and what result.*

Omission

Downplaying by omission is common since the basic selection/omission process *necessarily omits* more than can be presented. All communication is limited, is edited, is slanted or biased to include and exclude items. But omission can also be used as a *deliberate* way of concealing, hiding. Half-truths, quotes out of context, etc. are very hard to detect or find. Political examples include *cover-ups, censorship, book-burning, managed news, secret police activities*. Receivers, too, can omit: can "filter out" or be closed minded, prejudiced.

Diversion

Downplaying by distracting focus, diverting attention away from key issues or important things; usually by intensifying the side-issues, the non-related, the trivial. Common variations include:"hairsplitting," "nit-picking," "attacking a straw man," "red herring"; also, those emotional attacks and appeals *(ad hominem, ad populum)*, plus things which drain the energy of others: *"busy work," "legal harassment,* etc. Humor and entertainment *("bread and circuses")* are used as pleasant ways to divert attention from major issues.

Confusion

Downplaying issues by making things so complex, so chaotic, that people "give up," get weary, "overloaded." This is dangerous when people are unable to understand, comprehend, or make reasonable decisions. Chaos can be the accidental result of a disorganized mind, or the deliberate flim-flam of a *con man* or the political *demagogue* (who then offers a "simple solution" to the confused). Confusion can result from *faulty logic, equivocation, circumlocution, contradictions, multiple diversions, inconsistencies, jargon* or anything which blurs clarity or understanding.

DOWNPLAY

The three most common ways to intensify are **repetition, association,** and **composition.** Their counterparts, the three most common ways to downplay, are **omission, diversion,** and **confusion.** These categories and terms may be useful, but are arbitrary (created by observers); recognize that many parts often function simultaneously.

Pattern recognition is important. No one can keep up with new items in an information explosion. Nor can anyone predict the future: what specific new products, new inventions, new advertising campaigns, new social and political issues will appear. But, we can learn some basic patterns and categories which will help us to cope with incoming information. Recognize the easy patterns first.

Repetition

Repetition is _comforting_. People love the familiar, the known, the predictable. As children, we enjoy listening to the same nursery rhymes and stories over and over. Most of these have built-in repetition devices (Three Little Pigs), formula openings ("Once upon a time"), and strong rhyme schemes (end rhymes, internal rhymes). In folk tales, "circular" or "endless" tales are common; in folk songs, "rounds" ("row, row, row") and "endless" songs ("100 Bottles of Beer") are common; many more songs have repeated _refrains_ after every chorus. People have "favorite" TV programs and most people like TV _series,_ continuing programs in which the same characters and format are repetitious and predictable. People have "favorite" books, play "favorite" games, watch "favorite" sports: the common attraction is a _repeated_ pleasurable experience. While there is some truth in the old folk adage that "familiarity breeds contempt," this saying emphasizes the negative aspects of repetition—the irritation and boredom factors. But, familiarity also breeds comfort. When we _recognize_ something, we feel emotionally at ease. Franchise stores (e.g., McDonalds, Holiday Inns) may be "boring" to some people because they are so similar, repetitious throughout the country. But, it is this very standardization which makes many people feel comfortable and attracted to the "known."

Repetition is _useful_. All education, training, indoctrination, and propaganda is largely based on repetition, and is concerned with the receiver's memory: the ability of the receiver to identify or recognize, and _respond_ appropriately. Human learning depends much on our memory, comparing past experiences with the present; repeated experiences are much easier for us to handle than new situations. Some scholars believe that a certain redundancy is necessary in any language simply because there are so many noisy distractions that messages would get missed without a built-in repetition factor. Formal schooling, in any society, relies heavily on repetition. At the extreme, some people complain about the abuses of rote memory work (multiplication tables, word drills), yet every classroom and textbook involves some kind of reiteration, repetition, and review.

Commercial advertising recognizes the effectiveness of repetition. Every American knows that Budweiser is the King of Beers and that Coke is the Real Thing, simply because we've been told that a million times by such saturation campaigns. Other important uses of repetition by advertisers include "putting words in our mouths," almost literally; TV commercials, for example, present dramatizations of typical situations in which viewers are taught ready-made scripts, stock responses, on what to say, or how to respond: the friendly bartender smiles, asks for the order, and the hired actor replies "Make mine Miller," or "I'll have a Bud." These often-repeated scenes are meant to give us familiarity with the situation, to take away fears or doubts, to give us the confidence of knowing what to do, what to say.

Bonding the group together is an important function of repetition. All cultures have chants, prayers, litanies, rituals, and dances based on repetition. By such repetition, groups are able to organize the energy of individuals into a unified, more powerful whole. Such bonding is most obvious in work chants or work songs in which the vocal rhythms are needed to coordinate the physical labor of pulling or lifting. Or, in large groups at sporting events, the bonding effect is also apparent as cheerleaders can bring the group together with rhythmic clapping, footstomping, or simple cheers. Most repeated chants and prayers are short, simple formulas of praise or petition (Praise God, Glory Be, Amen, Hallelujah, Kyrie elison, Ora pro nobis, Lord have mercy, Save us), especially useful in group prayer. Most religious groups and social organizations have some kind of distinctive clothing or badge traditionally worn by the leaders during important rituals. Furthermore, all traditions and customs within a group involve a repetition in time: "We've always done it this way." Group bonding is most important in times of crisis. In wartime, in political campaigns, in periods of social unrest, and before the "Big Game," we are likely to see mass demonstrations organized—"pep rallies" or "protest rallies"—in which the group is bonded together more closely by the verbal repetition of chants and cheers, and the nonverbal repetition of uniforms, flags, banners, signs, pennants, armbands, badges, and so on.

Slogans. The word "slogan" originally came from Gaelic, meaning a war cry or the gathering call of the Highland clans, but today the word is widely used in advertising and politics. William Safire, for example, defines a slogan as "a brief message that crystallizes an idea, defines an issue, the best of which thrill, exhort, inspire." Slogans are concise, crafted, and purposeful. Frequently, they are consciously planned and promulgated by a group or a sponsor in order to persuade some audience to know, to like, or to do something. In the distant past, slogans were exclusively associated with the causes of church and state: "For God and Country." During the past century, the new phenomena of corporate enterprise and commercial advertising introduced new uses for slogans. An effective slogan says a lot, and suggests a lot, in a few words. Often, much more is implied than stated. After frequent repetition, the accumulation of such suggestions increases as audiences keep associating the phrase with the other times and situations in which they have heard it. Slogans are meant to have an emotional impact, not a rational one. They are not meant to explain or to analyze a problem, but to persuade or to give a solution. "A slogan is strong," says the French analyst Olivier Reboul, "when one cannot find any retort, when the formula defies response, eliminates dialogue, reflection, and questioning; when the only possibility is repetition." This repetition, *by the audience*, is important. Persuaders may generate, produce and *send out* millions of words in one direction. But, possibly, the most effective ones are those few which are picked up, and repeated, by the receivers.

Association

Intensifying by association is a technique of persuasion which links (1) the idea, person, or product with (2) something already loved or desired—or hated or feared—by (3) the intended audience. Thus, it is very important to know the audience. Today, millions of dollars are spent by advertisers in such "market research" ranging from simple polls, surveys, questionnaires, and contests to sophisticated psychological and sociological research. Politicians have advisors, and governments have agencies, whose function it is to provide such "target audience" information so that political persuasion campaigns can be based on an assessment of the audience.

Although there are an almost infinite number of possible combinations of subject matters and intended audiences, some patterns of human behavior are predictable (for example, attitudes toward God, country, nature, etc.) and are commonly exploited by the persuaders. Variations occur in different cultures, different eras, but essentially the subject matter of the association technique extends to all of the pleasures and ideals for which people live and die.

Any list of human "needs" suggests *what* people desire. The techniques of association, the ways *how* to make links, can be divided roughly into three major concerns: (1) the choice of *words* and *nonverbals* (pictures, etc.); (2) the choice of the *source*, the speakers and the statements; (3) the choice of *support*, references to others and to what others have said.

Words & Nonverbal Associations. Some words have limited *denotations* (rather specific, exact meanings); most words are rich in *connotations* (suggested or implied meanings). To persuade others, people can choose words with the appropriate connotations or associations. Just as certain words have favorable or unfavorable associations, so also do certain sounds, sights, smells, tastes, gestures, facial expressions, and background settings. A sound or a smell, a photo or an object seen, or a touch against the skin, may trigger our memory to recall past experiences. Many of these associations are *common* to most people, linked with standard conventions within a culture. We learn, for example, what the "appropriate" music is for a wedding or a football game. Such social conventions can be violated; some people are deliberately unconventional, but this only points out the strong social bonds within a group which establish a regularity of what is expected. By knowing the conventions of a group, it's easier to predict what kind of associations would be most common in both verbal and nonverbal communication.

Choice of Source. Everyone gets information from other people. We often believe a message simply on the basis of our belief in, or liking of, the speaker. If we already like the speaker, it's likely we'll like what the speaker says. Aristotle claimed that the *most effective* way to persuade was to build up the "image" of the persuader as being *sincere, knowledgeable,* and *friendly.* In modern advertising the emphasis may be on *knowledgeable* for certain informational advertising (also newscasters and political persuaders) and on *friendly* for most advertising which promises non-tangible "added benefits." In the past, the study of rhetoric has focused on the *individual.* Today, the presentation of "self" is often a *corporate* process as committees within large corporations select the kind of people to be used *to present* or *to endorse* their products.

Presenters. Presenters are the people who deliver the messages on television and radio. Basically they say "*Buy* this"; they need not endorse or explicitly say "*I like* this" or "*I use* this," but usually such an endorsement is implied. Every era has its beautiful people, admired and envied by millions: beauties, fashion models, sports heroes. Such people can be "rented" by corporations who know that pretty faces sell products. Fictional characters can be created to present or identify a product. Often much cheaper and easier to control than real celebrities, such *continuing central characters* (advertising jargon) can be planned for their usefulness in both television and print advertising. Well-known "plastic people" include: Ronald McDonald, Betty Crocker, Charlie Tuna, the Pillsbury Doughboy, the Jolly Green Giant, and Speedy Alka-Seltzer. Some modeling agencies specialize in providing "plain folks" for certain commercials designed to avoid the "slick" look associated with beautiful models. Large corporations, for example, often seek to "humanize" their image, to make it more credible or trusty, by using such "plain folks." Radio announcers and the people who do the television *voice-overs* are carefully chosen for their "voice signatures," voices which seem "sincere," "folksy," or "sexy" depending on the product being sold.

Endorsers. Endorsements or testimonials are statements of recommendation or approval in which the speaker explicitly says "I like this" or "I use this." Advertisers do *not* expect many people to make *conscious* decisions based on such testimonials. But we do *subconsciously* imitate, or model after, other people we admire. Politics as well as advertising makes extensive use of testimonials, relying on the transferring of a favorable "aura" or "overtones" from one person to another.

At political conventions, for example, the nomination speech and the seconding speeches are good examples of a careful selection of people chosen to endorse the candidate. Usually there will be token representatives from every geographic area, every ideological segment of the party, racial and religious group, all selected to show widespread support. Later, during the campaign, successful politicians will be in local areas, speaking on the behalf of lesser-known politicians. The political party currently in office will take its unknown candidates to the White House where they will be photographed individually with the President—smiling, talking, handshaking—trying to transfer the aura of the office. Such ritual blessings have long been with us: the favorites of kings and monarchs have always been displayed publicly as a symbolic gesture of approval. In wartime or crisis, political leaders will always gather as many endorsements and testimonials as they can to support their position.

Choice of Support. People add support to their own presentation by bringing in *references* (direct, clear, explicit, specific mentioning) or *allusions* (indirect, implied, implicit mentioning) to other people well regarded by the intended audience. For example, in a political speech, a Democrat will "pay homage" to Thomas Jefferson, Franklin D. Roosevelt, or John F. Kennedy, thereby associating self with these political heroes by such *references*. The background music ("Happy Days are Here Again") might be an *allusion* suggesting F.D.R. References and allusions are common in literature, especially in poetry where the right choice of a few words can add dimension, extend the meaning, increase the richness or suggestiveness. In music, also, a borrowed phrase, a "musical quotation" can be an allusive echo suggesting other composers or concepts. In everyday conversation, such references and allusions are often called *name-dropping*. People also *place-drop* ("When I was in Bermuda last winter . . .") and *event-drop* ("At the concert last night . . .") to their advantage. Whether such name-dropping is really effective or not depends on the skill and cleverness of those who do it.

Attribution. In addition to mentioning others, we can also repeat *what others have said,* adding their authority to our presentation, claiming that the source is outside. A *quotation* is an exact repetition of someone else's words; a *paraphrase* is a re-statement, in different words, of someone else's ideas. It is unethical to *misquote* someone else, or to quote *out-of-context,* thus misrepresenting what another has said. Ideally, we expect accuracy; in practice we recognize that sometimes people do *deliberately* misquote others (usually by omission) and sometimes *accidently* misunderstand others. If we see that such problems can occur with quotations, the *most specific* kind of attribution, then we can understand that problems will also occur when attributions are *vague.* One kind of vague attribution is the "mind reading" done by some persuaders, and some reporters, who make casual generalizations about the *inner feelings* and *beliefs* of others, the buried emotions and concealed thoughts, the motives and goals of individuals, small groups, large crowds, entire geographic areas, whole ethnic groups. We are so accustomed to it that we hardly notice the TV commentators offhand remarks that "the Germans feel . . . the French believe . . . Southerners think . . . Blacks feel. . . ." Folk sayings, maxims, and adages are a special kind of vague attribution to *anonymous authority in the past.* Folk sayings are very effective because they have a sense of tradition and wisdom about them. But, such wise sayings exist for practically *any* position, even contradictions. For example, if we want to praise *speed,* we can say "Strike while the iron is hot"; to take the opposite position, "Fools rush in where angels fear to tread." Such contradictory pairs of folk sayings are so common that we should realize that any use of folk sayings to add outside support is simply a selection by the speaker. Vagueness or specificity of attribution is not intrinsically good or bad. Few people would object to the *vague* attribution that "the Bible tells us to be good" (a generally-held idea), but if someone said "the Bible tells us to stand on our heads" (an unusual idea), most people would want a *specific* chapter-and-verse citation. The *degree of specificity* should be appropriate to the situation. For example, a reporter could attribute routine business to "White House sources" or "Pentagon officials," but a significant story might need a more specific attribution.

   Guilt by Association. The phrase "guilt by association" is often used in formal logic to describe an error in linking ideas, a fallacy also known as the "undistributed middle term." In political usage, the phrase has been used to describe reckless implications or innuendoes made against someone without explicit, direct or formal charges: "smear campaigns." Such statements may be false, invalid, illogical, and in error; yet at the same time they may be very effective psychologically or emotionally. Just as a persuader can add a little "gilt" by association with favorable things, so also the persuader can use the association technique as an attack weapon, associating the opposition with things already hated or feared by the intended audience.

Composition

Composition is the putting-together process. We can intensify communication by the words and images we choose, by the patterns and arrangement. All human creative activity (including music, painting, architecture, literature) can be described in terms of the composition process. But, in this book, there are some arbitrary definitions imposed to stipulate some limits and to emphasize certain things. Repetition and association, for example, which could be described as sub-categories under the whole composition process, are given extra emphasis here and in the Intensify/Downplay schema. So also, that schema focuses much more attention on things which are unsaid (omission) and on strategies of diversion and confusion. This section on the composition process basically deals with *verbal* communication, moving from the smaller parts (word choice) to the larger decisions about structure.

Words. Persuaders choose words and images to gain attention, to build confidence, and to urge a response: but the main body of most messages are those words which intensify the "good": the desirable qualities of the product, the benefits to be gained. Some of these words are specifically related to the product itself, but some words are more related to the "added values," the emotional associations suggested. (*The Pitch* contains 40 pages of word lists covering all of these common categories, not only itemizing the *praise words,* but also noting the less-frequently used *attack words; The Pep Talk* adds four other categories common in political rhetoric: unity, loyalty, quality, endurance.)

Nearly everyone notices the choice of favorable or unfavorable *adjectives* and *adverbs,* words which are obviously describers. Fewer people notice the choice of *verbs* used by persuaders. Verbs are less noticeable, but are often more important because these are the key words to make a statement, ask a question, give a command or direction. For example, verbs used by the endorsers in testimonials emphasize their *possessing* (I have . . . own . . . possess . . . got . . .); their *belonging to* (is a member of . . . is one of . . .); their *favoring* (I like . . . love . . . favor . . . approve . . . encourage . . . endorse . . . support . . . commend . . . recommend . . . agree . . . concur . . .); or their *desire* and *satisfaction* (I want . . . need . . . desire . . . satisfy . . . please . . .). Of the 50,000 or so verbs in the English language, a foreigner need learn only a few dozen to understand our advertising: buy . . . get . . . use . . . try . . . enjoy . . . select . . . choose . . . eat . . . drink . . . taste . . . smoke . . . drive . . . wear . . . see . . . listen . . . feel . . . shop at . . . go to . . . come to . . . stay at . . . travel on . . . play with . . .

Figures of Speech. Traditionally, this term described any out-of-the-ordinary wording; Quintillan defined a *figure* as any kind of speech "artfully varied from common usage." We may not know that "Hot Diggety Dog" is an example of *tmesis,* the interjection of a word between parts of a compound word, a figure commonly used by Shakespeare. But hundreds of these possible variations in wording have been categorized and labeled by scholars in the past. Readers need not know all of these names, but it is useful to know that the language patterns of today's persuaders (on Madison Avenue, in the Pentagon or the Kremlin) can be analyzed basically using the same principles which were first stated by Aristotle, Cicero, and Quintillan. In the past, this intensified language was used by writers—poets and preachers—primarily in praise of church, or state, or their beloved. But today the "patron of the arts" is different. Who could have imagined, a thousand years ago, that in the twentieth century, writers would be well paid for praising a tube of toothpaste, or would earn their living writing metaphors about mouthwash or similes about soapsuds? However, while the *content* of persuasive messages may have changed, the *form* remains the same. Some teachers today use the language of advertising as a way to interest students in traditional rhetoric. Professor Don Nilsen, for example, (in *En-*

glish Journal, Feb., 1976) relates: "Students 'turn on' to advertising language where the same literary device in a text leaves them cold. We may bemoan the fact that we live in a commercial era where everything is valued in terms of how much it costs, but students nevertheless respect language and the language skill that is a part of that commercial world. If they see a clever slogan on a billboard or on TV, they know someone valued it enough to pay out a great deal of money, and hence they value it more."

By sheer numbers, the figures of speech most commonly used in advertising would probably be *hyperbole, metaphors, similes,* and *puns.* Hyperboles are either extravagant overstatements ("millions of uses") or the favorable subjective opinions of the speaker ("greatest car ever built"). In advertising, such vague superlatives are usually called "puffery." Metaphors and similes are fictional conventions by which we make comparisons, saying that one thing *is* another (metaphor) or *like* another (simile). Metaphoric language has two functions: to explain and to associate. It can explain the *unknown* by comparing it to the *known.* Metaphoric language, however, can do much more than mere information transfer; because it also *transfers the emotional overtones,* metaphoric language is very important in the *association* technique, that linking together of (1) the idea or product, with (2) something already held favorably by or desired by, (3) the intended audience. The choice of words, of similes and metaphors, is one of the key ways by which these links are made.

Variations in word *order* basically involve adding, subtracting, rearranging, and repeating elements. In addition to repetition devices (*alliteration, anaphora, assonance,* etc.), some of the most common variations in word order are: *parallelism* (similarity of structure), *isocolon* (very precise parallelism), *antithesis* (opposing ideas set close together), *climax* (in increasing order of importance), *anastrophe* (a reversal of normal order), *parenthesis* (inserting ideas, or interrupting the order), *apposition* (adding explanatory modifiers), *ellipsis* (omitting items), and *parecbasis* (digressing off topics). Other writers may use different labels: antithesis may be explained in terms of *juxtaposition,* or may be described metaphorically as being a *"sugar sandwich"* or a *"poison sandwich."*

One of the classic campaigns demonstrating the power of advertising was the Thisotex automobile undercoating product which came out of obscurity with a name change, creating a "central continuing character" (Rusty Jones) and an effective slogan "Hello Rusty Jones, Goodbye rusty car" (an isocolon). Ziebart, their main competitor, also uses an isocolon for a slogan ("It's us, or rust") which is logically invalid (*either/or* fallacy) but rhetorically effective.

The ideal construction combines form and content; the structure reinforces or adds to the meaning by making the idea more memorable. For example, Ben Franklin's epigram, *"Little strokes fell great oaks"* is a tight, well constructed sentence: five words (adj./noun/verb/adj./noun) pivoting on the verb in the middle, a parallel structure, balanced, in antithesis, with internal rhyme, and expressing a meaningful idea—endurance, patience, hard work will conquer obstacles. In contrast, the sentence *"Little croaks sell great blokes"* has all the same structural qualities, but has no significant meaning. Thus, a mere mechanical tinkering with structure is not enough.

Larger Structures. Thus far, this section has focused on the smaller matters of composition, such as the choice of words and images, and the patterns within sentences. Most of our formal schooling in "language arts" focuses on these aspects, and perhaps much of our everyday experience in composing also deals with tactical decisions. However, the composition process starts with some kind of grand concept, some kind of general strategy, directed toward a goal. Composition is a purposeful behavior: we put things together for a purpose. In a well-composed thing, the final purpose should have a close relationship with the overall design, the basic structure. In architecture, the slogan has been: *"form follows function."* One of the best ways to understand the larger structures of written composition is to focus on ultimate purpose.

Advertising, for example, is often criticized by outsiders for being *annoying,* or *boring,* or *not informative* enough. Such criticism is based on the implied criteria that the purpose of advertising is entertainment or information. But the primary goal of advertising is *not* to entertain or to inform, but to persuade. When the ultimate goal is *persuasion,* then the patterns of "the pitch" and "the pep talk" (as they are called here) are much more appropriate as the major organizational "superstructures" than the patterns of induction, deduction, or narration.

Induction or deduction, for example, might lead to truth. But the purpose of persuasion is not the quest for truth, but for *assent,* for *response.* The goal of persuasion is not "information-sharing," but to stimulate a response. This isn't to say that an ad cannot give us information, or provide entertainment. Many ads are very informative and delightful. But this is not their reason for being. The first consideration about the superstructure of any composition should be related to its purpose.

Non-Rational Persuasion. Even though Aristotle's Rhetoric gave much attention to the use of the emotional appeal and the *ethos* (the "image"), later rhetoricians tended to focus more attention on the *rational* means of persuasion, especially when dealing with the arrangement, or organization, of the oration. The gulf between theory and practice widened: most analysts and scholars were dealing with the patterns of rational persuasion, most persuaders "in the real world" were actually using *non-rational* means of persuasion, appealing to the emotions of the audience and manipulating the "projected image" of the speaker. Some scholars simply scolded persuaders for doing things "they shouldn't do." That is, instead of analyzing *how* the advertisers, for example, were using the available means of persuasion, some scholars were making moral judgments condemning non-rational persuasion as being "bad."

In recent years, the greatest interest in the dynamics of non-rational persuasion has been in advertising texts, in books designed to train the future persuaders. <u>The most widely known device used here is the</u> <u>"AIDA" formula, an acronym</u> for *Attention, Interest, Desire, Action*. Future advertisers are told they should get the attention and interest of the audience, stimulate their desires, and prompt their action. The most fully developed analysis of the pattern of non-rational persuasion is Alan Monroe's "motivated sequence" appearing in his widely used textbook *Principles and Types of Speech*. Minor variations of sub-sorting and labeling the parts can be seen in other texts, but all of these attempts to describe patterns share some similarities. <u>All agree that the message must start</u> <u>with an attention-getter, develop a "desire" or a "need," and end by</u> <u>moving the audience to some kind of action.</u> *The Pitch* and *The Pep Talk* are the first books to describe patterns of non-rational persuasion from the vantage point of an observer interested in instructing the *persuadees,* average citizens and consumers, about the techniques of the persuaders.

In contrast to the easily seen ways of intensifying elements of communication (by repetition, association, composition), it is more difficult to recognize the techniques of downplaying. We don't even have an adequate vocabulary to label or to identify the various kinds of downplaying. Omission, diversion, and confusion are suggested here as three major categories of downplaying. If one intensifies by repeating things frequently, then one can downplay by omitting them. If one intensifies by association, which brings things together, then one can downplay by diversion, which splits things apart. If one intensifies by composition, which lends order and coherence, then one can downplay by confusion, which creates disorder and incoherence.

Omission

The basic selection/omission process in communication necessarily *omits* more than can be presented. For example, look around the room, now: you see and experience everything, *simultaneously*. But, if you were to communicate what you see, you must do it *sequentially:* first one thing, then another. No matter where you start listing or talking about the things you see, everytime you make a choice to say one thing, you have omitted others. Thus, *all* communication is edited, is limited, is slanted or is biased to include some items, exclude others. But, in addition to this natural process, we also recognize that omission can be a deliberate, calculated, strategy of silence, usually to downplay the "bad." Such systematic omission can be encountered anywhere in private or public life. Despite recent interest in political cover-ups and deceptive omissions, no one has made a comprehensive analysis of the techniques of omission. However, there are *some* useful things to be said, some useful ways to approach this difficult subject.

Omission is perhaps the most difficult aspect of communication to analyze. Literally, there's nothing there. How do you know *what* has been omitted, withheld, concealed, hidden? A listing of omissions and negatives—things which are *not said* or *not included*—could be infinite. Most omissions are not relevant, not harmful, and not deceptive, either by intent or result. An advertisement for an automobile, for example, does *not* mention the price of tea in China, or the untold billions of other things which are *normally omitted* as being *not relevant to the ad*. In analyzing omissions, the problem is to determine which omissions are *relevant*. Focus first on consequences: be concerned with any harmful *effects* to yourself, and also with the *causes* related to those harmful effects.

Concealed Causes. In seeking out what has been omitted, our primary concern is with those *effects* which may harm us. But the related *causes* of these harmful effects are often concealed because if people are aware of a "bad" cause, they'll often correctly infer it leads to a "bad" effect. For example, if we see a restaurant with a filthy kitchen, decaying food, and coughing cooks (potential *causes* of a harm to us), we need not wait for the "proof." Our decisions and choices are often based on discovering a cause-and-effect *relationship:* when we see a probable cause, we infer the future results.

Determining the cause of something is often difficult, both in theory and in practice. Causes are often complex and interrelated, but there are some common sense ways to clarify the problem. We can apply the traditional theory of causality (using Aristotle's basic four-part division of efficient, material, formal, and final causes) as a useful way to analyze the various possible causes.

Aristotle's folksy example of the shoemaker and the shoes identified the **efficient** cause as the doer of the action, the person involved, the shoemaker. The **material** cause, in this case, would be the leather, the nails, and so on; the **formal** cause would be the design or blueprint or the plan that gives it form; the **final** cause, the purpose or intent involved, would be to protect the feet; or, perhaps others would say, to beautify the feet, or to pay the shoemaker's rent, or to make a profit.

If we assume that people (including advertisers, politicians, and governments) *downplay their own "bad,"* Aristotle's theory of causality gives us a pattern useful to suggest where to look for omissions, for *concealed causes* relating to harmful effects, as a way of determining *relevant* omissions. For example, we can apply this pattern to a systematic analysis of the omissions to be expected in advertising.

Ads omit unfavorable information about the "maker," the **efficient cause** (the manufacturer, the workers, the sellers, the distributors) including such things as: bad reputation, financial insolvency or instability, mismanagement; incompetent or inexperienced workers; unsanitary workers (communicable disease); unbonded and uninsured repairmen; unaccredited schools; a "fly-by-night" company; a "front"; and so on. Ads omit unfavorable information about the **material cause.** Materials can be unsafe or unhealthy, poisonous, contaminated, flammable, fragile, breakable, sharp-edged, etc. Economic loss or harm can result from materials which are inferior, substitute, shoddy, sub-standard, imitation, adulterated, or any aspect which results in less quantity or less quality. Ads omit unfavorable information about the design, the **formal cause.** Errors, mistakes, flaws, and weaknesses in the planning or design will be concealed or minimized. Sometimes a design can create an unsafe, life-threatening situation; more commonly, many poorly-designed products are simply inconvenient, uncomfortable, unwieldy, difficult to use. Planning and organizing errors in providing services (airlines, mail orders, auto repairs, home repairs) are common: complex or complicated procedures, "red tape," delays, and interruptions. Ads omit unfavorable information about the intended use or purpose, the **final cause.** With some products there is an inherent risk or danger in the use; for example, anything with a saw, a blade, heat or flame, or electricity. In addition to safety hazards and misuse, some items have other inherent problems in use: energy-wasting, time-wasting, inefficient, very costly to operate, not compatible with other systems, limited usefulness, skilled operators needed, and so on. (Consumer protection laws try to prevent harmful effects by requiring "warnings" and "disclosures" of the concealed "bad" so that consumers may estimate the risk and make informed choices.)

　　Omission of relevant things influences our decision-making process. "Free choice" depends on knowing all of the options, the advantages and disadvantages, as we weigh and balance these various factors, good and bad. Thus, the information we have must be both *truthful* and *adequate*. The function of "disclosure laws" in advertising, for example, is to help provide such adequate, relevant information; here, people use government as their agent to counter the advertisers' omissions. In political propaganda, people (in some places) may have a "free press" as their agent to counter the governments' omission. The function of investigative reporting is to seek out those "bad" things (usually errors, corruption, abuses) being downplayed by the politicians and governments. Official news releases from the White House, the Pentagon, the Governors' Mansion, and City Hall can be expected to tell of great achievements, victories, progress, and promises: to intensify the "good." Reporters who simply re-write these "public relations" handouts become "lap dogs of government," as Jack Anderson put it, "instead of the watchdogs over government." Anderson, a veteran Washington journalist, related some of the difficulties that investigative reporters have in searching for that which has been downplayed: "There are no press secretaries to brief those who search after concealed facts, no hucksters to package the suppressed details in attractive press kits. We have never known a government official to call a press conference to confess his wrong-doing, nor a government agency to issue a press release citing its mistakes. Men in power, and men seeking power, do not relish having their cozy relationships exposed, their sources of money bared, and their blunders brought to light. Rather than cooperate, they obstruct investigative reporters. Doors are closed; files are locked; phones are slammed back into receivers. The last thing people at the top of government want to see are stories about government wrongs. For they know that exposure can bring an end to power.''

In practice, the use of omission techniques is neither ''static'' nor simple. Many techniques can be used simultaneously and there is a commonly-seen **sequence.** It's almost as if people were working with a simple branching diagram; if one option fails, the next one is used. The first step is **to omit:** people downplay their own ''bad.'' Assume that no one, including advertisers and politicians, is likely to reveal that which is unfavorable, unless they are somehow forced by others. Omission is the first line of defense, whether it's an individual, a corporation, or a government seeking to conceal the ''bad.'' (In addition to concealment, those who have *power* can prohibit or discourage others from access to the ''harmful'' information.) If the ''bad'' is discovered, there are several options (including destruction or revision—if one has the power), but commonly the next step is **to deny** that it is ''bad'' (''There's nothing wrong with that.''); or to deny responsibility (''I didn't do it—''); or to deny intent (''I didn't mean it''). If denial doesn't work, the next step is **to minimize,** to downplay the degree of harm: ''it's only a little harmful . . . only a few people involved . . . not very important . . . not very common . . . not very frequent . . . the lesser of two evils, etc.'' Frequently, the next step is **to divert** attention away from the main issue. The most common kinds of diversions are *ad hominem* attacks against the other, *ad populum* emotional appeals, and a wide variety of diversionary tactics which intensify ''side issues'' and downplay the main issue. Thus, the ''bad'' gets hidden or lost unless the opposition can re-discover or re-focus. If so, then the cycle repeats: **omit, deny, minimize, divert.**

This sequence is most commonly seen in political arguments, but seldom in commercial advertising because the advertiser buys the time and space to present a one-sided favorable message. However, the sequence can be seen in some ad campaigns for controversial products, such as cigarettes and sugared cereals, and in the public controversies over nuclear energy, automobile safety, and so on. The ''offenders'' would prefer that nothing be said about the problem; but, once raised, the ''bad'' is denied, minimized, and attention diverted away from it.

Diversion

Diversions *downplay* the important things, distract focus away from the main issue, by *intensifying* side-issues, non-related, or trivial things. Diversions are so common that people have given many metaphoric names to the various techniques used: red herrings and nit-picking, smoke-screening and hair-splitting, poisoning the well, and playing on the heart-strings. In addition, several key descriptors (*ad hominem* attacks, *ad populum* appeals) have been with us for centuries.

Are diversions "bad?" Not necessarily, not intrinsically. Because this book deals with commercial and political propaganda, *some* examples of diversion here might be judged by most people to be "bad," and, in other books, diversions are usually discussed (correctly so) as errors in formal logic. However, if one agrees that value judgments about human activities should be made in the context of the whole situation *(who is saying what, to whom, under what circumstances, with what intent and what result)* then there are times when diversions are useful and humane behaviors. Consider, for example, a child sick or in pain (a "main issue") and parents seeking to divert attention, to provide pleasant distractions; or consider that when people are deeply involved in arguments, it's often wise to take a break, a cooling off period, and divert attention away from the problem for a while.

Consider also the great variety of nonverbal diversions, all of which intensify something less important while downplaying (hiding, concealing, diverting attention away from) the more important: for example, when athletes fake or feign one way, then make the major move in another; in football, the draw play, the screen pass, the reverse; in basketball, the head-fake; in soccer, the false-kick. So also, the magician diverts attention away from where the action really is. In animal behavior, biologists speak of "decoy behaviors" when animals deliberately create a diversion to lead predators away from a nest or den. In military maneuvers, the *defense* seeks to lure the enemy into attacking a dummy position or unimportant sector; the *offense* uses small diversionary forces to create the illusion of an attack in one area, when, in reality, the main attack will take place elsewhere.

Ad hominem. To speak of an *ad hominem* attack means that someone is diverting attention away from the issue and focusing on the person, "an argument directed against the man." This is a *logical* fallacy because personality is not logically related to the truth or falsity of what a person says. Logically, we have to separate the argument from the person: "bad" people can make sound rational arguments, and "good" people can be very illogical in their thinking. But the *ad hominem* attack is often used because it is a powerful *psychological* and *emotional* way to persuade people. People do have prejudices and do respond emotionally. It is a logical error, for example, to argue that something is false simply because the idea is held by a *communist* (or a *fascist*); but such an irrational argument may sway the emotions of an audience. Some people have closed minds. They simply will not listen to or believe what is said by people in other groups. Thus, as soon as a speaker is identified as being a Democrat or a Republican (a black or a white, an advertiser or a consumerist, and so on) some people are so prejudiced that they will not judge the merit of the issue. Propagandists exploit this tendency by using *ad hominem* attacks which divert attention away from the issue and focus on the person or source. Such personal attacks, usually using emotionally intensified language ("name-calling"), are sometimes called "character assassination." "Poisoning the well" is another phrase for this, suggesting that once the source has been discredited, no one will trust that which comes forth.

In politics, *ad hominem* attacks are often called "smear campaigns" or "mudslinging." Such tactics are frequently used, especially by means of planted rumors and anonymous gossip to spread suspicion and doubt. When the Watergate investigation widened to include other facets of the 1972 election, Donald Segretti was found guilty of being in charge of "dirty tricks," the author of some malicious anonymous letters, printed during the campaign, containing vile charges about the morals of the Democratic campaigners Humphrey, Jackson, Muskie, and McGovern. It's rare that such secret *ad hominem* attacks can be pinned to a particular person, but it's rather common that such attacks do occur during campaigns. Therefore, it's wise for an audience to be very skeptical of any personal charges made in such situations.

Ad hominem attacks are rare in commercial advertising, partly because of laws against slander and libel. (But, in person-to-person situations, it's fairly common for merchants to communicate some nasty things about their competitors by means of gestures, voice tones, or subtle hints.) Comparative ads—in which a product was compared specifically with another product by name—were long avoided by advertisers fearing costly law suits. More recently, the FTC has encouraged comparative ads as long as advertisers can substantiate their claims. This isn't working too well because it's a big complicated mess of claims and countercharges within the industry and the regulatory agencies. But such comparative ads have generally intensified *minor* issues, and have avoided the main issues that parity products are basically the same. Furthermore, many people do not *like* comparative ads, such as the Pepsi or Burger King ads; thus, comparative claims are risky. Most advertisers don't want to rock the boat, don't want to erode *any* confidence in advertising.

Most national advertising money today is spent on selling *parity products*—those goods and services which have little or no difference from their competitors, including things such as: gasoline, detergents and cleaning products, cosmetics, cigarettes, over-the-counter drugs, beer and whiskey, soft drinks, snack foods, breakfast cereals, airline services, fast-food restaurants, and so on. Most of these are high-profit items, with the potential for frequent or repeated purchase by consumers; many are "luxury" items, non-essentials, appearing only in affluent societies. Some economists believe that one of the functions of advertising, in a society which prides itself on "free enterprise," is to create the *illusion* of competition, to downplay the reality that a few large corporations have a near-monopoly on the market. For example, the many "competing" brands of cigarettes, soaps, and breakfast cereals are really made by only a few corporations. With parity products, the advertisers' job is to make the minor differences seem important. Thus, we're apt to see ads in which the characters are excited that a toothpaste has a new color, or a cigarette has a new box, or a detergent has exciting new green flakes in it, or that the shape of a container has been improved. Advertising of parity products tend to emphasize the trivial, thus diverting attention from other things.

"Bait and Switch" describes a diversionary tactic often used in deceptive advertising, especially in *local* advertising (car dealers, furniture and appliance stores). A product is advertised at a very low price, but when the customer comes to buy it, the seller tries to switch the customer into buying a higher-priced item. It is illegal to advertise one thing with the deliberate intent to sell another; but it's very hard to catch, very hard to prove. Many people are never aware that they've been "switched" because the seller uses so much *flattery:* "*You* have better tastes than most people, so you'd like a better model. . . . *You* recognize value." Diversion intensifies a side issue, downplays the main issue. In "bait and switch," the original *main issue* (the reason the buyer was attracted to the store) was the advertised low cost. At the store, the seller *intensifies the side issues* (e.g., quality, or immediate availability) *which were downplayed* (in small print, or omitted) in the original ad. The basic defense against this fraud is awareness of our own priorities.

"Second Thoughts." Many consumer complaints are caused because the *buyer* is at fault. At first, the buyer intensifies one aspect (e.g., beauty) and ignores or downplays other aspects: e.g., "details" about installation, price, or availability. Later, the buyer may be most concerned about these items. Buyers, too, have obligations. Most businesses are honest. It is unfair to them for customers to change their minds—switch priorities, and then start complaining because they feel they have been treated unjustly. Many complaints received by consumer agencies are from people who are dissatisfied, but who have no legal claim. Laws may help to protect buyers from fraud or deception, but not from their own errors in judgment.

Ad populum. Instead of focusing on any rational aspect of the issue involved, an *ad populum* appeal diverts attention by playing on the emotions or prejudices of the audience. As the rational issues are downplayed by this diversion, the emotional aspects are intensified—usually by the language used ("name-calling" and "glittering generalities") and by the association technique. Thus, the persuader must know the attitudes, feeling, prejudices, and values *already held* by the audience: the "dreams and nightmares" of the audience.

The *ad populum* technique basically works with some kinds of promises or threats involving the desires or fears of the audience. Promises, for example, can range from subtle flattery to blunt bribery. Speakers can flatter an audience in many ways, praising their intelligence or saying something the audience likes to hear about themselves. Bribery and threats are extreme forms of the *ad populum* appeal in which no attention is given to the intrinsic merit or the rational aspect of the issue. Bribery can involve money, sexual favors, drugs, influence-peddling, any kind of kickbacks. Threats can range from a frown of disapproval to the serious crimes of extortion (shakedown), blackmail, or violent force. All of these things were included in Aristotle's category of the "non-artistic" means of persuasion.

Ad misericordiam. Another diversionary technique is a focus on the self, rather than the issue, sometimes called the "appeal to pity" *(argumentum ad misericordiam)* or, simply, the "poor me" technique. Lawyers, for example, may "play on the heartstrings," may try to influence a jury to acquit a client out of pity. Most teachers are familiar with the appeal to pity; some students try to divert attention away from academic issues (poorly done work, late assignments, being absent or tardy, etc.) by appeals to pity. Politicians know the value of winning pity from their audience. Sometimes, a personal handicap or a family tragedy may even be exploited deliberately to win a sympathetic vote. But the most common political technique is using the appeal of being the "underdog." Many people sympathize with the "underdog"; politicians often exploit this by picturing themselves as the "underdog" in a great crusade against "the big guy" or the Establishment.

Side Issues

"Red herring" is a term used commonly to describe a noisy controversial side issue, not related to the main point. The term comes from the folklore that a person being pursued by bloodhounds could distract the dogs by dragging a smelly red herring across the track so that the dogs would lose the scent.

"Hair-Splitting" and **"Nit-Picking"** both refer to a constant quibbling over definitions, fine points, or side issues: *reductio ad absurdum* — that is, reducing to the absurd by a constant subdividing or over-precision of terms. Here again there is the problem of degree. Definitions are important and key terms do need to be defined clearly. But this can usually be done effectively by both parties agreeing to a "working definition" (an operational or stipulative definition).

"Fault-Finding" or **"Nothing But Objections"** are closely related as diversionary tactics. Life is so complex that there are no human plans which cannot be objected to for some reason or another. No matter what decision is made, one can always find fault with it. One can always raise objections for any course of action. Very few human arguments are simple. Most significant arguments involve "the lesser of two evils" or "the greater of two goods." Choices and decisions are hard, but often have to be made at a certain time. Otherwise the lack of decision is a decision itself. Constant objections can be used as a delaying technique by those who wish to slow down or obstruct change.

Perfection. A call for perfection is a diversionary maneuver because it calls for an impossible condition; for example, if people were to argue: "if men were taught to be good, we'd have no need of jails." Such arguments get nowhere because they have no basis in human experience. Arguments must be based on observable human nature, on what people actually do, not on what they should do. It would be nice if all people were good, honest, trustworthy, and kind; but it would not be logical to assume that this were the real situation. If one did so, then this false assumption of premises could well be a hidden diversion, distracting from the real issue.

Pointing to Another Wrong. To point to another wrong, or to claim that "everybody is doing it," is often used as a diversion, avoiding the main issue. Two wrongs do not make a right. If a citizen complains that "our inflation rate is high," the politician who responds "it's worse in India" is simply pointing to another bad situation and not facing the issue.

"And now, for something completely different . . . ."

Humor. Everyone has heard a serious argument interrupted by one of the speakers who remarks, with a little laugh, "that reminds me of a story," and then proceeds to tell a joke. A good story-teller, or joke-teller, can amuse and entertain an audience, sometimes diverting it from the main issue. Some jokes or anecdotes, of course, may be used as illustrations or examples directly related to the issue. But, when humor is not related, then it can be considered a diversion. In some situations, humor downplays main issues by diversion; at the same time, humor can intensify by building up the image of the speaker as a pleasant, friendly, jovial person. Other kinds of humor (satire, caricature) intensify by attacking (mocking or ridiculing) the opponent's "bad." Humor is a very complex, sophisticated communication act (perhaps, uniquely human); one of the possible uses of humor is diversion.

"Bread and Circuses," as used here, suggests diversion on a grand scale such as the ancient Roman emperors did in providing entertainments (gladiators, lions and tigers at the Circus Maximus) which diverted people's attention away from the serious social and political issues of the day. Some commentators today suggest that much of our attention now is taken up with modern versions of bread and circuses: sports, radio, television, movies. If citizens are so pre-occupied or satisfied with entertainments, then the genuine issues and problems within our society are often ignored or neglected. A century ago, Karl Marx charged that religion was the "opium of the people" because it focused on an afterlife, thus diverting people's effort away from solving the problems of life. Today, some critics claim that TV is the opium of the people. Anytime a major catastrophe or political event interrupts regular television programming, the networks get thousands of angry calls from viewers who are disturbed that their favorite soap opera or situation comedy isn't on the air.

Degree is an important consideration. Everyone enjoys entertainment; everyone needs a break at times. But, at what degree, in what proportion do these pleasant entertainments become harmful diversions from more significant issues? Cultural assumptions are often hard to recognize within one's own society. In this country, for example, few people see anything wrong with 200 reporters in a press box covering a televised football game while there are only a handful of reporters in the nation assigned to cover the intricate affairs of the Pentagon.

"Draining" and **"Busy Work."** Practically everyone has had the experience in which repeated or persistent petty distractions or annoyances have had the cumulative effect of "wearing down" or "draining"—diverting attention from one's occupation or goal. Our language has many verbs to describe such petty actions: to tease, to harass, to bother, to vex, to pester, to harry. Recognize that such "draining" can be a deliberate strategy, a diversionary device, which anyone can use; yet, it works most efficiently for those who possess wealth or power. Legal harassment, for example, is possible. Corporations and governments can retain large staffs of attorneys to file suit and to argue against their opponents. During the Vietnam war, for example, the federal government started hundreds of cases against protestors who disagreed with the administration's foreign policy. Very few ever got to court, but for years these lawsuits drained away the time, money and energy of those individuals and small groups. Citizens in a democracy ought to be aware that such techniques have been used by many governments in the past as a way of silencing opposition. "Busy Work" is another way to drain, to divert energy. In modern society, we live in systems built by words (laws, rules, etc.) with many people working in groups and committees. Idealistically, some standard rules and procedures are meant to encourage efficiency and justice; but these idealistic purposes can be distorted by manipulation. It's possible to divert and drain the energy of people by misusing *Robert's Rules of Order*, for example, or by creating endless "busy work" in committees and sub-committees in which all of the efforts are diverted and wasted.

Multiple Diversions. Sometimes it's possible to identify one major diversionary technique; but, in many cases, it's difficult or impossible to make such a simple identification because there are so many diversions going on at once. For most people, it's more important to get a general sense, and to recognize the general patterns, of diversionary and confusion techniques. Metaphoric labels such as *"cloud the issue," "muddy the waters," "smokescreen," "shotgun attack"* are used to suggest the generally confusing pattern of multiple diversions.

Thus far, diversion has been analyzed in terms of *intensifying a minor issue* while *downplaying the major.* But, who is to say what is a minor issue and what is a major one? What if people disagree about the relative importance of things? People do disagree, in good faith. If this happens in our person-to-person relationships, we have to have a mutual understanding and respect for others' opinions. Sometimes we have to ask others what they mean, or how they define a word, in order to understand them. So also, we sometimes have to ask what they consider more important or of lesser importance. We have to stipulate our priorities. We may not reach agreement, but at least we'll know what the real issues are.

Confusion

Confusion can *downplay* key issues by making them so complex, complicated, or vague that a receiver cannot understand, or comprehend them. Earlier, the term "composition" was used to refer to the purposeful "putting-together" *process,* the choice and arrangement of elements. Confusion, as used here, refers primarily to the *result* of either (1) a poorly-composed message, unintentionally confusing the receiver, or (2) a well-composed message *deliberately intended* to confuse the receiver.

Confusion can be accidental. People can make errors, can ramble and be disorganized, without malice. On the other hand, confusion can be deliberately planned as a way of deceiving others, misleading people away from key issues, or hiding things. The *con man,* for example, uses confusion as a way of getting money from those who are being fleeced or gulled. Political demagogues have used confusion as a way of gaining power. When people are confused, they have often turned to strong leaders offering simple solutions. Governments can use confusion as a way of hiding secret information from external enemies, or of hiding unfavorable information from internal critics. When we are confused, we are more likely to be deceived. By reducing confusion, we reduce some of the risks of being deceived.

Omission, an important factor related to confusion, is probably the most common way people downplay their own "bad": unfavorable information is omitted, hidden, concealed. If receivers lack information, especially relating to harmful effects, they can be confused. Confusion can also result from the *absence* of structure, organization, sub-divisions, boundaries and limits, links and transitions, directional cues and signals. Anything that is unplanned, unsorted, and unorganized is likely to be confusing. Most crucial is the absence of *goals* or purpose: things literally become "senseless" and "meaningless."

Confusion can also result from *unclear* goals (vague, unspecific), *unfamiliar* goals (new, strange, or foreign), *variable* goals) shifting priorities), and *complex* goals. Consider, for example, large organizations, such as universities and democratic governments, with *many, vague,* and *shifting* goals resulting from the pressures of diverse interest groups. It's easy for a trade-school (or a private business) to have one, clear, specific goal; but universities, for example, are always involved in the shifting priorities among their multiple, abstract goals: "liberal education," "career preparation," "cultural enrichment," and "research."

Confusion is frequently caused by too many *senders* of messages: too many people talking at once, too many bosses, too many cooks. Sometimes confusion is caused by the unrelated quality of this experience: in committees or meetings, for example, often speakers go off on unrelated tangents. In other cases, multiple speakers may send *contrary* or *contradictory* messages: workers getting conflicting orders from different bosses; different government agencies issuing conflicting reports.

Conflicting and contradictory claims by *different* speakers (such as opposing political parties, economic ideologies, religious beliefs) are common in a free society. Free people must learn to cope with a multiplicity of conflicting views.

After recognizing the role of *omission,* and the importance of the *efficient* and the *final* causes (the senders and receivers, and their goals), the rest of this section will focus on confusion *within the message* itself, on the *material* and *formal* causes (the words and images, their patterns and arrangements). From observation, here we stipulate that confusion is likely to occur when things are (1) **unclear,** (2) **unfamiliar,** (3) **too variable,** (4) **too complex.**

Unclear. Confusion can be caused by unclear messages. However, when people advise us to "be clear" or "write clearly" or "speak clearly," there are several different things they may mean; two of the most commonly suggested problem areas are *carefulness/carelessness* in the "basics" of encoding, and *ambiguous/unambiguous* elements.

Messages have to be understandable, that is: *visible, audible, legible, readable,* or *recognizable.* Confusion can be caused in the basic encoding/decoding process if there are such things as errors in speaking, penmanship, typing, spelling, grammar, punctuation, diction, translation, math, or technical and mechanical problems in transmission. Errors in "basics" can cause confusion. In addition, such errors are often seen (rightly or wrongly) as indicators that the speaker/writer lacks information, training, education, experience, practice, or discipline. Many of the problems relating to errors are extensively discussed in Mina Shaughnessey's *Errors and Expectations;* her common sense approach focuses on trying to sort out errors and to establish priorities in dealing with them. Ignorance of words and of their connotations can cause errors leading to confusion; for example, a speaker with a limited vocabulary lacks precision in expressing meaning and feeling. Shaughnessey further argues that an inadequate vocabulary also leads to wordiness, circumlocution, and awkward sentences. In ordinary conversation, if we make an error, we can frequently get feedback from our audience, so that we can clarify ourselves. In conversations, we often have a constant informal exchange of nonverbal cues (head nodding, etc.) and phatic communications ("uh-uh, uh-uh . . . you know what I mean?") to keep our words and meanings clear. In writing, we don't have such aids. Thus, to reduce misunderstandings when we write, we usually need to give more attention to our choice of words.

Sometimes the call for "clarity" refers to specificity and seeks to restrict the meaning of a word or image to one single unambiguous meaning. Ambiguity exists whenever any word image, or signal can be interpreted in more than one way. Many words are intrinsically ambiguous because they are *generalizations* (covering broad categories) or *abstractions* (referring to *intangible* concepts, ideas, qualities) in contrast to words which are more *specific* and/or *concrete.* Nonverbal ambiguity is common. Gestures and facial expressions are frequently misinterpreted or misunderstood because the "vocabulary" of nonverbal communication is often even more ambiguous and less defined than our verbal communication.

Specific language is often very useful, necessary, and appropriate, but it is not better than more generalized and abstract language. We need to abstract and to generalize as much as we need to be specific. There's a great deal of criticism leveled at vagueness, as if it were wrong or "bad" in itself. But there are situations when the deliberate use of vague language is appropriate: for example, when a child asks "What am I getting for Christmas?" and the parent replies, deliberately evasive, "Something nice." Diplomats often try to avoid forcing their opponents into a corner. Instead of using a specific threat ("If you do that, then we'll bomb Moscow.") it is often better to be vague and general: "We'll take *appropriate actions.*" This is not an endorsement of all vague, general statements by politicians and diplomats, or advertisers. There are times when firm, precise statements must be made. But some people seek certitude and demand precision *all* of the time, perhaps because such precision implies some kind of control. If we wish to reduce ambiguity, senders can stipulate definitions, give examples, use specific concrete language, and use modifiers and cue words; receivers can seek out key terms, clarifying examples, context cues, and, often, ask questions: "What do you mean?"

Unfamiliar. Confusion can be caused when the message, or parts of it (such as the words or images) are *unfamiliar to the audience. The message may be clear, but still not understandable because the receiver lacks necessary background information.* We need not confine ourselves to a Me-Tarzan-You-Jane vocabulary, nor restrict ourselves to the Dolch List of 800 Words of Basic English, but we should recognize that the potential for confusion increases with any unfamiliar, atypical, or uncommon words, including *slang, jargon, euphemisms,* or any *"fancy" words. (Eschew Obfuscation!)*

"Fancy words," as used here, describes those words which exist within the vocabulary of the language, but are *uncommon* or *unfamiliar* to most speakers. Many of these words have a marginal existence, living on precariously in only the largest of dictionaries and on Spelling Bee lists. Many of these words are polysyllabic "big" words, with Latin, Greek, or French roots (in contrast to curt Anglo-Saxon words); many have precise meanings, being the accumulated bits and pieces of various specialized jargons in the past. There's a great amount of criticism and mockery of such inflated language (as being strained, artificial, ornate, pompous, exaggerated, extravagant, pretentious, affected, high-faluting, ostentatious, flowery, grandiloquent, showy, bombastic, exotic, esoteric, obscure, obsolete, archaic, and pedantic); yet, this human foible of using big words to "impress" people has always been with us, and despite all the practical advice given by those who warn us away from polysyllabic claptrap, it's likely to remain.

Jargon, in its narrow sense, refers to the language peculiar to a group or a class. Every trade and profession has its jargon: a specialized vocabulary, a shop-talk, or in-language of commonly used words, often shortened to abbreviations, acronyms, and nicknames. (By adding the -*ese* formation to a root, writers have coined a whole variety of words to suggest the jargon of specific groups, Bureaucratese, Pentagonese, State Departmentese, Legalese, Educatorese, Journalese.) Jargon is very useful, perhaps essential, *within a group:* we need a "shorthand" for practical purposes. Among equals, where everyone *knows* what the words mean, jargon is appropriate. However, jargon used with "outsiders" leads to confusion.

Discussions of jargon (slang, "fancy words" and euphemisms) eventually have to focus on the *intent* of the sender and the *result* to the receiver. Vanity is one reason people use jargon with outsiders. It's a form of showing off, a "badge" to show others that the speaker *belongs,* is a member of some elite or special group. Jargon is so used to intensify our own "good." However, jargon can also be used to downplay the "bad," to hide or conceal things by using words unfamiliar to the receiver. It's this use of jargon that receives the most attention from critics because it can confuse or deceive. It's difficult to judge another's *intent* in using jargon or other unfamiliar words with outsiders: conscious or unconscious, deliberate or accidental, vain or malicious? It's more useful to focus on the possible *result or consequences* of such language.

Euphemisms are words which downplay the "bad." A euphemism can be a new word (slang), a technical term or specialized word (jargon), an obscure word ("fancy word"), or an ambiguous word; many euphemisms are simply words which are more abstract or more generalized than the concrete specifics they replace. Examples of euphemisms in the Vietnam war, for example, include both the soldier's common *slang* ("waste a gook," "barbecue party,") and the Pentagon's official *jargon* (protective reaction strike, selective ordinance). Many critiques about the American military manipulation of language during that war have used George Orwell's 1945 essay on "Politics and the English Language" as a starting point for their analyses. In that, Orwell wrote:

> In our time, political speech and writing are largely the defense of ·the indefensible. Things like the continuance of British rule in India, the Russian purges and deportations, the dropping of the atom bombs on Japan, can indeed be defended, but only by arguments which are too brutal for most people to face, and which do not square with the professed aims of political parties. Thus political language has to consist largely of euphemism, question-begging and sheer cloudy vagueness. Defenseless villages are bombarded from the air, the inhabitants driven out into the countryside, the cattle machine-gunned, the huts set on fire with incendiary bullets: this is called *pacification.* Millions of peasants are robbed of their farms and sent trudging along the roads with no more than they can carry: this is called *transfer of population* or *rectification of frontiers.* People are imprisoned for years without trial, or shot in the back of

the neck or sent to die of scurvy in Arctic lumber camps: this is called *elimination of unreliable elements.* Such phraseology is needed if one wants to name things without calling up mental pictures of them.

Orwell was accurate in describing the use of euphemisms by contemporary warmakers, but it would be inaccurate to restrict this to a *modern* practice (the "decay of language" bit), or to one side ("good guys/bad guys"), or to make an *absolute* condemnation of euphemisms. Familiarity/unfamiliarity is the crucial issue. Euphemisms *per se* are not bad; it's whether the audience *understands* the message being sent. Many euphemisms are familiar and common conventions within a language community. For example, our standard euphemisms for death and dying (passed away, eternal reward) and bodily functions (going to the bathroom, the washroom) are well understood within our society. It's only when the *meaning* is obscured that euphemisms cause problems. When the Pentagon uses euphemisms, technical jargon such as "low yield, clean thermonuclear device," most people do not get an accurate mental picture of the reality because the words sound rather pleasant: it's *low* yield, *clean,* and only a *device.* By words, the military has downplayed the reality that these bombs are more powerful, more devastating, more catastrophic than any weapon ever used before in human history.

Unfamiliar patterns, procedures. Confusion can be caused by any kind of unfamiliar pattern whether it's an atypical sentence pattern, or configuration of images, or a new procedure. Anything that isn't part of a long established routine has the potential to be confusing; anytime a new product, a new service, a new form is introduced, there is the need for instructions, directions, rules, or guidelines. Most people adapt quickly and are flexible enough to handle change, but still the possibility for confusion increases when we are dealing with any unfamiliar situation, process, or procedure. The most costly error in financial history, for example, occurred (Oct. 5, 1979), when a person at Hanover Manufacturers Bank made an error on a *new* reporting form providing data to the Federal Reserve Board. Because of that erroneous report, the Fed increased the interest rate by a full point, triggering the worst stock market panic since 1929, and investors lost over $200 billion dollars in a few days. Confusion is likely to occur anytime people deal in mathematical systems, whether "simple" math, algebra, statistics or computer languages, because these are very sophisticated systems which relatively few people understand. Familiarity may breed contempt, but unfamiliarity breeds confusion.

Too variable. If things are "too variable," that is, if there are constant or frequent changes, variations or irregularities, confusion is likely to occur. Any changes or shifts, any inconsistencies or incongruities, within a message (including *contradictions, paradoxes, double messages,* and *qualifiers*) increase the possibility of confusion. The potential for confusion exists anytime things are unstable (irregular, erratic, unpredictable, uneven, unsteady, transient, ephemeral, spasmodic, inconstant, random, fluctuating, or different) in contrast to things which are stable (steady, lasting, permanent, uniform, constant, even, regular, unchanging, fixed, standard, predictable, unvariable, the same). Changes may appear under many different *labels:* revisions, amendments, updates, corrections, emendations, exceptions, substitutions, changes, alterations, modifications, and variations. In terms of *motion* or *movement,* for example, variability may be thought of in terms of *continuity/discontinuity* using the analogies of "traffic flow" in a complex highway system or in computer flowcharting. The risks of confusion are low as long as there's no delays, slowdowns, interruptions, breakdowns, stoppages; but the potential for confusion increases with intermittent, erratic, sporadic, jerky, stop-and-go irregularities.

Qualifiers. Words which express *qualifications,* in contrast to words which express *absolute certainties,* are related to "change": qualifying words allow for variations. Several critics of advertising have damned such qualifiers as "weasel words." In Paul Stevens' exposé of advertising, *I Can Sell You Anything,* he elaborates on the use of such key words as *helps . . . like . . . virtual, . . . virtually . . . acts like . . . works like . . . can be . . . up to . . . as much as . . . the feel of . . . looks like . . .* and a variety of commonplace puffery words *(refreshes, comforts, smells, tastes)* relating to taste and subjective opinions. However, most of the qualifiers he notes are those words *required* by FTC and FDA regulations designed to reduce deceptive advertising claims. Drugstore remedies may no longer categorically claim, as they once did, that they can *stop pain, cure* or *heal.* If the drugs have some effects, they are permitted to advertise that they may *help* to reduce pain, or *aid* in healing, or some other qualified claims (such as *"temporary relief"*) as specified by the regulators. Stevens is correct in his basic point that confusion can result from the use of such qualifiers. Certainly consumers do need to be aware of the meaning and implications of such qualifiers. But calling them "weasel words" suggests that qualifiers are "bad" in themselves.

However, qualifying words serve an extremely important function in our language and reasoning. Qualifiers help us to express the realities we perceive: sometimes we're unable to predict or estimate future results, unable to measure or to verify past facts, unable to have certitude, unable to make general or universal statements. If we had to speak in absolutes all the time, firm assurances, unqualified and categorical, we would distort reality. Yet, in a world of uncertitude, many people still seek certitude and highly value those speakers (the "strong leaders") who project such assurances and condemn those who lack such "certitude" as being wishy-washy, vacillating and wavering, hesitant and hedging.

Change. In one sense, change is simply natural and normal: all things change. Change can be accidental, unintentional. Wavering, uncertainty, and inconsistency in our everyday life can be caused by a subconscious shifting of goals or premises. But, in another sense, change can be a deliberate strategy. For example, in most *conflicts,* whether in warfare or in sports, the elements of change and irregular movements are basic both in offense and in defense. Combatants seek to deny predictability: to keep their opponents "off guard" or to avoid "telegraphing their punches." Armies avoid static positions; nuclear submarines and SAC bombers prowl in unpredictable routes. Boxers dance and weave; football and basketball players feint and shift; baseball pitchers mix their pitches—all with the intent of gaining an advantage over the opposition. Thus, we commonly see change—shifts, movement, variations—used as an important part of such physical conflicts. Change can also be used deliberately to create confusion in more subtle conflicts. A government, for example, that sends out a dozen different versions ("revisions" or "updates") of economic statistics or budget reports is apt to confuse most observers. The CIA's term "disinformation" refers not only to creating false cover stories, but also to producing multiple and contradictory news releases to create confusion.

Change without rationale, without rhyme or reason, disturbs many people. If change is arbitrary and capricious, it violates our sense of order. Accidents and catastrophes often cause sudden and violent changes; sometimes survivors of catastrophes are most shocked by this element of inexplicable disorder. We want to be able to predict, to foresee, to anticipate. We want regularity, predictability. In a world of change, we seek stability; in a world of complexity, simplicity.

Too complex. Confusion can be caused if things are too complex, that is, if the *quantity* is too large (e.g., the amount of information, the number of parts) or the *process* is too complicated or too fast. Complexity, quantity, and speed need not be confusing in themselves; a well-designed computer operation, for instance, demonstrates that a great quantity of information can be processed at great speed. However, it's still a reasonable generalization to say that confusion commonly occurs in complex situations when people are confronted with too many things too quickly. Conversely, we are not likely to get confused when things are simple, slow, orderly, clear, familiar, and unchanging. (They may be dull, but not confusing.)

Confusion can be "accidental" in the sense that certain situations have inherent problems: large organizations (including governments, their bureaucracies, corporations), democratic systems (including committees), quickly changing conditions (including accidents and catastrophes), unorganized groups (including mobs), and organizations with multiple goals (including governments and universities). However, confusion can also be a deliberate strategic maneuver. In politics and government, for example, confusion can be used as the smokescreen to cover up errors and mistakes, crimes and violations, aggressions, unpopular ideas and vote-losers. By those in power, confusion can be used as a defense measure: if critics are confused about the processes and prodedures, if critics get the "run around" or a "wild goose chase" or get "lost in the maze" or "snarled in red tape," then it's hard to change a system. As one reformer noted: "You can't fight City Hall if you can't find it."

Advertising offers many examples of calculated confusion. Consider, for example, the non-standardized jumble of *sizes* and *shapes* of packaging grocery items. Together with the verbal confusion of names and labels (GIANT, LARGE, SUPER, ECONOMY SIZE, FAMILY SIZE), the overall effect of such confusion makes it almost impossible for a consumer to *compare* items. Comparisons are also difficult in any product or service in which there are massive or complex listings of all of the possible variations. Airline fares, for example, have so many different possible combinations of services that one literally needs to be an expert in order to figure out the cheapest fare. Sellers of hi-fi sets, home computers, stereo components, and automobiles also use a mass of statistical information so that it is almost impossible to make an accurate comparison of prices. The number of models, plus accessories available, is so confusing that a buyer has great difficulty in comparing prices or shopping around for value. Sellers know this and are there to offer a simple solution ("buy this one") usually after some flattery about the buyer's wisdom.

A large number of items, a great quantity of information, in itself is likely to contribute to confusion. Humans have varying limits to the amount of material they can handle, but, for everyone, there's a saturation point. Our most common problems in dealing with information is the sorting and re-sorting process as we impose structure and organization, as we put things together, as we *compose*. In rhetorical terms, the criteria usually applied here are *unity* (the relation of parts to the whole), *coherence* (the relation of parts to each other), *proportion* (the relative amount, or degree, of the parts appropriate to the purpose).

Not only could a structure be too complex, because there are too many parts, but also a *process* could be too complex, too difficult, too hard for a person to achieve. Daniel Bell, in *The Coming of Post-Industrial Society,* in speaking about the new "information society," listed four problems new to contemporary society: the sheer amount of information; the increasing technical nature of such information; the need for mediation or journalistic interpretation of it; and, finally, the human limits: "There is an outer limit to the span of control of the bits of information an individual can process at one time. There is equally an outer limit to the amount of information about events one can absorb (or the fields or interests one can pursue)." Whether we're talking about a political procedure or a how-to-do-it assembly plan, a process can be too complicated if it has: (1) too many *steps;* (2) too many *decisions* (that is, options, alternatives, possibilities, branching points); (3) too many *simultaneous* sequences going on; (4) too many *intersections,* points at which simultaneous sequences must be in "sync." None of these factors necessarily creates confusion, but the potential for confusion increases as the number of these factors increase. In addition, relating to the sequence of a process, there are such commonplace errors as: *non sequiturs, wrong cues, circular reasoning, false choice* (either/or), and *circumlocution.*

Closely related to the *amount* of items involved in an overload situation is the *speed* at which they appear. Confusion is more likely to occur when people are rushed, in a hurry, in a crisis situation. Haste makes waste. The urgency plea in "the pitch" is designed to encourage fast action, quick response, without contemplation, or second-thoughts. But the greater the speed, the more probable the error. To reduce confusion caused by such urgency, prior planning is necessary. Hospitals and military organizations, for example, routinely practice disaster plans or emergency plans already laid out in preparation for a crisis. People have to anticipate the possible scenarios of what will occur, and prepare appropriate structures and sequences to respond to the various options. Then, such advance plans have to be rehearsed, tried out at a slow speed in a non-crisis situation. The accelerating speed of change is the theme of Alvin Toffler's *Future Shock:* "For education the lesson is clear," Toffler says, "its prime objective must be to increase the individual's 'cope-ability'—the speed and economy with which he can adapt to continual change."

Overload. Extreme confusion can cause a kind of mental paralysis, a stasis, an inability to act or to decide. Such a feeling of *overload* has a debilitating effect on people; commonly we describe our feelings in terms of being *stalled, stuck, stranded, bogged down, frozen, mired, hung up.* Complexity of thought leading to a mental paralysis is not a new problem (e.g., Shakespeare's Hamlet, Dostoevsky's "underground man"); yet, such overload in some respects is a uniquely modern problem because before television never have so many people been exposed to so much information and so many conflicting views. In the past, literacy and education were necessary for anyone to encounter uncommon ideas or a large body of information. Today, the "information explosion" doesn't simply mean that more information is being *produced,* but that it is also being *distributed* to new audiences of millions of people.

Red Tape. "Red tape" has become the symbol of confusion in the modern world, suggesting any kind of delay or confusion involving the processes or procedures in governmental bureaucracies or large organizations. Usually the term implies two characteristics, *quantity* and *obliqueness:* too much of something (paperwork, forms, copies, steps, procedures, revisions, waiting periods, people involved, etc.) done too indirectly (runaround, wild goose chase). "Red tape" is an easy target to criticize, a scapegoat. Not only do cartoonists have a heyday (paperwork piles, maze diagrams, etc.), but any outsider can criticize the current administration as having "too much" paperwork. In addition, some corporations (e.g. Mobil Oil) affected by regulations keep up a steady stream of anti-regulatory advertisements stressing the horror stories of "red tape" and bureaucratic bungling. Waste and inefficiency are almost universally condemned by business leaders and politicians who plead for the elimination of "red tape." But it's not that easy. Because, as Howard Kaufman points out, in *Red Tape: Its Origin, Uses and Abuses,* much of the paperwork that the federal government generates is not an abnormal growth, which can be cured or pruned away, but is a direct result of some of the ideals of our society: compassion and representativeness.

Compassion leads government to prevent people from hurting each other. In the marketplace situation, a mass of regulations seeks to assure the purity of food, the safety of drugs, the honesty of advertising, the safety of toys, cars, railroads, airplanes, and so on. Compassion also spawns programs to help the poor, the aged, the blind, the disabled, the old, the unemployed, the victims of storms and droughts, and so on. Once the mandate is given, the "red tape" will follow, as Kaufman says: "The moment a government program for a specified group gets started, legislation and administrative directives and court battles proliferate. It is essential to define who is in the group and who is not. The amounts of benefits and the criteria for determining who in the group is eligible for which amount must be established. Procedures for requesting benefits, for processing such applications, for distributing the benefits, and for settling disputes with applicants over their entitlements have to be set up. Preparations must be made to defend actions in court and to justify them to legislators representing disappointed constituents."

Representativeness leads government to be responsible. Procedures for due process (e.g., Affirmative Action, Equal Opportunity) create a great deal of paperwork and red tape to insure equity. Disclosure regulations and public access rules make up another major body of regulations. Finally, the needed controls against dishonesty (theft, bribery, payoffs, embezzlement) account for many rules. Kaufman emphasizes: "Much of the oft-satirized clumsiness, slowness, and complexity of government procedures is merely the consequence of all these precautions."

Confusion will exist in any democratic group (committee or nation) in which the various elements are free, and vying for power. In such situations, the compromises and tradeoffs among the various groups will result in: (1) multiple goals, (2) ambiguously-stated goals (vague enough to please everyone); or (3) shifting goals and priorities as different factions stress differently; (4) procedures and laws with multiple exceptions, changes, amendments, and revisions. Democracy by its nature produces such confusion, waste and inefficiency as "red tape." One answer to such confusion is simply to abolish choice and freedom, impose order. To eliminate "red tape," get a dictator, get a government which doesn't have to account to anyone where the money goes, or if its plans are fair to all groups involved, or doesn't have to justify anything. Dictators can cut through "red tape" by fiat. But another response can be to recognize the problem, tolerate the trade-offs, and work to decrease the *degree* of confusion: operational definitions can be agreed upon, routine processes can be standardized, jargon can be discouraged. The real challenge today is to learn how to cope with the reality of a growing amount of paperwork and "red tape." Without expecting miracles, quick cures, or easy solutions, people need to keep trying to reduce waste, inefficiency, and confusion in such large organizations. Maintenance and housekeeping tasks like this are not very glamorous, but are essential to sustaining any system.

To recap: The Intensify/Downplay schema is a useful device to sort out and focus on the various ways people intensify some elements of communication and downplay others. **Repetition** is comforting to the audience, useful in any learning, helpful in bonding groups; simple repetition is the basis of many persuasion campaigns. **Association** techniques intensify by linking (1) the idea, person, or product with (2) something already loved or desired by (3) the intended audience (In attacks, with something already hated or feared); thus, the importance for audience analysis: polls, surveys, market research. Such associations are most commonly done by the appropriate choice of words and nonverbals, the speakers used (presenters, endorsers), the references, allusions, and attributions made. **Composition** intensifies by the choice of words (including figures of speech), the patterns and variations of words in sentences, the arrangement and strategy of larger structures (as in "the pitch" in advertising, or "the pep talk" in some political rhetoric). People downplay elements of communication: **Omission,** especially, by concealing "bad" effects and their causes, influences the audience's choice and decision-making process. **Diversion** downplays the main issues by intensifying side-issues; trivial, irrelevant, or deliberately distracting, ranging from nasty *ad hominem* attacks to pleasant humor. **Confusion** downplays key issues by making them too obscure or complicated to understand. Confusion is caused when things are unclear (through error or ambiguity), unfamiliar (words, procedures), too variable (frequency and speed of change), and too complex (quantity of information or parts; the intricacy of a process), often causing overload. Although the symbol of modern confusion is "red tape," it needs to be seen as a necessary evil if we are to operate in a complex society.

5

"THE PITCH":
THE MOST COMMON PATTERN
OF PERSUASION IN
ADVERTISING

"The pitch" is an old American slang term, variously defined as "a set talk designed to persuade" *(American Heritage Dictionary);* "an often high-pressure sales talk; advertisement" *(Webster's New Collegiate);* "a line of talk, such as a salesman uses to persuade customers" *(Webster's New World).* Now, "the pitch" is my term for describing a five-part strategy as the *basic pattern* of persuasion in that large quantity of advertising emphasizing *non-rational* elements.

Using the pattern of "the pitch" is the *easiest way* to analyze ads: a fingertip 1-2-3-4-5 sequence, easy to memorize, simple to use, complete here with cartoon balloons; yet, sophisticated, elegant, and accurate. Some people will recognize that "the pitch" is akin to the traditional pattern emphasizing *rational* persuasion, the classical oration *(exordium, narration, confirmation, refutation, peroration).* Other formulas (such as "AIDA") and other analyses (such as Monroe's "Motivated Sequence") have focused on the patterns of persuasion in advertising. But none are as complete and systematic, nor designed for the *receivers* of the messages: the average citizen and consumer.

ATTENTION-GETTING

Hundreds of thousands of ads compete for our attention. Today, over 42,000 *new* TV commercials are produced each year, making up only a small portion of the total number of ads we see and hear. Billions of dollars are spent on a process of persuasion in which a very critical step is the initial point of contact between the persuader and the audience. The first part of "the pitch" is the *attention-getter: Hi!*

You can't persuade if no one's listening or watching.

First, an ad has to get attention; *finally,* an effective ad has to get response. But *first,* an ad has to be heard or seen.

Attention-getting can refer to: (1) *Physical attention-getters*—the simple signals to our senses—lights, colors, sounds, motions; (2) *Emotional attention-getters*—words or images with strong emotional associations—such as pretty faces, pets, babies and cute kids, and natural scenery; (3) *Cognitive attention-getters*—a wide variety of things appealing to our intellect and curiosity, such as news, lists, displays, advice, and stories. Anytime our attention has been focused on *one* ad, or anytime we can remember the brand name, corporation name, logo or signature, of any item, among the hundreds of thousands of competing ads, then the attention-getters have been effective.

All three of these categories involve a focusing, or selective narrowing, of our thought and consciousness. All three aspects often coexist and are interrelated. Most effective ads have many things going at once, multiple and simultaneous appeals. In order to understand ads better, we have to take them apart in smaller bits.

In analyzing any ad, remember that the typical 30-second spot television commercial is the *synthesis,* the end result, of months of work by a skilled team of people putting it together: writers, artists, designers, camera crews, a whole host of technicians and specialists, and often, market researchers, behavioral psychologists, advisors, and consultants. Thus, much has gone into the making of an ad, and much could be said about any ad. One way to start analyzing an ad is to look at the openers, the attention-getters.

CONFIDENCE-BUILDING

Everyone gets information from other people. We often believe a message simply on the basis of our belief in, or liking of, the speaker. If we already like the speaker, it's likely we'll like what the speaker says.

Establishing trust is basic. All persuaders ("good" or "bad," public or private) can be analyzed in terms of what "image" they project. We believe in, and we buy from, people we trust. Aristotle, over two thousand years ago, claimed that the most effective way to persuade was to project the image *(ethos)* of being: the most effective way to persuade was to project the image *(ethos)* of being:

1) **expert,** that is, knowledgeable, informed, competent, wise, prudent, a person of good judgment and good sense;

2) **sincere,** that is, honest, trustworthy, truthful, open, candid, a person of integrity and good moral character;

3) **benevolent,** that is, friendly to the audience, a friend, an ally, a benefactor, a person of good will, with your interest in mind: "on *your* side."

It would be nice if these qualities were really genuine, but Aristotle points out that it's still *very effective* for the persuader even if there is only the *appearance* of these qualities of expertise, sincerity, and benevolence. In the past, the study of rhetoric focused on the *individual* as a persuader, often discussing how the individual can present the best image. Today, the presentation of "self" is often a *corporate* process as committees within large corporations select the kind of people to be used to present or to endorse their products.

The basic strategy of establishing an *ethos,* or building confidence, is to put the audience in a good mood, trusting and receptive, toward the speaker before the main part of "the pitch" begins. Sometimes this may take place *within* a single ad or message; however, in much advertising today, image-building often takes place in a *wider context*. Frequently, we already know or like the speaker and the brand name. A great deal of long-term conditioning propaganda (various forms of "public relations," "corporate advertising") usually occurs within a society, functioning as a solid base on which to build any specific ad campaign.

DESIRE-
STIMULATING

After *getting attention* ("Hi!") and *establishing confidence* ("Trust Me"), the main part of "the pitch" intensifies *desire* by promising benefits: a pleasure to be gained, a pain to be avoided, a possession to be safeguarded, a problem to be solved. Advertisers often call *this reason why* people want something, the "main selling point." The body (the content, the substance) of most ads involves the *stimulating* and *focusing* of specific human needs and wants: *"You Need."*

The traditional view of advertising, still held by many people, stressed the concept of a "Maker" praising the product; an auto manufacturer, for example, might focus on the "economy" or "utility" of its products. Such a business concept was closely related to the "better mousetrap" idea that all a business had to do was to build a better product and the world would eagerly seek it out. Prior to World War II, most American advertising was thus, **product-oriented.** At best, it informed the public about the genuine merits of products; at worst, it made false and deceptive claims. But, most commonly, it was characterized by superlatives and self-praise: "puffery."

However, by the 1950s, a major shift developed as advertising became increasingly **audience-oriented,** that is, more focused on human desires, the needs and wants of the target audience. This view of advertising emphasizes the concept of the "Persuader" seeking the audience's response. The emphasis shifted away from a focus on the *intrinsic* merits of the product (product-as-hero ads) to a focus on the benefits desired by the buyer. Often, these benefits were the intangible **"added values"** —the status or prestige of a name brand, the promise of popularity or sex appeal, the various dreams and fantasies, hopes and wishes of the audience.

Thus, persuaders must first know what the intended audience likes and dislikes. What *do* people need? Want or desire? No one knows for certain. There's no absolute, fixed list of human needs. Philosophers and psychologists have long tried to analyze such human motivation and behavior. More recently, advertisers and market researchers have spent billions in a search to find out what people like and dislike, why people act.

Such **"market research"** (also called "consumer behavior research," "motivational research," "audience analysis," etc.) is a very important part of the persuasion process. Not all individuals or groups will respond the same way, but researchers seek predictable patterns of behavior by studying specific audiences. What's a "good thing" for one audience may be a "bad thing" for another: ads in *Playboy* are geared differently than those in *Good Housekeeping*. Advertisers try to target a specific audience—by age, sex, race, occupation, income, area, etc., which can be easily measured.

Advertisers thus spend millions each year in opinion polls, surveys, questionnaires, sociological and psychological studies to find out what motivates human behavior, what people like and dislike. Although this extensive research has not produced *exact* answers, we do know enough to predict *probable* patterns and *common* reasons for human behavior.

(The companion book, **The Pitch,** lists and discusses some two dozen categories of human needs and wants, covering nearly every kind of desire analyzed by various psychologists and philosophers: *food, health, sex, security, certitude, territory, belonging, esteem, play, curiosity, creativity, etc.* Furthermore, this book lists and discusses general categories of advertising claims covering nearly every conceivable thing which can be said about the **intrinsic merits** of a product: *Superiority, Quantity, Beauty, Efficiency, Scarcity, Novelty, Stability, Reliability, Simplicity, Utility, Rapidity,* and *Safety.* In addition, these word lists are cross-referenced showing specifically how these are used by some forty kinds of products and services—soft drinks, beer, cosmetics, cars, stereos, home repairs, airlines, etc.—representing thousands of brands today, and billions of dollars worth of advertising. For an overview and brief summary, see "The 30-Second-Spot Quiz" at the end of this book.)

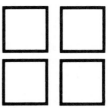

URGENCY-STRESSING

Creating a sense of **urgency** is common in some, but not all, advertising. Some people distinguish between *"hard sell"* and *"soft sell"* advertising depending whether or not there is an urgency plea. Others use the term "hard sell" more broadly to suggest any kind of aggressive techniques, such as intimidating salespeople who brow-beat customers in person-to-person transactions.

The five-part pattern of "the pitch" is presented as the *basic* pattern of advertising, even though many ads *do not use* an urgency plea (#4: "Hurry") or a specific call for action (#5: "Buy"). However, using this five-part pattern emphasizes that the ultimate purpose of advertising is some kind of *response*. By trying to apply this full pattern, the more likely you are to notice when there are omissions, to distinguish between "command propaganda" and "conditioning propaganda."

When the urgency appeal is used, whether in advertising or in political situations, it tends to stress the emotions rather than thoughtful contemplation. Although some urgency claims (such as *real* emergencies, *actual* time limitations) are genuine, many are artificial. They are designed to rush us into action: to buy something, to do something, or to believe something, without adequate thought or critical judgment.

The urgency plea usually seeks to force an issue into a crisis, and to narrow the options to *two: yes or no, stop or go*. Although such a tactic probably forces some people to choose "no" (to decide against the persuader), it also forces a certain number to choose "yes." Logically, the urgency appeal seeks to create a *contradictory* relationship instead of a *contrary* relationship (in which other options are available); psychologically, such urgency seeks to increase our anxiety about losing a benefit.

Advertisers and politicians are not the only ones to use urgency pleas. Poets and lovers have traditionally urged their beloved ones to "seize the day": this *"carpe diem"* theme is common in poetry. No matter who uses the urgency appeal, there's a risk; persuaders are always concerned with the relative effectiveness, in different situations, of the relaxed "soft sell" or the urgent "hard sell."

RESPONSE-
SEEKING

Response is the goal, the basic intent and the final purpose of "the pitch." Advertising, for example, is meant *to sell* a product; attention-getting may be the first important step of the process, but an *effective* ad, ultimately, must provoke a response. Some ads may be clever, witty, humorous, entertaining, informational, or educational: but if they don't achieve their intended goal, if they don't *sell* the product, they are not effective.

Making the response *easy* is one of the persuader's most important jobs. *Skilled persuaders know that it's not very useful to call for a difficult, complex, or impossible response.* Advertisers will seek to make response easy, to limit options, and to use triggering words, simple directives telling us what to do. Mass media response devices include a variety of coupons, contests, blow-in cards, and (800) phone calls. Removing obstacles to the response also includes the removal of *fears* which can be accomplished in the early part of the pitch: establishing confidence in the speakers and products.

"Closing the sale" is the important part in person-to-person selling. Most people have participated in these transactions, in roles both of buyers and sellers. But some people are especially skilled in the art of closing a sale. In selling houses and cars, for example, some sellers are the "closers" who are best able to get the customer to say "yes" and to sign the contract. There's a whole range of nonverbal techniques of salesmanship available: making people feel obligated to buy, or embarrassed not to buy; filling out paperwork for the sale *as if* consent had already been given, ringing up the cash register, or asking about "extra" information ("What color do you want?"; "Will it be cash or charge?") *as if* consent had already been given. In person-to-person selling, the persuader can change tactics and can use different techniques if the buyer doesn't respond. But in advertising in the mass media, the persuader doesn't have the same kind of feedback. It's much *more difficult* to get response, but it's also much *more economical*.

pep talk *n:* usu. brief, high-pressure, and emotional talk designed to influence or encourage an audience.

Webster's New Collegiate Dictionary

6

THE PEP TALK

The term "pep talk" is most commonly associated with the pep rallies before the big football games, or the coach's inspiring speech at half-time in the locker room, or the sales manager's enthusiastic meetings instilling a competitive spirit encouraging the staff to greater efforts to sell more, to do more, or to beat their rivals. But in this book, the term "pep talk" is going to be used more broadly and metaphorically to suggest a very common pattern in a great deal of social and political persuasion.

Political, as used here, suggests not only our domestic party politics (Democrat, Republican; national, state, and local politics) and international political issues (Communism, etc.), but also, in the broadest sense, any grouping together for a goal, a purpose, a cause. Thus, this pattern can usefully help to analyze civil rights and environmental issues, party politics and neighborhood citizen's groups, union strikes and company sales meetings, picket lines and protestors, special interest groups and "single issue" candidates, and often rumors and "junk mail."

The "pep talk," as used here, is that pattern of persuasion used to organize and direct the energy of a group toward *commited collective action:* commonly a sequence of (1) the Threat, (2) the Bonding, (3) the Cause, (4) the Response.

Whether the cause or the group is "good" or "bad," important or trivial, the pattern will be basically the same. The *intent* of a "pep talk" may be the persuader's malicious exploitation of the naive, or it may be the most genuine altruism and benevolence, but the pattern will be basically the same. The *content* of the "pep talk" may be true or false, accurate or erroneous, but the pattern will be basically the same. The *consequences* may be beneficial or harmful, to the individual or to others, but the pattern will be basically the same.

In reality, the "pep talk" is not as tidy, nor as sequential as this 1,2,3,4 pattern. Observers come in at different times, or hear only brief fragments. On one hand, we're probably accustomed to the bonding efforts of our own group (nationality, religious, ethnic, etc.), on the other hand, watching the TV news, we're apt to see only a brief exposure of some other group's "cause" without really knowing much about their whole set of beliefs and attitudes, hopes and fears. Typically, we see bits and fragments of the "pep talk," odds and ends.

Here's a basic structure to help sort out these fragments of political language and relate them to their part in a process of purposeful communication. Consider first some of the possible benefits and dangers involved in such "pep talks," then note the qualifications and variations: for example, the differences and overlaps between "the pitch" and "the pep talk." Then, the four subsequent chapters will explain more and illustrate the various parts.

Using simple terms such as "pep talk," (and later, "horror stories" and "atrocity pictures") helps to clarify a complex process. Some people may feel that this informal language is flippant or frivolous. But the intent here is not to minimize the genuine human pain and suffering often related to such "pep talks" in the past, but to innoculate for the future. If, by the use of a simple pattern and memorable phrases, it is possible to clarify and to simplify these basic techniques for large audiences, especially younger audiences, then it would be cynical *not* to do so, or to restrict such information to an elite few.

For the past few generations, for the first time in human history, broadcasting can link persuaders with a mass audience. Not only do many corporations seek after this audience, using the "pitch" to sell their products, but also many political groups and "causes" would like to organize and direct the energies of this large audience.

In the future, as in the past, people will be asked to join in a good cause, or to fight for God and country, or to defend themselves and to protect others from an evil threat. A "cause" can involve mankind's most noble sentiments. But, our altruistic impulses can also be exploited, manipulated, abused by others.

Young people are always the prime target for such a "pep talk":
they have a great deal of idealism, enthusiasm—and inexperience. It's
useful to know some patterns of persuasion, and to teach them to the
young. It helps to clarify choice and decisions. There are times when
we may wish to commit ourselves to a cause. If we are aware of some
patterns, our decisions may be more based on the merit of the cause
rather than on the slick delivery, the skill, the cleverness or the cha-
risma of the persuader. If we know the form, we can concentrate on the
substance.

The propagandist does not want our thought, our contemplation, our
analysis, our advance awareness of the techniques; the propagandist
wants a response, action.

Some persuasion emphasizes the positive or upbeat: some conservative persuasion, for example, would stress joy, contentment, and satisfaction for the "good" possessed, for the blessings received, as we often
hear on Thanksgiving Day, Christmas, Fourth of July; some progressive
persuasion, for example, might stress growth, progress, and achievement,
the optimistic hopes and dreams of a situation getting better ("I have a
dream . . ."). There's a great deal of such ceremonial rhetoric, appropriate to many situations, and we expect it and hear it in many instances in
which the audience is to be inspired or praised, calmed or consoled.
Similarly, in religious persuasion, some preachers might focus on the
glory of God, the beauty of the universe, or heavenly delights. But, other
preachers have been known to talk about hellfire and damnation. Perhaps
the "pep talk" might be the secular equivalent of such hellfire preaching:
starting with a problem, working on the emotions, and leading to solutions being suggested.

If there are varieties of religious experience, so also there are varieties of secular experience. Some people would prefer hearing "good
news" all the time; others would object to such a thing as being unrealistic and Pollyannish. Some people may not like a "pep talk"—some may
object to its negative emphasis, others to its emotional intensity, others to
its seeming artificiality. Without denying the virtues of positive inspira-
tional rhetoric, the emphasis in this book is on the negative: the conservative rhetoric stressing anxiety and fear of losing the "good" and the
progressive rhetoric stressing anger, resentment, and frustration about not
having the "good" or seeking relief from the "bad." The attempt here is
not to endorse or condemn what persuaders do, but to observe and
describe it.

Good results, good intentions.

"Pep talks" can be beneficial, can be the means to good effects.
There are, genuinely, many "good causes." Many things which need to
be done in order to make this a better society can only be done by
organized group effort. Individuals working alone simply cannot do some

things which people can do collectively. Various methods of organizing people are possible: a business corporation can offer financial rewards, for example; or a powerful government can simply command by force. Yet, even without such inducements as money or guns, human energies can be organized toward collective action simply by skillful combination of words and images, a "pep talk."

Assume that all or most "pep talks" are made with *good intentions,* that is, the speakers are sincere believers in the merits of their "good cause." (Some persuaders may not be so; some may be manipulators or con men.) However, "good intentions" do not necessarily guarantee good results. But, if it is assumed that everyone (even scoundrels and rascals) can justify their actions as being based on "good intentions," one need not waste effort trying to establish the persuader's motives; be concerned instead with the *consequences.* More specifically, be aware of the potentially *bad* effects of "pep talks."

"Pep talks" can cause harm to great numbers of people. In a world with very real danger of wars among nations, terrorist assaults by individuals and small groups, and sophisticated weapons easily available, it's very risky to stimulate fears or incite quick responses based on emotional feelings. The obvious, overt danger is that of stirring up hatreds and triggering off the Crazies. The more subtle danger is the general conditioning within a wider society in preparation for officially-sanctioned wars.

"Pep talks" can be harmful to individuals. What may benefit the group, may harm the individual. All of us owe some debt of loyalty to the many groups to which we belong because we inherit or share in their benefits. Yet, any time a person gives up responsibility to any group, the person risks a loss of self. Yet, it happens. Some people with low self-esteem find their comfort in belonging to a group, identifying with it, and following it with unquestioning loyalty.

Self-righteousness is another danger. People who are "true believers" in the absolute virtue of their own "cause" are, at best, obnoxious; at worst, dangerous. The world has seen too many wars, slaughters and massacres carried out in the name of God or the cause of Justice. The "pep talk" encourages polarized thinking, dichotomies, the "good guys/ bad guys" mentality; it encourages people who are narrow and rigid authoritarians to believe that they are the "good guys," the Truth-Possessors with an authority to impose the "right way" on others.

Individuals can be harmed emotionally by a constant repetition of the "threats" and warnings given in "pep talks." Just as some young people, for example, can be overstimulated by the acquisitve demands ("buy this . . . get that") of commercial advertising, and end up being always dissatisfied and frustrated, so also some people can be overstimulated by a constant repetition of threats, warnings, bad news, and urgent pleas. A sensitive young person, for example, encountering a daily dose of environmentalist pleas (pictures of dead seals, dead whales, dead birds, dead dogs, etc.) can be overwhelmed by this depressing sight.

Often these are undue fears, unreasonable anxieties, because the degree, proportion, or relationship of the harm has been exaggerated out of context. Even though any single ad or any single "pep talk" could be defended as being tolerable, the *cumulative impact* of thousands of single-issue "cause" group ads, each intensifying their own warnings and problems, can be harmful to the sensibilities of the audience which receives them all. Our children grow up not only blitzed by commercial advertising pleasantly promising dreams of the good life, but also saturated with horrible warnings and nightmare images.

Cynicism is one result. Sometimes young people completely accept a "pep talk" at face value, literally, without reservations. Later, they may feel that they had been deceived, duped, or exploited. Such disillusionment often causes a bitter reaction: cynicism, apathy, a total rejection of previous beliefs. Problems of credibility also exist when so many extreme warnings are made about so many things that some people simply overload and discount everything. Many people scoff at FDA warnings about cancer-causing chemicals ("next thing they'll say is that *everything* causes cancer" is the cliché) without recognizing the real complexity. Many people simply disregard, block out, any warnings about nuclear war as being either unthinkable or unbelievable.

We not only live in an age of real problems and real threats, but we also live in an age in which the professional persuaders are right with us, daily and constantly, often to warn us about these problems and ask us to do something about them. A hundred years ago, even sixty years ago, the average citizen would seldom experience a skillfully constructed "pep talk" during the course of a lifetime. Today, the average citizen is likely to see bits and fragments of one every time the TV is turned on, and is likely to get a complete "pep talk" daily in the mailbox.

The Pitch, the Pep Talk, and other persuasive attempts

Both the "pitch" and the "pep talk" seek a response, but the basic difference between the two is that the "pep talk" seeks a *committed collective action*. That is, the "pitch" leads to a simple response (usually, to buy); the "pep talk" asks a person to *join with others, for a cause.*

To relate these techniques with other persuasive attempts, consider first the *timing* of the response, using the terms *Command* propaganda which seeks an immediate response *(Now!)* and *Conditioning* propaganda which seeks to mold public opinions, assumptions, beliefs, attitudes on a long-term basis as the necessary climate or atmosphere for a future response *(Later!)*

Both the "pitch" and the "pep talk" are *Command* propagandas, seeking immediate actions. The chart (below) relates these two concepts with terms used by others to describe other kinds of persuasive attempts.

"Command propaganda" is the easiest to recognise. Here both the "pitch" and the "pep talk" are types of such persuasions seeking an immediate response.

"Conditioning propaganda" is more subtle, harder to analyze or limit; many different names have been used to describe persuasion which seeks to create, shape, mold basic opinions, assumptions, beliefs, attitudes, myths, worldviews.

	NOW!	LATER
Timing of Response	(Command)	(Conditioning)

Kind of Response		
action	"THE PITCH"	"soft sell" "public relations" (PR) "publicity" "institutional advertising" "corporate advertising" "image building" "promotion" "goodwill" advertising
committed collective action	"THE PEP TALK"	"political education" (Lenin) "basic propaganda" (Goebbels) "sub-propaganda" (Ellul) "pre-propaganda" "education" "indoctrination" "awareness" "consciousness raising"

The persuader's goals
are to get others...*to do* the "right" acts...and *to think* the "right" way.

In reality, such neat categories do not exist. Borderline cases are common, between command and conditioning propagandas, and between the "pitch" and the "pep talk." Adding to the complexity of any real situation are some common basic factors which can be described in terms of *multiples, mixtures,* and *mistakes.*

Multiples. Multiple persuasion attempts are usually made at the same time, either to the same audience using different pitches, or to different audiences using the same pitch. In auto ads, for example, there may be a dozen different sets of ads prepared for different audiences: some ads stressing a "safety" angle for old folks, "sporty" for young folks; some ads with urban backgrounds, some with rural; some emphasizing economy, others stressing prestige, and all could be talking about the same car. In such an advertising campaign, a basic premise is that most people only notice ads directed at "them" in such smaller sub-categories, and ignore the ads directed at other sub-categories.

Multiple association devices are also used in politics. In a typical political campaign, for example, the major parties will create and fund a whole host of various committees and "front organizations" and sub-groups (such as Farmers For Reagan, Polish-Americans For Reagan, Italian-Americans For Reagan, Union Members for Reagan, etc.) not only to give the illusion of widespread support, but also to appeal to those specific ethnic, occupational, or interest groups. Political protest movements also have a multiplicity of propagandas going on at the same time (e.g., Vietnam Veterans Against the War, Another Mother for Peace, Clergy and Laity United for Peace, Students for Peace, etc.); such diversity is sometimes a genuine grassroots movement, sometimes manipulated by others.

Mixtures. In any political campaign, there's likely to be a mixture of the "pitch" directed at an outside public, and the "pep talk" directed at an insider audience—the party regulars. In religious persuasion, there's likely to be one kind of evangelizing, spreading the good news, to others, and another kind of preaching to the saved. In both of these examples, we are likely to see a "recruiting sequence": first, the "pitch" to bring in new members, converts; then, the "pep talk" to keep them bonded and to direct them toward a new action. Or we might find a re-directing sequence: first, a "pep talk" to bond for one cause; then, once bonded, re-directed to another cause. Or we might find an escalation sequence: a series of "pep talks" leading to increasingly more difficult actions, "raising the ante."

Thus far, we've been assuming that these patterns and variations can be applied to *truthful* and *sincere* attempts at persuasion; but they can also be applied to *deceitful* and *insincere* "pitches" and "pep talks." A scoundrel, for example, may use a "pep talk" to bond people for a political or religious cause, simply as a prelude to a "pitch" to get the audience to buy something or donate money. Sometimes this is obvious and recognizable—if the politician or minister walks away with bulging pockets stuffed with money. But, more likely, it's difficult to detect, and the real borderline cases will be between clever scoundrels and true believers.

Mixed motives are common in almost every human action. Multiple goals are possible, simultaneously, in almost every human endeavor. Consider, for example, the many *reasons* for, and the *results* sought in, "corporate advertising" in such organizations as Mobil, U.S. Steel, Dow Chemical, IBM, Xerox, Union Carbide, and other corporate giants. Such "corporate advertising" (*not* ads for specific consumer products) is also called, by various writers, "public relations," "institutional advertising," "image building," "goodwill advertising," and other related synonyms.

Mixed Motives in Corporate Advertising

label	purpose	audience
synonyms: "corporate advertising"	to sell, indirectly, consumer products by building awareness (Hi!) and reputation (Trust Me) of parent corporation, brand names, logos.	consumers
"institutional advertising" "public relations"	to encourage new stockholders to invest money, existing stockholders to retain stock.	investors; financial community
"image advertising" "goodwill"	to increase employee morale, higher productivity and work quality; to attract good new employees.	employees; potential employees
"publicity"	to influence, indirectly, legislation and regulation; to get citizens and their representatives friendly and favorably disposed toward the corporation; to ward off taxes, controls, regulations, limits, etc.	citizens: voters, legislators & regulators
"advocacy advertising" is the closely related *Command* propaganda here seeking a specific immediate response.	to influence, directly, legislation or regulation: "seeking specific actions, explicit directives: "Write your Senator . . . Vote for . . . "	citizens: voters, legislators & regulators

Note that all four general purposes (above the line) could exist at the same time; most corporations defend their expenditures (to their stockholders and to the general public) with such explanations. In actual practice, there are no problems with the overlaps among these four categories. Serious "borderline" problems occur however in that vague area between *command* propaganda and *conditioning* propaganda, between "advocacy advertising" and "corporate advertising." Just where is the boundary between spending money to have the public "like" (tolerate, accept) the corporation (or the policies, the goals of the corporation) and spending money to have the public "advocate" (support, endorse) the goals and policies of the corporation. Clarifying the issues at this borderline involves high stakes because of the tax laws and the problems of corporate influence—complex legal problems which do not fit neatly into any existing jurisdiction, but are overlapping concerns of the FTC, FCC, and IRS. (As the first step in approaching this problem, the Senate's Subcommittee on Administrative Practice has published a whopping, 2133 pp., *Sourcebook on Corporate Image and Corporate Advocacy Advertising*.)

Another factor which makes it difficult to deal with the borderline between command propaganda, seeking an immediate response, and conditioning propaganda, preparing the way for a future response, is that all of this is an *ongoing process,* constantly in motion. Any particular piece of information may be "news" to the *receivers* or may call for an urgent action, but the *sender* may know months or years ahead about the content and timing of a long-term propaganda campaign.

The "pitch" and the "pep talk" may be useful to help understand some of the persuasive messages we receive, but we must be prepared to see the variations and the "surface texture." In the United States alone, for example, there are literally several hundred thousand commercial products which advertise, and there are probably more than that number of sources of political, religious, ethnic, and social propagandas. We live in this environment of competing propagandas, and the hubbub of this marketplace of ideas can get confusing at times.

Mistakes. Because of all of this complexity, persuaders can make mistakes. Every persuader seeks to be effective, but this is not always the result. Sometimes ads come "too close" to us, get palsy-walsy, treating us as if we were already friendly, assuming our interest and involvement, taking our assent for granted. This kind of error in persuasion causes the audience to back off, to reject the overfriendly advances as being offensive, cloying, too saccharine. Sometimes this is caused by a mishandling of the "confidence" (Trust Me) part of the "pitch." Sometimes it's caused by using a "pep talk" instead of a "pitch," in a situation which is not appropriate. Sometimes, in a "pep talk," errors in persuasion can occur because of an incomplete bonding or a premature "response" plea.

Delivery. Although this book concentrates on patterns and the structure underneath, the "surface" tactics of delivery or execution are equally important. Simply to point out the pattern doesn't mean that everyone has the skill to do it well. Effectiveness varies with the speaker, the audience, and the situation. Sometimes an attempt at a "pep talk" falls flat; the audience may not be moved or may react against it as being too "gung ho" or too "rah-rah" or as "laying it on too thick."

If the bonding is incomplete, if the audience doesn't genuinely feel a part of the group, feel threatened by the outside, then the pep talk may be ineffective or backfire. In the example below, an outsider (the reporter who labels city employees as "payrollers") writes for other outsiders describing a "pep talk" given by Mayor Michael Bilandic campaigning for re-election in Chicago in 1979:

BILANDIC LIKENS WOES TO JESUS' CRUCIFIXION
By William Griffin

Mayor Bilandic exhorted Democratic precinct captains Wednesday to get out and work for his re-election, likening criticism of his administration to the crucifixion of Jesus, the mass murders of Jews, and the recent collapses of foreign governments.

His voice frequently cracking with emotion, Bilandic warned 500 payrollers attending the precinct captains luncheon in the Bismarck Hotel that his critics were out to destroy the Democratic party here.

"We've withstood challenges in the past," he said. "They've tried to take it away from us before, but they couldn't."

Bilandic then compared the criticism of him and the party organization with the persecution of Jesus and his disciples.

"In the early history of Christianity, you see a leader, starting with 12 disciples. They crucify the leader and made martyrs of the others.

"And what was the result"?

"Christianity is bigger and stronger than it was before."

The mayor went on to make similar comparisons between his administration's problems and the killing of six million Jews by Nazis in World War II, the oppression of Poles, and the enslavement of blacks. . . .

Bilandic told the captains that his re-election was not so important to him personally as it was for the Democratic Party to keep control of city government. He then pledged his allegiance to the machine:

"I'm proud to be your friend. I'll stand side by side with you, shoulder to shoulder and face any task, fight any foe, solve any problems. I'll go from here to hell and back for you. That's what we're going to do. And we're going to do it together."

Bilandic credited the party organization for the elections in recent years of blacks, latinos, and women to high offices. They were elected, he said, without the endorsements of newspapers or by becoming a "darling of the media."

Bilandic then cited the recent collapse of governments in Iran and Cambodia as examples of what could happen to Chicago.

"The same seeds of subversion are being planted right here in Chicago," he said. "The same attempt to destroy is just as strong here today as it is in the foreign intrigue situations."

"The people of Chicago are too smart to let it happen. They won't let it happen. I won't let it happen."

As he made that final vow, Bilandic's voice cracked to a falsetto. At that point, some of the precinct captains, who had been looking at one another incredulously as Bilandic made his dramatized comparisons, lowered their heads to conceal laughter.

The high voice and excited delivery contrasted with the cool and confident-appearing Michael Bilandic shown in a 15-minute campaign film that preceded his speech.

Several veteran politicians said it appeared that Bilandic's speech was nothing more than a page borrowed from the late Mayor Daley, who gave excited speeches at precinct captains luncheons to work up the workers. . . .

A Borderline Case: the "Scare-and-Sell" Ad

In contrast to most advertising which deals with our dreams, promises, and hopes, some health and safety products (such as fire and life insurance, travelers' checks, burglar alarms, over-the-counter medicines, deodorants, etc.) often start from our nightmares, threats, and fears: the *"scare-and-sell"* approach.

Thus, the ad may begin with a "threat," and in this way is similar to the beginning of the "pep talk." But the "scare-and-sell" approach *does not* ask for bonding or commitment to a cause. It's a pitch, a simple sales transaction: "You have a problem; here's the solution."

The problem is emphasized, then the solution is offered ("anxiety arousal and satisfaction"), but there is no demand on us to give anything other than our money. It's easiest to recognize this in ads which dramatize physical fears (death, fire, loss of money, etc.), but we also have emotional fears (loneliness, rejection, etc.) that are stirred by many ads. The basic "translation" of many ads might read: "You'll be unloved, unwanted, rejected . . . unless you buy our soap, toothpaste, deodorant, hairspray, etc."

A Borderline Case: The Selling of the Candidates

Following the lead of books such as Daniel Boorstin's *The Image* and Joe McGinnis' *The Selling of the President,* and movies such as *The Candidate,* there has been increasing criticism about the packaging or marketing or selling of modern political candidates as if they were commercial products: bars of soap, tubes of toothpaste. Critics cry that "Madison Avenue" has taken over: slick professionals, crass manipulators, PR specialists and media technicians who know how to create and manipulate an "image," a "television personality," a "plastic person" who looks like and talks like what the polls say the voters want. There has been a great deal of commentary about these media mercenaries or rented rhetoricians.

Usually such complaints about modern political campaigns are set in contrast to romanticized images of old-time party politics—of Fourth of July speeches, political rallies, orators on the gazebos, friendly waving crowds, torchlight parades and bandwagons, handprinted homemade signs, and all the hoopla and ballyhoo which we associate with political campaigns in the days before radio and television. Most of this old time politicing can best be described in terms of the *"pep talk":* the great emphasis was on the bonding of the group, for a cause. Party politics emphasized the group; later, "issue politics" of the 1960s also could be described in terms of the "pep talk" because of its emphasis on "principles," on the "cause."

But the approach of those who are creating the "image" candidates can best be described in terms of the *"pitch."* Most of these ads are *not* asking the voters to join the party, work for the party, commit themselves to a cause, but are simply asking for a one-shot "purchase"—a vote. (And if that purchase isn't satisfactory, there'll be a new improved model for the next election.)

We are likely to see more of the "pitch" in future political campaigns because of the decline in political party membership, party loyalty; the increase in uncommitted "Independent" voters; and because it is ultimately cheaper and easier to use the technology of the mass media than to sustain an ongoing organization.

In the future, we're still likely to see the "pep talk" given to insiders (usually by means of meetings, rallies, letter mailings, in-house publications), but the use of the "pitch" will increase in messages directed to outsiders—to the uncommitted public—seeking only their vote on election day.

However, this new kind of "image" campaigning may always be considered a borderline case between a "pitch" and a "pep talk," because it is likely such "pitches" will have the surface appearance of a "pep talk" by using such *commitment words* ("dedicate yourself . . . join us . . . in our noble cause"), but in fact seeking or specifying *no other response than voting.* When somebody asks us to canvas a neighborhood, ring doorbells, fold envelopes, work hard and give time for the cause, we are likely to be hearing part of a "pep talk"; but when we see the 30-second-spot on TV, we're likely to be seeing the "pitch."

Hired Hands and True Believers. No one yet knows the full implications of this new "image" campaigning. Those who use the "pitch" in political advertising are open to charges of being cynical, calculating manipulators; those who use the "pep talk" are feared as zealots, fanatics, extremists. But some political observers are saying that we have passed the era of conflicts between political parties, and of conflicts between opposing ideologies, and now are witnessing the conflict between technicians: which team of specialists can best package the product and sell it.

To recap: The "pep talk" is used here to label a common pattern of persuasion used to organize and direct the energy of a group toward committed collective action; commonly, the sequence: (1) the Threat; (2) the Bonding; (3) the Cause; (4) the Response. Regardless of intent, consequences, significance, or content, the pattern is basically the same, albeit we often see only bits and fragments as reported and edited by others. "Pep talks" can be beneficial as aids to directing human effort; but "pep talks" can also be harmful to society (inciting hatreds, wars) and to the individual (irresponsibility, self-righteousness, undue fears, cynicism). The "pep talk" is similar to the "pitch" in that both are *command* propagandas seeking a response; but the "pitch" leads to a simple transaction while the "pep talk" asks a person to join with others for a good cause. A static diagram is limited in suggesting the reality of multiple and mixed persuasion techniques and motives (illustrated by the mixed motives of "corporate ads") and in the reality of mistakes in planning and in delivery (illustrated by Mayor Bilandic's speech). Borderline cases exist: some commercial products using ads stressing fears, the "scare-and-sell" technique; some slick political ads "selling candidates" as if they were commercial products.

7

THE THREAT

The first part of the "pep talk" is *the warning:* alerting the audience, by means of words and images; "making problems" for them by intensifying the "bad" of an immediate or potential danger, harm or threat.

People have predictable fears. We can identify in advance a whole cluster of common kinds of fears that most people are likely to have. Persuaders know these and can intensify these fears, stirring us up emotionally to an excited state of readiness: ready to be bonded into a group, channeled and moved to action. This chapter presents first some *general* ways of intensifying words and images (name-calling, "horror stories", "atrocity pictures") and then at some *specific* applications to a group of common predictable fears: death and destruction, domination, invasion, restriction, inequality, and chaos.

People aren't *controlled* by outside persuaders, but audiences can be *influenced.* People aren't *limited* to emotional responses, but audiences can be *moved.* In reality, our world is filled with many persuaders in conflict, vying for our attention and seeking our assent, with a great variety in their credibility and effectiveness. Audiences, too, have different degrees of susceptibility and immunity to these various persuaders.

Yet, the fact remains that people are persuadable by emotional appeals based on their fears. Other writers may create different lists or use different labels, but the basic point is that humans do have a set of *predictable* fears. If persuaders want to get our adrenalin flowing, they know how to do it. They know the things which are likely to stir the emotions and arouse the passions.

Audiences and their Fears

"Pep talks" are directed at audiences with the *same* relationship to a benefit; for example, a conservative "pep talk" is directed to an audience of Haves; a progressive "pep talk" is directed to an audience of Have-Nots. In either case, the bonding of the group and the antagonisms against the opposition may be very effective *within the group* itself, but may sound strange or offensive to outsiders. Sometimes, in fact, a group's "pep talk" is overheard by unfriendly audiences and creates a backlash, inspiring the opponents to do more. Different audiences have different perceptions of what is "good" and what is "bad" as far as specific examples are concerned. However, there are some general statements which are applicable for all.

Absence of the "good" is the basic fear. Haves are afraid of losing the "good" they already possess; to this audience of Haves, conservative persuaders stir up fears of loss: someone else is going to take away what they have, invade their nation or their neighborhood, destroy what they own, take away their "just rewards," upset the existing order. Likewise, Have-Nots are angered at being deprived of the "good" they desire, and fear they will not get relief from the "bad." To this audience of Have-Nots, progressive persuaders intensify their awareness of deprivation and suffering: they point out all the "goods" they don't have, the restrictions placed upon them, the injustices in being denied a "fair share," the corruption and the mismanagement of the existing System.

Haves fear that things will change; Have-Nots fear that things won't change. Haves fear future evils, that things will get worse. Have-Nots fear existing evils, that things won't get any better. Both conservative and progressive rhetoric share the same basic problem/solution pattern. Both stimulate the fears of their audiences on this basic theme of the absence of the "good."

Situations and Problems. Books about problem-solving usually stress that problems only exist within the mind of someone, when that person feels some kind of conflict between *what is* and *what should be*. This "felt difficulty" or "cognitive dissonance" is not the same for everyone. Two people can experience the same situation: for one, it may be a problem; for the other, no problem. Driving in heavy traffic or flying in a plane may be a great problem for some people, nothing at all for others. Millions of people on earth today live without TV sets or indoor plumbing, but this situation may not be a problem if there's no felt difficulty. Yet, an affluent suburbanite with two cars and a swimming pool might feel beset by problems. Problems exist only within the mind of the perceiver.

Persuaders are often "problem makers." Often, their first task is to try to make their audience *aware* of a situation, then to *perceive* it as a problem, *fear* it as a threat to self or group, feel a *responsibility* for doing something, the *ability* to do it, and the *desire,* will, or commitment to do so. Persuaders want to move an audience from a position of ignorance, unconcern, and apathy to that of knowledge, concern, and action. The persuaders job is to create the problem in the audience's perception so that they feel a threat exists, a wrong should be righted, a "bad" should be corrected, a flaw should be repaired: "There's a problem which threatens me; it can be changed; I ought to do something; I'm able to, I want to, and I will."

Many people "don't know they have a problem" until persuaders define it for them; that is, persuaders can give an audience a new insight into an existing situation so that the audience becomes more keenly aware of both the existing realities and the ideal possibilities. Consider the women's movement in the 1970s, for example: a *situation* (unequal pay, discrimination, etc.) had existed for a long time, but not many people saw it as a *problem* (something that shouldn't be, and that could be changed) until there was a great deal of "consciousness raising" by feminists.

Some people have vague anxieties and free-floating anger. "Something's wrong," they think, but they can't put their finger on why they feel dissatisfied or discontented, fearful or angry. Working on this kind of audience, skilled persuaders can stimulate these feelings, channel them and offer suggestions so that the audience accepts the persuaders' definition of the cause of their difficulties.

Thus, persuaders are often problem makers: creating dissonances, stirring up emotions, getting the adrenalin flowing. Or when the tensions and the emotions are already high, the persuaders are concerned with directing and channeling, suggesting problems and offering solutions.

Intensifying the seriousness of the danger, the magnitude of the problem, and the urgency of the situation are common techniques. The greater the problem, the more the need for the solution. In reality, *some* things are very dangerous, but recognize that persuaders usually tend to overstate the danger. We know, for example, that a sure sign of a Pentagon budget request is the flood of preparatory press releases pointing with alarm at growing Soviet strength. Whether saving souls from hellfire, or saving seals from extinction, persuaders know that the greater the threat is intensified, the greater is the need for their remedy.

Powerful governments can intensify a crisis, can "fan the flames," by systematically planting rumors, or releasing news reports of "horror stories" and "atrocity pictures." Agitators, outside of the Establishment, can also use this tactic of deliberate rumors and gossiped "horror stories" to keep the threat intensified. (In contrast, sometimes goverments seek to downplay issues, to calm and soothe, to cool inflammatory rhetoric, by managing the news, withholding information, imposing censorship and restraints, creating "rumor control" centers, etc.)

Accidental arousal of fears is possible. Many racial and ethnic conflicts, for example, have been spontaneous and unplanned; crises have occurred by accident, triggered haphazardly by unpremeditated acts. But such randomness is different, both in kind and degree, from an organized propaganda campaign such as Hitler's persecution of the Jews.

Deliberate, systematic, and intentional manipulation of human fears and hatreds is also possible. Today, because of technological advances, the *potential* danger is far greater than ever in the past. Today, persuaders with the intent to manipulate have better tools to do so. The psychological techniques are more sophisticated to identify what people fear, as are the methods to target audiences precisely and to deliver messages to them instantly and constantly.

Giving the Warning

The "warning alert" of a threat can be made by an official leader of an established group or it can be made unofficially by anyone ("self-appointed"), or by an outsider, someone from a counter-group seeking to re-form a group. If we wish to praise these warning-givers, we can call them "patriots" or "prophets"; if we wish to attack them, we can call them "rabble-rousers" or "agitators."

Within or outside the established order, warning-givers point out a threat to intensify the danger or the evils involved, usually try to blame these problems on one identifiable person or group, the *scapegoat,* on which all of the fears and hatreds can be focused. The warning about a present danger is usually built upon a past history, an accumulation of fears and hatreds, a series of charges, a list of grievances.

Many social animals have warning cries to alert the group to danger. Humans have a much more sophisticated warning system because we perceive so many different kinds of danger. At the simplest level, we have some very explicit warning words (beware, danger, look out, be careful, be alert, attention, watch out) and we can also warn others by using simple sounds and sights (cries, yells, sirens, whistles, bells, flashing lights, waving flags). But most of our more sophisticated warnings also involve (as they will be called here) *"name-calling," "horror stories,"* and *"atrocity pictures."*

"Name-calling"

"Name-calling" is used here to suggest the attack words used to intensify the "bad" of others: emotionally-charged words, slanted, biased, used to express fear and anger and to stir them up in others. If spoken, the tone of voice is often angry or enraged, sneering or mocking.

Everyone has experienced or witnessed such use of language as a spontaneous, unpremeditated response to some situation. Yet, here we point out both some common generic name-calling and some name-calling which specifically intensifies the bad *effects* feared and the *causes* related to them.

Generic name-calling. Several kinds of all-purpose attack words can be used in many contexts. Some are simply the derogatory names, slurs, and insults applied to *other groups,* ethnic, national, or religious. All cultures have such pejorative terms for the various sub-groups within, but the United States is uniquely rich in such a vocabulary (niggers, wops, kikes, chinks, spics, japs, krauts, hunkies, dagos, etc.) because of the complex immigrant experience with so many groups so quickly thrown together. Another large body of generic attack language relates to *sexuality* and *bodily functions;* "dirty words" considered vulgar or taboo, forbidden in polite society, are commonly used as all-purpose insults and invectives. A third major category of generic name-calling relates to words which suggest that the other is *non-human* (monster, brute, savage, animal, dog, rat) or *less-than-fully human* (stupid, ignorant, dumb, jerk). If spoken with great vehemence, the most common word linked with all of these generic insults is the all-purpose adjective, "dirty." The intensity of such name-calling varies; war propaganda is usually the most intense, but there are other "gut issues" such as racial and religious conflicts which stir up intense emotions.

Political name-calling usually focuses on three categories, the opposites of the desired "image." When politicians intensify their own "good," their positive *claims* are that of being competent, trustworthy, and benevolent ("on your side"). Conversely, when politicians intensify the others' "bad," the negative *charges* relate to the undesirable qualities of being *incompetent, untrustworthy,* and *self-seeking* (or, being "owned" by some special interest). Thus, during election campaigns, most name-calling exchanged by candidates for office will seek to discredit a person's image of being competent, trustworthy, and benevolent. Opponents will expose the ignorance, catch the errors, and bring up the scandals of the past. Opponents are likely to focus on a vulnerability, a weak spot, and exaggerate it, by caricature, by satire, by rumors, and by constant repetition of charges in order to destroy credibility, to "poison the well." Expect that the three key charges will be: *incompetency* (e.g., ignorant, unprepared, lazy, unfit, impractical, weak, indecisive, etc.); *untrustworthiness* (e.g., dishonest, unjust, unpredictable, disloyal, etc.); *not benevolent* (e.g., unfriendly, uncaring, selfish, opportunist, working for others, etc.).

If these charges are true and verifiable, they are legitimate criticisms and logically valid. For example, if someone *is* incompetent for the job, it is reasonable for opponents to attack that fault. But, usually the charge of incompetency is simply a general *assertion* of the opponents' opinions and feelings, not a verifiable fact. In most cases, such attacks against the person are invalid, illogical and irrelevant to the issue. But there are some cases in which criticism is valid, logical, and relevant: when the person is the direct, efficient cause of the undesired effect. To provide *evidence* demonstrating that an opponent is incompetent is a legitimate issue in a campaign; to criticize an opponent for physical appearance or some irrelevant factor is an *ad hominem* attack, a logical fallacy, usually defined as an attack against the person rather than on the issue. In the heat of a campaign or a crisis, it's not easy to separate legitimate criticism from invalid *ad hominem* attacks. Large audiences seldom make fine and careful distinctions, especially in stirring situations. Past experience warns us that much of the "name-calling" is likely to be *logically invalid,* but often *rhetorically effective*.

In American politics, although much of the name-calling and *ad hominem* attacks are spontaneous expressions by zealous advocates, there are certain semi-official roles related to the sending and receiving of personal attacks. Usually the candidate or the leader has "clean hands" and does not get involved in such *mudslinging* and *smear campaigns*. Often the "hatchet-man" is a subordinate who does the dirty work of the personal attacks against the opposition; in Nixon's administration, for example, Vice-President Agnew was a notorious "hatchet-man." In contrast, a "lightning rod" is a subordinate who attracts much of the opponents' criticism, diverting it away from the boss; for example, in Reagan's administration, Interior Secretary Watt took much of the criticism for Reagan's policies.

Abstract issues are hard to grasp. Propagandists often focus attention on, and specify some visible, *identifiable* person or group, as the "scapegoat" to blame. Hitler, for example, systematically scapegoated the Jews and orchestrated verbal attacks against them. Some Americans scapegoat other ethnic groups (the blacks, the whites, the Mexicans, the Cubans) which can be easily identified and verbally abused. Very commonly the threat is *personified* in the leader of the opposition. Hatred is directed against the specific person as being the symbolic embodiment of all evils. Fist-shaking mobs, chanting the name of the opponents' leader, or burning the effigies, are common sights on television now. Name-calling usually exists in a full context of verbal and nonverbal abuse of the opposition. One of the most ways of making abstract issues vivid and concrete is to focus on one example and tell a "horror story."

"Horror Stories"

"Horror stories" is the term used here to describe the narratives, the specific examples, the "gory details," about what the evil villains did, or what happened to the poor victims (or, what will happen *if . . .*). Instead of an abstract analysis (of *effects* produced by *efficient causes*), such "horror stories" present concrete details, often told in vivid exciting sequences. "Horror stories" can vary widely in length and scope, in truthfulness and accuracy, and in the sophistication of the narration.

In length and scope, "horror stories" can range from fragments of gossip and rumor ("Did you hear what the dirty guys did . . .") to elaborately-planned propaganda movies and novels. "Horror stories" can be those tales told by the preacher in the pulpit, those horrible examples of sin and sinners. Or the narratives can be dramatized, as in the movies, plays, or even (as the Chinese do) in ballets. In American literature, a listing of some famous "horror stories" about social injustice would include such novels as Harriet Beecher Stowe's *Uncle Tom's Cabin,* Upton Sinclair's *The Jungle,* John Steinbeck's *The Grapes of Wrath,* and Richard Wright's *Native Son.*

Literary critics might refer to fictional "horror stories" as *didactic literature:* writings designed basically to teach or to instruct. Although there's much disagreement among critics over different kinds (e.g., "proletarian literature," "problem plays," "allegory," "exemplum," "satire"), there is a large body of narrative stories in all languages, which is intended to teach us about threats (evildoers, villains, and bogeymen) and how to behave in response to them. In contrast to the fragments of rumors (which only intensify the bad), these crafted "horror stories" usually present positive *role models* of behavior: we learn to be heroes, or how not to be victims.

In truthfulness and accuracy, there can be great differences. The horrors of some real events, such as the bombing of Pearl Harbor or the tortures at Dachau, can be told in great detail with great fidelity to truth. Propaganda writers who used these events as part of a revenge theme in WW2 propaganda simply had to re-tell and re-emphasize true stories to stimulate audiences. Other episodes, based on real events, may have been fabricated or manipulated by government officials seeking a crisis to rally public opinion in their favor; for example, the Tonkin Bay "attack" on the U.S. Navy during the Vietnam war. "The first casualty of war is truth," observed Senator William Borah in 1917 and historian Philip Knightley's book *The First Casualty* (1975) has well documented the chronic manipulation of war stories by all governments involved in the wars of the past century. Some horrible atrocity stories commonly used in war propaganda (such as babies being chopped up, and the "bucket of eyeballs") date back to the Crusades without ever being substantiated. Nations have always tried to unite their own people by depicting the savagery and barbarity of their enemies.

The sophistication of the narratives and the overtness of the propaganda varies. Some of the WW2 John Wayne movies, for example, seem very blunt and heavy-handed propaganda today when seen on the late, late show. Didactic writing can sometimes be very obvious and explicitly labeled: traditional animal fables and medieval morality plays, for example, usually end with a specific "moral to the story." Sophisticated novels often imply their message, rather than make any explicit statement, allowing their readers to complete the connections.

"Atrocity Pictures"

"Atrocity pictures" are the *visual* counterpart of "horror stories": drawings, paintings, photographs, or movies which show scenes of the horrible effects caused by the threat. In war, for example, we see the pictures of dead bodies, burning cities, bombings, explosions, and concentration camps. But all "Cause" groups, from anti-abortionists to vivisectionists, will show pictures of dead bodies (babies, dogs, seals, whales, birds, etc.) as visual evidence showing the victims.

Juxtaposition, putting extremely contrasting examples right next to each other, is a very common tactic used in "atrocity pictures." Earlier propaganda films have given us some classic visual images of poor people looking through the windows of the rich who are feasting at a banquet; of starving beggars, arms upstretched, being rejected by sneering bullies; of poor Russian sailors being served maggoty meat while their haughty Czarist officers humiliate them; of fiendish enemy soldiers lurking near sweet innocents. To later observers, such techniques may appear blunt and heavy-handed, but this tight juxtaposition of good guys/bad guys is a very effective technique. Closely related to juxtaposition is the use of *"foil characters,"* whether in written literature or in movies, who are two characters with some similarities (in birth, appearance, situation), but whose differences contrast more noticeably.

"Atrocity pictures" might even be extended to include other *nonverbal* items, such as relics from the martyrs and victims. Here, the most common is something *blood-stained*. "Waving the bloody shirt," a phrase used after the Civil War, described the way the Republican Party kept suggesting to Northern voters that the Democrats were responsible for the war. In Russia today, the Soviets still focus much attention on war memorials and sites of Nazi atrocities (statues, pilgrimages, ritual ceremonies) to keep reminding people of the evils of Fascism. So also the Israelis memorialize the Jewish Holocaust victims: many complex human motives are involved in such memorials, but certainly one effect favors the propagandists concerned with stimulating and bonding a group ("Never again!")

Stereotypes are usually defined as "standardized mental pictures held in common by members of a group" which represent an oversimplified opinion or attitude about others. Stereotypes can be favorable, intensifying the "good" (such as the Dutch being "neat and tidy"); but, most stereotypes (or, at least, the most noticeable ones) are pejorative and unfavorable. Most stereotypes are created by those words and images discussed here as "name-calling," "horror stories," and "atrocity pictures"—all ways of *intensifying the "bad"* of the other.

Stereotypes are easily recognized in poster art for wartime propaganda and in the caricatures drawn by editorial cartoonists. Some propaganda posters intensify the "good"; we commonly describe them as *idealizing, romanticizing,* or *glamorizing* certain qualities. Heroic-size figures, for example, are common: paintings of strong, handsome, muscular men and beautiful, determined-looking women, marching shoulder-to-shoulder, faces thrust forward, arms raised, are clichés of propaganda posters designed to glorify one's "own." Audio stereotypes exist too: military march music or villainous laughs and sneers can be associated and clustered with the visual images in our mind.

Caricatures intensify the "bad" and are the graphic or pictorial equivalent of attack words. The artist selects certain features, distorts them by exaggeration, or associates them with something already hated or feared by the audience. The enemy is often seen as an inhuman monster (werewolf, lots of teeth, fangs, claws ripping with blood), or a fearsome, repellent animal (snake, shark, spider), or as a sub-human, animalistic brute. In 19th century American caricatures, for example, both the despised Negroes and the despised Irish immigrants were drawn as ape-like, gorilla-like, baboon-like brutes. Dozens of other stereotypes exist and are used by editorial cartoonists as a graphic short-hand to intensify the "bad" of the enemies they attack: sinister intruders, evil foreigners, traitors, back-stabbers, bloated bureaucrats, profiteers, exploiters of the poor, fat cats, gluttons gorging themselves, misguided naive dupes, bumblers, incompetents, officials snarled in red-tape, buried in paperwork, prudes, bluenoses, prissy fussbudgets, rigid authoritarians, machine-like robots, unthinking order-followers, hand-wringing do-gooders, and so on. But the most intense visuals are likely to appear in war posters using the theme of enemy-as-inhuman-monster.

Scripts & Scenarios. A single word, a brief phrase, a picture or a cartoon drawing sometimes suggests a complete *script* or *scenario* for some people, mental dramas in the imagination, often recalling sermons or speeches heard long ago. The "Fall of Rome," for example, is a favorite scenario for conservatives. This phrase conjures up vague visions of decadent toga-clad, lazy laurel-leafed Romans frolicking with lithesome lasses in unspeakable orgies while the Huns/Vandals/Barbarian Hordes are about to sweep down upon Civilization in a Cecil B. DeMille mob scene. People who respond emotionally to the "Fall of Rome" scenario often see themselves as Prophets ("Wake Up, America!") or as Defenders of the Faith, ready to Hold the Fort, at the Last Outpost, ready, to do battle with the foe outside, but most irritated about their own colleagues—The Enemy Within!—who do not accept their ideas of their version of the impending Armaggedon.

More seriously, consider that scripts and scenarios are the result of *conditioning propaganda*—longstanding, low-keyed accumulation of ideas and feelings which become assumptions. Hitler, for example, for nearly a decade before the actual imprisonment of Jews in Germany, exploited existing anti-Semitism and made the Jew a "scapegoat" responsible for all problems. The German propaganda machine repeated a constant tirade against the secret "Jewish conspiracy" to take over the world. During the 1930s, Nazi Germany passed scores of seemingly petty laws harassing the Jews: in retrospect, we can see the escalation from the first petty attack to the horror of the Holocaust.

In the United States today, consider the vast vaguely-defined scripts and scenarios associated with black and white race relations, with accumulation of "bad" stories and unfavorable stereotypes both groups have about each other. Note the potential danger if the federal government, controlling all the mass media, were to deliberately and systematically *intensify the "bad,"* using a minority group as a scapegoat.

Generic Threat Metaphors. When the threat of danger doesn't seem too bad or too serious to the audience, the warning-giver commonly uses certain metaphors and allusions to intensify the threat. In addition to the language of *sensory alertness* ("open your eyes"; "Wake up, America!"), the most common metaphors, which can suggest a whole scenario in some peoples' minds, are:

Hidden Danger	**Beginning Sequence**	**Contamination**
(Little threat seen; most hidden)	(Little threat seen; most coming)	(Little, but lethal)
Tip of the iceberg	"Domino" theory	Drop of poison
Undercover agent	Slippery slope	Poisoned well
Internal rot	Opening wedge	Bad apple
Under the veneer	Foot in the door	
Waiting in ambush	Lit fuse	
Setting the trap	Timebomb ticking	
Evil cabal	Snowball effect	
Secret conspiracy	Little bit pregnant	
Snake in the grass	For want of a nail	
Wolf in sheep's clothing	Fall of Roman Empire	
Pandora's box	Fertile soil/seedbed	

The "beginning of a sequence" is probably the most popular imagery used because (1) it deals with *future* effects, which cannot be as easily challenged as the conspiracy or contamination appeals; (2) it is easily coupled with an *urgency* plea: "Stop it now . . . before it's too late!"

When the threat involves external forces, local enemies are often attacked by using metaphors of *hand manipulation:* the locals are the *puppets* (marionettes), *pawns* (chess), or *tools* of the evil-outsider. For example, if a priest in a Latin American nation speaks in favor of the Establishment, the opponents call him a "tool of the CIA"; if he speaks in favor of the Left, the opposition calls him a "communist dupe." If he remains silent, both sides can attack him for his apathy or lack of concern. (An observer, who *wants* to attack, can always criticize: for *kind* ("did the wrong thing") or *degree* ("too much . . . too little . . . too soon . . . too late).

Categories of Common Fears. Earlier, in discussing the benefits promised by commercial advertising, there were lists of a dozen kinds of intrinsic qualities commonly mentioned and two dozen categories of good things commonly associated with the product. Such lists, although arbitrary, were based on observation, as is this listing of some common human fears often intensified in political rhetoric. Of the many possible things people fear, and of the many possible ways of categorizing them, here's a brief useful list:

> **We fear that our life, our possessions, our territory, our freedom will be lost or taken away by someone stronger; or that someone else has more, or that a human system will break down.**

In the following 6 pages these fears are discussed in terms of: **(1) Death & Destruction; (2) Invasion; (3) Restriction; (4) Dominance; (5) Inequality; (6) Chaos.** These categories differ some, such as: ''Death & Destruction,'' relate to all the physical threats against the human body and the possessions we own. Other categories, such as ''Inequality'' and ''Dominance'' relate to often vague and subjective relationships; although these are less tangible and hard to specify, they are still *real:* people who have suffered an injustice or who have been humiliated or ''put down'' know that these are conditions to be avoided even though they can't be objectively measured. The basic point is that whatever (thing, quality, or condition) we define as ''good,'' the absence of it is ''bad.'' Thus, these predictable things which will stimulate the fears and anxieties, angers and resentments of an audience are discussed in the following pages.

These categories often cluster. A war, for example, often involves fears, simultaneously, of Death & Destruction, Invasion, and Restriction. Fears of Dominance or Inequality are about relationships which can occur in many different contexts. In practice, much political discourse has mixed and multiple messages; the degree of intensity also varies, shifts, and changes. Again, with such preliminary warnings here to avoid pigeonholing, rigidity, and oversimplifying, here's a useful set of categories which helps us to recognize patterns and to sort out some very complex and emotional arguments.

DEATH & DESTRUCTION

Conservative rhetoric of those who HAVE benefits (life, health, property, possessions) stresses *protection* (keep the "good") and *prevention* (avoid the "bad"). HAVES fear loss (death, injury, illness; theft or destruction of property).

Progressive rhetoric of those who HAVE-NOT benefits (life,* property) stresses *acquisition* (get the "good") and *relief* (change, get rid of the "bad"). HAVE-NOTS fear continued deprivation (death,* suffering, pain, poverty).

The feared threat in this broad category includes any physical harm or loss to the person or possessions. Commonly, people fear the violence of war (bombing, shooting); most of our attack imagery relates to such active aggression. But lethal dangers also present in famine, starvation, plague, radiation. War propaganda is most intense, but "death and destruction" theme also appears in domestic politics: "crime in the streets" imagery, any fears of attacks against persons (assault, robbery, rape), animals (cruelty, killing), or property (theft, looting, arson, vandalism, neglect).

---

*Dead people obviously do not use these techniques; but by "extending the self," many living persuaders speak *on behalf of* the dead. Common themes — revenge for past deaths, or prevention of future deaths.

WORDS common in name-calling & "horror stories":
(naming & describing the *threats,* the feared *actions,* and the *agents*)

death	kill	multilate	ruin	vicious	killers
destruction	murder	massacre	raze	ferocious	murderers
loss	injure	destroy	wreck	ruthless	butchers
harm	harm	demolish	spoil	malicious	criminals
pain	maim	annilhilate	rape	cruel	robbers
injury	slaughter	devastate	sack	deadly	thieves
suffering	torture	plunder	loot	fierce	muggers
misery	mangle	pillage	rob	ravaging	rapists
distress	batter	ravage	steal	marauding	vandals
	deface	deform	smash		

& IMAGES common in "atrocity pictures":

Blood, bloodstained relics of victims; dead bodies (children, babies, animals); fire, smoke, burning houses and cities; explosions, bombings; desolation, wasteland scenes; air pollution, chemical spills; sounds (cries, screams, moans, shrieks, sobs, gunfire); consider persuaders' graphic use of real attacks (Alamo, Luisitania, Pearl Harbor); massacres (Dachau, My Lai, Sabra, Korean jet 007); lynchings, gang fights, police brutality, etc.

INVASION

Conservative rhetoric of those who HAVE benefits (land, territory, space) stresses *protection* (keep the "good") and *prevention* (avoid the "bad"). HAVES fear loss of land (eviction, dispossession) and others moving into their area (intruders, invaders).

Progressive rhetoric of those who HAVE-NOT benefits (land, territory, space) stresses *acquisition* (get the "good") and *relief* (change, get rid of the "bad"). HAVE-NOTS fear continued deprivation (exile, displacement, homelessness); in land conflicts, HAVE-NOTS are angry either at being dispossessed from the space, or denied access.

The feared threat is loss of territory or space to another. Many people have strong sense of possession or ownership of the area around them, ranging from the close "personal" space ("My room . . . my house . . . my seat . . . my place in line . . . my parking place") extending outward to their region (neighborhood, hometown, state) and to the often-artificial political boundaries of a nation. Border wars, disputed boundaries, and conflicting claims of land ownership are common (Palestine, Northern Ireland, Saar, Sudetenland, China, Russia, Poland, South Africa) with both sides seeking "justice" for past generations. In addition to border competition, *invasion* fears also occur when "outsider" groups are introduced into a group, as in immigration (e.g., 19th century USA, anti-immigrant xenophobia; racial integration—"there goes the neighborhood"). Future population increase will intensify these fears as more people compete for limited territory.

WORDS common in name-calling & "horror stories":
(naming & describing the *threats*, the feared *actions*, and the *agents*)

invasion	invade	dispossess	invaders
intrusion	intrude	evict	intruders
infiltration	trespass	meddle	trespassers
dispossession	penetrate	interfere	strangers
eviction	breach	exile	foreigners
exile	infringe	displace	outsiders
expulsion	encroach	exclude	aliens
exclusion	attack		imperialists
homelessness	raid		colonialists
landlessness			blockbusters
			carpet baggers

& IMAGES common in "atrocity pictures":

Images and metaphors of *tension* (straining, resisting, trying to hold back); of *disintegration of barriers* (dam bursting, gates breaking, doors being smashed in, walls crumbling, home-invaders; of being *overwhelmed* by hordes, crowds, throngs, troops, refugees; of *water* —flooding, unstoppable tide, seeping through cracks. Scenes: bordercrossers, riverwaders, climbing the fences, scaling the walls; refugee camps, shelter huts, long lines, migrant camps, boat people, wanderers, DPs.

RESTRICTION

Conservative rhetoric of those who HAVE benefits (freedom, liberty) stresses *protection* (keep the "good") and *prevention* (avoid the "bad"). HAVES fear loss (capture, seizure, enslavement, limitation).

Progressive rhetoric of those who HAVE-NOT benefits (freedom, liberty) stresses *acquisition* (get the "good") and *relief* (change, get rid of the "bad.") HAVE-NOTS fear continued deprivation (slavery, restriction, restraint).

The feared threat is any restraint on our freedom, ranging from slavery, bondage, or imprisonment, at one extreme, to any restriction imposed upon us by any rule, law, or limit established by society. Imprisonment of ourselves is greatly feared; of others, is defended or justified as a means to a greater end to protect society. In international politics, the imagery of slavery is applied to the USSR (Iron Curtain, Berlin Wall, Captive Nations) in contrast to the "free world." "Free enterprise" advocates often use intense slavery imagery to equate any laws or regulation with oppressive bondage.

Censorship is the attack word to label those laws or restrictions which are disagreeable to us; to defend restrictions which we favor, we emphasize that they are necessary, prudent, reasonable, for the common good: "there ought to be a law."

WORDS common in name-calling & "horror stories":
(naming & describing the *threats*, the feared *actions*, and the *agents*)

slavery	enslave	restrict	slavedrivers
bondage	imprison	constrain	enslavers
captivity	jail	seize	oppressors
prohibition	capture	limit	regulators
censorship	arrest	confine	censors
limitation	restrain	prohibit	prudes
restriction	curb	ban	prigs
regulation	check	censor	puritans
	bind	regulate	
	inhibit	contain	
	hinder		

& IMAGES common in "atrocity pictures":

Images of slavery and imprisonment are most common: chains, bonds, handcuffs, fetters, prison bars, walls, barbed wire fences, guardtowers, searchlights, police dogs, chaingang; Berlin Wall, Gulag Archipelago, Iron Curtain. Anti-regulatory cartoons depict government regulations choking, strangling, ensnaring, encircling Business. Censorship cartoons: (political) "Big Brother is watching you"; TV monitors, spy satellites, other surveillance agents; book-burning; (social bans) Puritan clothing, "A"; stocks, witchhunting, scolding postures.

DOMINANCE

Conservative rhetoric of those who HAVE benefits (power, control, strength) stresses *protection* (keep the "good") and *prevention* (avoid the "bad"). HAVES fear loss of control (submission, powerlessness, impotency).

Progressive rhetoric of those who HAVE-NOT benefits (power, control) stresses *acquisition* (get the "good") and *relief* (change, get rid of the "bad"). HAVE-NOTS fear continued deprivation (submission, lack of control).

The feared threat is dominance by, or submission to, a stronger other; we don't fear the weaker. Dominance and submission are relationships possible between two parties, or among several in a hierarchy, a "pecking order." Degree varies from absolute domination to relative co-existence; audiences differ in their standards of feeling "humiliated"; some take affront at slightest insult, overreact; others underreact. Kinds of dominance vary: physical strength, social status, ideological "moral" dominance. Power, like money, may be a "common denominator," a means to all other ends.

WORDS common in name-calling & "horror stories":
  (naming & describing the *threats,* the feared *actions,* and the *agents*)

defeat	win, lose	surrender	abdicate	arrogant	aggressors
submission	defeat	submit	yield	domineering	oppressors
subjugation	conquer	succumb	serve	haughty	antagonists
impotency	beat	capitulate	obey	insolent	enemies
humiliation	vanquish	defer	control	overbearing	foes
disgrace	subdue	bow	dominate	tyrannical	tyrants
dishonor	surmount	cede	degrade	condescending	competitors
shame	overcome	relent	subordinate	disdainful	rivals
subservience	overwhelm	give up	subservient	supercilious	
dependency	humble	give in	patronize	snobbish	
degradation	humiliate	resign	condescend		
		relinquish	command		

& IMAGES common in "atrocity pictures":

Images emphasize large size and huge number (huge flags, banners; massed troops, large crowds, demonstrators); bodily strength (giants, muscular bodies, heroic-size statues, paintings); fierce and powerful animals (lion, tiger, bull, horse, dragon); powerful natural forces (lightning, thunder, storms—stormtroopers, blitzkrieg); powerful machines (tanks, trains, battleships, dynamo); monumental architecture as symbol and evidence of power. Victims of power abused: the weak, defenseless, poor, women, children, elderly, fragile.

INEQUALITY

Conservative rhetoric of those who HAVE benefits (justice, equality) stresses *protection* (keep the "good") and *prevention* (avoid the "bad"). HAVES fear loss (decrease, getting less) than their "just desserts."

Progressive rhetoric of those who HAVE-NOT benefits (justice, equality) stresses *acquisition* (get the "good") and *relief* (change, get rid of the "bad"). HAVE-NOTS fear continued deprivation (injustice, inequity, not getting their "fair share").

The feared threat is that someone else has more, or something better *undeservedly,* or that someone is trying to take away our "fair share." In a world of obviously unequal distribution of benefits (money, possessions, skills, virtues, beauty, etc.), there is also a widespread human desire for justice. Everyone seeks, or defends, their "fair share," thus causing a basic tension between the HAVES and the HAVE-NOTS. Those who HAVE seek to keep the existing relationship; those who HAVE-NOT seek to change. When HAVES are challenged that they have more benefits in one category (e.g., more money), they respond with a Justice argument: that they deserve it because of another related category (e.g., work harder, longer; more skill, more experience). Inequality threats always involve *degree* (more good or less bad) which people seek to *preserve* or *change,* for their own benefit. When people are "fighting for the principle involved," it's often the principle of justice: people feel that they "deserve" something better, or that others are getting something they don't deserve.

WORDS common in name-calling & "horror stories":
   (naming & describing the *threats,* the feared *actions,* and the *agents*)

inequality	unequal	(too much)	(too little)	exploiters
inequity	unfair	excessive	insufficient	cheats
injustice	unjust	immoderate	inadequate	
imbalance	inappropriate	inordinate	deficient	
unfairness	improper	extravagant	meager	
	unsuitable	exorbitant	scant	
	undue	extreme	skimpy	
		superfluous	lacking	
		surplus		

& IMAGES common in "atrocity pictures":

Inequality involves a more/less *relationship*. To show this, the key visual device is juxtaposition: putting the extremes or opposites close together, side by side, to intensify the differences, heighten the contrast. Pairs of photos are common. Graphic devices are often used to help visualize abstract concepts. "Horror stories" about injustice often use "foil characters" for extreme contrasts; plotting themes often lead to "poetic justice" at the end: "tables turned," "last laugh," etc.

CHAOS

Conservative rhetoric of those who HAVE benefits (order, efficiency, integrity, a well-run system) stresses *protection* (keep the "good") and *prevention* (avoid the "bad"). HAVES fear loss (disorder, breakdown, corruption).

Progressive rhetoric of those who HAVE-NOT benefits (order, integrity) stresses *acquisition* (get the "good") and *relief* (change, get rid of the "bad." HAVE-NOTS fear continued deprivation (disorder, corruption).

The feared threat is any breakdown of a human system which can affect our well-being. Here, chaos will be used to suggest any problems of socio-political-economic systems, but most especially those associated with *domestic politics*. The threat may be intangible or indirect (such as in inflation, or devaluation of currency), but the harmful effects are nevertheless real, and felt. Mismanagement of the political system or the economy can produce a loss of money or possessions to the individual. In most political campaigns, the *incumbent* administration claims the systems work well; the *opposition* party charges that the systems do not work well, and there should be change, reform. Each side often provides supporting evidence for such claims and charges. Systems breakdowns are basically either *intentional* (corruption) or *unintentional* (incompetence); thus, the basic claim made by any candidate can be summarized in one sentence: "I am competent and trustworthy; from me, you'll get more "good" and less "bad.""

WORDS common in name-calling & "horror stories":
   (naming & describing the *threats*, the feared *actions*, and the *agents*)

mismanagement	waste	corrupt	unqualified	incompetents
incompetence	squander	crooked	incapable	wasters
waste	abuse	greedy	wasteful	spendthrifts
corruption	misuse	avaricious	stupid	crooks
graft	mismanage	dishonest	ignorant	grafters
inefficiency	steal	deceitful	inefficient	liars
incoherence	cheat	untruthful	ineffective	
disorganization	defraud	mendacious	incoherent	
inability		devious	disorganized	
negligence		tricky	negligent	
confusion		lazy	confusd	
carelessness		inept	careless	

& IMAGES common in "atrocity pictures":

Imagery of *systems confused* (red tape, paperwork piles, stuffed files, runarounds, maze, puzzles, knots); of systems *not working* (garbage in streets, potholes in roads, pollution, blackouts, bridges broken, crime, riots, looting, arson, muggers); of *waste* (lazy workers, shovel-leaners, cobwebs on sleepers, clock-watchers, "frills"); of *stealing* (money-stuffed pockets, "fat cats," bags of gold); of *secrecy* and *conspiracy* (back room deals, under the table bribes, pals, cronies); *taxpayer as victim:* overburdened, overworked (carrying heavy load, climbing hill), overtaxed (empty pockets, pauper, beggar, naked in a barrel), poor John Q. Public, often juxtaposed next to politician's luxury bought by "hard-earned dollars" of taxpayer.

To recap: Persuaders know the predictable fears of people and these fears can be deliberately stimulated. Absence of the "good" is the basic threat. To an audience of Haves, the conservative persuader stirs up fears of the loss of the "good" they already possess. To an audience of Have-Nots, the progressive persuader stirs up anger at being deprived of the "good" and fears of not getting relief from the "bad." Persuaders are often problem-makers, encouraging an audience to see a situation as a problem, then proposing a solution. Accidental arousal of emotions is possible; but intentional manipulations are possible, also, and quite potentially dangerous today. The process of a "pep talk" begins with some kind of *warning*. The threat is intensified by means of attack language: *name-calling* (both generic and specific to certain threats); *"horror stories"* (narratives, widely ranging in scope and sophistication) and *"atrocity pictures"* (visuals and other nonverbals). Of the many possible things people fear, six common categories are illustrated by the words and images used to intensify the "bad" of: death and destruction, invasion, restriction, dominance, inequality, and chaos.

8

THE BONDING

In preparation for committed collective action, an important part of the "pep talk" is the bonding: bringing the group together, keeping it together, and building pride in the group.

No matter what threats or causes are involved, the bonding actions are basically the same, involving: **unity** ("united we stand"), **loyalty** ("be true to your . . ."), and **quality** ("we're number one . . .").

Unity words, important in all political persuasion, stress the idea that the individual is not alone, but is (or should be) *part of* a larger whole. Unity words often appear in the names of many groups, such as the United States of America, United Nations, Union of South Africa, Soviet Union, United Kingdom, United Auto Workers, etc. Unity slogans are probably the most widespread of all political rallying cries: As we go arm-in-arm, hand-in-hand, shoulder-to-shoulder, forward together, we will rally 'round the flag.

> "United we stand, divided we fall"
> "All for one, one for all"
> "One nation, under God, indivisible"
> "Solidarity forever"

"Workers of the World, Unite"
"Ein Volk, Ein Reich, Ein Fuhrer"
  (One people, one nation, one leader. —1930's)
"Ein Kampf, Ein Sieg" (One struggle, one victory. —1940's)
"Bring us together" (GOP, 1972)
"Party and People are One" (USSR)
"People United to Save Humanity" (PUSH; 1980's)

Bringing the group together, the gathering of the clan, often involves an invitation, a welcoming; asking people to join, to enter, to come into, to affiliate with the group. Key words, common to all groups, which are used to bring the group together are:

Bonding Actions

join	*belong*
support	*give*
favor	*donate*
back	*aid*
boost	*help*
enlist	*subscribe*
keep	*send*
stand up for	*endorse*
demonstrate	*commit*

We enter some groups naturally, at birth, and are entered into other groups by proxy (e.g., early baptism in some churches), but some of these groups will have a ritual (puberty rites, Confirmation, Bar Mitzvah) by which the individual can re-affirm or confirm membership. Frequently we are asked to show our affiliation and support by donating money, not only for the economic welfare of the group, but also for the symbolic significance: "to put our money where our mouth is." Affiliation with a group can range from formal (dues, membership card, initiation rites, etc.) to informal (sharing the opinions of others), but often there are some visible signs of membership identifying the individual with the group: a pledge, a salute, a gesture, a uniform, a color, a badge, a bumper sticker, and so on.

Unity appeals *intensify the similarities* and *downplay the differences* of the individual members of the group. Every individual person belongs to countless groups, or categories, simultaneously. A person, for example, can be a female, black, college student, American, Texan, Democrat, Catholic, musician, stamp collector, and so on, infinitely. When any of these particular groups seeks to bond that individual, the group em-

Words which *intensify*
Unity

> alliance, ally
> associate, association
> belong, belonging
> brother, brotherhood
> coalition
> colleague
> combine
> common, commonwealth
> commune, community
> companion, companionship
> comrade, comradeship
> confederate, confederation
> co-op, cooperate, cooperation
> federation
> fraternity
> friend, friendship
> harmony
> incorporate
> integrate
> interdependence
> league
> mutual
> oneness
> organize, organization
> partner, partnership
> share
> sister, sisterhood
> solidarity
> sorority
> team, teamwork
> together
> union, unification
> unite, united

First person *plural* pronouns—*we, our, us*—(instead of *I, me, mine)* are important, shifting focus off the individual. Other plurals (such as, *Voters for . . . Citizens for . . . People for . . .)* suggest not only unity, but also strength in numbers, often attempting an illusion of wide support. "Attack words" intensify the opposite, undesirable qualities: disorganized, different, divergent, disaffiliated, alienated, eccentric, loner.

Unity appeals *intensify the similarities* and *downplay the differences* of the individual members of the group. Every individual person belongs to countless groups, or categories, simultaneously. A person, for example, can be a female, black, college student, American, Texan, Democrat, Catholic, musician, stamp collector, and so on, infinitely. When any of these particular groups seeks to bond that individual, the group emphasizes the similarities the person has with others within that group. Sometimes these similarities are obvious and permanent, such as race or sex; sometimes they are unseen and temporary, such as groups of like-minded people sharing the same artistic tastes, political opinions, or recreational interests. It is in the interest of the *group* (not necessarily of the *individual*) for groups to seek to intensify the degree of involvement and commitment of the members. In each of these different groups to which we belong, the degree of support may vary from active involvement ("bearing witness") to passive acceptance, tolerance, compliance ("bearing with it").

Partisanship in politics is often very emotionally intense. Some people do go to extremes, in any party, in any cause. We have dyed-in-the-wool conservatives, knee-jerk liberals, hidebound Republicans, Yellow Dog Democrats ("I'd vote for a yellow dog if he wuz a Democrat"), and all kinds of descriptive phrases relating to fiercely loyal partisans.

Groups often seek an increased degree of involvement in the group by telling individuals that they, as individuals, are important: "We *need* you . . . we *want* you . . . we're *depending* on you . . . your aid . . . your help . . . your support." Often the appeal to such altruism is very *explicit,* but is accompanied by an implicit, unspoken appeal to self-interest, that the individual will also gain a benefit from joining.

Such a double reward of "doing well by doing good" is often seen clearly in military recruiting ads: in addition to the altruistic service to country, the recruit is also promised personal benefits (adventure, excitement, travel, improvement, earning a skill): "Join the Navy and see the world"; "Be all that you can be . . . in the Army."

Keeping the group together is another important aspect of bonding. To insure such cohesion, it is to the benefit of the group that there is a stress on those *social* virtues of the individual's relationship with others. Courage and bravery can be *personal* virtues unrelated to anyone else; but faith, loyalty, trustworthiness, and other such *social* virtues always need someone or something outside of the individual.

The concept of duty and obligation, as a reciprocal for benefits received (either past or present) from the group, is also strongly encouraged. Public pledges, vows, oaths, promises of loyalty (e.g., "I pledge allegiance . . .") are common, often recited by groups in solemn ceremonies.

Words which *intensify*
Loyalty

allegiance
authority
commitment
deference
devoted
devotion
duty
faith
faithful
fidelity
guidance
homage
honor
leader
leadership
loyal
loyalty
oath
obedience
obedient
obligation
patriot
patriotic
pledge
promise
respect
reverence
true
trust
trustworthy
unchanging
unquestioning
unswerving
unwavering
vow

"Attack words" intensify the opposite, undesirable qualities: disloyal, treacherous, traitor, mutinous, rebel, disobedient, insubordinate, false, faithless, seditious, etc.

Loyalty is demanded, more or less, by every group to which we belong: sometimes asking for constant and increasing commitment; sometimes putting intense emotional pressure on us, guilt-inducing, if we do not follow the rules, fulfill our commitments to the cause. Sometimes these rules of behavior are *explicitly* expressed in lists of specific Do's & Don'ts; laws, or commandments. Sometimes these rules are *implicitly* suggested by the cultural assumptions of a society: the accepted customs, conventions, standards of behavior as to what is expected, typical, or normal; the traditional roles we play within unquestioned myths; the kinds of heroes and villains seen in our literatures: "Good Christians *never* do that . . . good girls don't do that . . . Scouts shouldn't . . ."

Most groups have *goals* (whether an explicit ideology or an implicit general direction); a *structure* of some kind, that is, a set of procedures for doing things; and *leaders,* or decision-makers, who influence or control the power of the group. Adjustment, "fitting in," "knowing one's place," or "learning the ropes" is a common theme in bonding appeals; for example, many war movies have sub-plots about the misfit or oddball learning teamwork.

Loyalty usually involves a submission to authority, or the acceptance of a guidance or control by a leader. Orders, commands, directives, imperatives ("Do this . . . Do that . . . You *should* do this") imply a leader/follower, stronger/weaker relationship. Loyalty to the group is often identified with loyalty to a particular leader. Very strong charismatic leaders, such as Hitler, have often been personified as being the very soul or essence of the group (e.g., "Hitler *is* Germany"; "Lenin lived, Lenin lives, Lenin will live"). In some situations, groups can bond well by focusing on a leader ("Long Live Chairman Mao!"); however, some (usually, rivals for power) have denounced such a "cult of personality" as working against group bonding.

Bonding favors the interests of the group over those of the individual. Bonding seeks an enthusiastic support of the group and its leaders, and discourages dissent, criticism, diversity, disobedience, and insubordination. In addition to any external threat, those who would disagree or disaffiliate are seen as a serious internal threat to weaken or disintegrate the bonding. Thus, groups often make extreme demands for loyalty, viewing any dissent as betrayal, treachery, or treason. In political affairs, this demand for orthodoxy has led to the countless purges and "witch hunts" throughout history.

Words which *intensify* Quality

> best
> champion
> choice
> excellent
> extraordinary
> fantastic
> finest
> first-class
> first-rate
> grand
> great
> greatest
> incomparable
> important
> magnificent
> matchless
> perfect
> prize-winning
> spectacular
> splendid
> super
> superb
> superior
> supreme
> top-notch
> top-rate
> top-quality
> tremendous
> ultimate
> unsurpassed
> ultra-
> victor
> victory
> win
> winner
> wonderful

"Attack words" intensify the opposite, undesirable qualities: poor, bad, inferior, loser.

Bonding can be done easier and more efficiently in dictatorships and closed totalitarian systems which can control the information flow, manipulate the media, and eliminate dissenters. "Spontaneous" demonstrations, for example, are easy to manufacture; so also, the rote repetition of propaganda *a la* Orwell's "Two Minute Hate" in *1984*. In contrast, in free and open societies which tolerate dissent, it's much harder to get unity from such diversity, a condition which may indeed have temporary disadvantages in quickly bonding a nation for concerted action. But such short-term problems are well offset by the long-term benefits of free speech in an open society.

Groups can manipulate the individual's need for esteem, approval by others, because groups have the power to confer or withhold esteem, to honor or to shame. Groups can manipulate the individual's need for a sense of belonging because groups have the power to accept or to reject. Thus, groups can exert great pressures for the individual to live up to the expectations of the group. On the other hand, if the group or cause doesn't live up to its own standards, or to the expectations of the individual, the disillusioned individual can do little except withdraw from the group.

Building pride in the group is an important aspect of bonding. Most people seek dominance; they want to be winners; they want to be esteemed; so also with groups. Sometimes individuals with low self-esteem are the "joiners" of groups and the fanatics within them because these individuals seek in the group that which they are lacking in themselves. These are the "True Believers," as Eric Hofer has called them, and they exist not only in every political group, but also in religious and ethnic groups, among athletic "fans," and so on: "Be proud of your . . . Race, Faith, County, School, Team. . . ." I'm proud to be American, Southern, Irish, Black, Chicano . . ."

While *individual* pride is often condemned as being improper, egocentric, selfish, or sinful ("pride goeth before the fall"), extravagant pride in the groups is encouraged ("We're Number One," ". . . our great nation," ". . . this grand and glorious flag . . .") as building morale, esprit de corps, school spirit, and so on. Thus, superlatives *intensifying the "good"* of the group are likely to be common.

Bonding actions within the group can include both the present and the past. In the present, groups can give rewards to individuals, can give encouragement and approval in many ways: words of praise, cheers and applause, awards and medals, titles and prestige, money and power. But, groups can also bond to the past by honoring the dead heroes and martyrs, by ceremonies and memorials, by re-telling "the lives of the saints" and "the tales of the heroes." Remembering the "good" of past glories and victories serves an important morale function in the present because individuals can hope that their heroic deeds will also be remembered in the future. Remembering the "bad"—the "horror stories," the atrocities committed against the group, functions as part of the "threat" and as a stimulus for revenge and retribution, to rectify an injustice, to settle the score, to even it up.

Bonding can be encouraged by any organized group activity: parades, demonstrations, processions, pilgrimages, picketing, marching, chanting, wearing uniforms, classroom pledge of allegiance. Team sports involving rules, hierarchies, teamwork, and controlled aggression ("Wars are won on the playing fields of Eton") may have a special importance in bonding; we even describe team supporters and boosters in intense terms of "fanatics": sports fans, avid fans, rabid fans, loyal fans, etc. During exciting sports events, observers can easily see the intensity of identification that individuals can have with their team or their group.

Music has a special importance in bonding. A group singing in unison is one of the most effective devices to increase morale and esprit de corps. In addition to the bonding to the immediate group, most music and songs have powerful memory *associations* which are triggered. Every country, for example, has patriotic songs which arouse the emotions: stirring marches and military music (such as the "Battle Hymn of the Republic," "Dixie," "Stars and Stripes Forever"), and slower music which suggests reverence and respect (e.g., "Star Spangled Banner," "God Save the King") or sentiment and nostalgia for the homeland ("America the Beautiful," "Back Home Again in Indiana," "My Old Kentucky Home"). We know this music from our childhood years and it has a powerful emotional effect on us. Not only does the Establishment use this music for bonding purposes, but also most protest movements have songs with simple lyrics (usually: the verse describing the conflict, the chorus emphasizing unity) based on well-known patriotic and religious melodies (We Shall Overcome, Solidarity Forever, etc.). Music is important in bonding religious groups and ethnic groups too. Negro Spirituals and gospel music, for example, have created a bonding in the black community that transcends any particular religious denomination. For centuries, the Catholic Church was bonded throughout the world with the use of Gregorian chant in Latin; recent reforms, whatever their other merits, have caused a serious break of this bonding.

Propaganda movies have traditionally placed a great emphasis on bonding scenes: *unity* and *loyalty* themes are usually expressed in scenes of camaraderie, friendship, often roughhouse fun and games, playing pranks, drinking together, and so on. Examples range from the earliest classic propaganda films, such as the camaraderie of the sailors on the Russian battleship Potemkin and the scout-camp atmosphere of the Nazi youths filmed in Reifenstahl's "Triumph of the Will," to the WW2 John Wayne movies and the good-natured gang at M*A*S*H. The *quality* theme ("We're #1") is also developed, often as the climax of the stories, as these happy-go-lucky friends get together "when the chips are down" for a methodical and efficient performance of their duties (marching, fighting, doctoring, and so on).

"Be Prepared." If quick response is a goal, groups must be in a state of readiness; thus, an emphasis on vigilance, alertness, and preparedness: "keeping in shape." Conditioning propaganda, in preparation for future action, often stresses *rehearsals* of responses so people know what to do. Such preparations are most systematic and are easiest to observe in *military* units, indoctrinated in certain values and trained in certain specific responses. Standing armies, for example, spend most of their time practicing and rehearsing various contingency plans.

In a less formal manner, civilian societies and other groupings get prepared for action by the slogans and clichés commonly used and accepted within the societies. For example, whenever some terrorist group or some small nation attacks American interests abroad, there's apt to be a wide spread spontaneous public response, using a predictable, limited number of clichés relating to retaliation and dominance: "They can't get away with that. . . ." Many slogans and clichés are *behavior instructions,* telling us what to do, how to behave: "When the going gets tough, the tough get going."

Conditioning propaganda acts as the necessary prelude to any specific response which could be called for later. Whatever the degree of intensity, there has to be a constant and sustained bonding of the group if it is to act effectively when it is necessary. If the group is well-bonded, it can respond to any new threat introduced.

Once a group is bonded, a structure and an organization comes into being and tends to perpetuate itself. People, especially the leaders, have *roles* to live, and often *jobs* to protect. Those in the organization now have a vested interest in keeping the group alive, moving, and even growing.

A sense of movement and progress is important to any progressive group: a sense of hope in achieving the goals, overcoming the obstacles, enduring the difficulties, of crossing the river Jordan and getting to the promised land. When this sense of progress stops, when movement is stalled or bogged down, then the group is in trouble.

Sometimes, when a group's goal is achieved, there is an anticlimax and the group falls apart. To prevent such disintegration, groups usually survive by creating new goals. When the March of Dimes organization achieved its goal of victory over polio, the staff and leaders did not disband, but transferred their techniques, experience, and organization to a new cause, birth defects. Communal groups and utopian societies usually succeed or fail depending on how long they can keep bonded for a specific cause. Typically, during the 1960s the many communes that were formed managed to survive only as long as they were actively progressing with a specific unifying cause (e.g., building a dome, winning an election, etc.).

One way to keep bonded is to keep introducing new threats and new causes. In politics, for example, both the Left and the Right have a cluster of overlapping causes—a movement. In such movements, people usually share the same goals or causes, and the same threats or enemies. It is to the advantage of any single group, left-wing or right-wing, to keep its members bonded by helping out its allies. Bonding can go on without a threat; there can be a great deal of emphasis on unity, loyalty, and the quality of the group. But, bonding is *easier* with a threat outside, or if the group has a "siege mentality."

People who donate to a charity or subscribe to a special interest magazine will soon begin receiving letters from other related organizations because mailing lists are rented out and shared, a useful way of bonding a movement, of keeping like-minded people informed of what's going on in other areas closely related to their special interests. Birdwatchers who join the Audubon club, for example, are likely to donate money to help "save the whales" or "save the wetlands" or other conservationist causes. In our enormously large and complicated society, these are good methods for individuals to pick and choose a few areas for their concern.

To recap: bonding is an extremely important part of the "pep talk"—bringing the group together, keeping it together, and building pride in the group. These key concepts are *unity, loyalty,* and *quality.* Conditioning propaganda frequently emphasizes keeping a group bonded together, simply in preparation for any future response. "Causes" often cluster; groups within movements share many overlapping goals and fears.

Dulce et decorum est pro patria mori. —Horace
(It is sweet and fitting to die for one's country.)

All wars are boyish, and are fought by boys,
The champions and enthusiasts of the state:
                                                            —Melville

9

THE CAUSE

Duty, defense, and altruism are key concepts here. People justify their involvement in a cause by a sense of obligation: they feel impelled that they "should" get involved, "must" do something, "ought to" do their duty, often expressed in *work* metaphors of a difficult, but necessary, job. Defense is viewed either as self-defense (survival, preservation) or, more commonly, as the altruistic defense of another who is often weaker or unable to defend self. Responding to a negative threat, a "cause" seeks a positive benefit. The basic concept of a "cause" can be expressed in the following formula: **a "cause" involves a sense of duty to defend another from a threat and gain a benefit.**

A "cause" involves a sense of duty to defend someone . . .

1	**2**	**3**

1.   **2.**   **3.**

It's our . . .	to	the
Duty	Defend	Nation
Obligation	Protect	Country
Responsibility	Guard	Homeland
Mission	Shield	People
Job	Safeguard	Workers
Task	Save	Common Man
Work	Secure	Proletariat
	Help	Oppressed
	Aid	Poor
	Serve	Children
		Future Generations
		Unborn
		Elderly
		Helpless Animals
		Environment

"If I know your sect I anticipate your argument." — *Emerson*

from a threat and gain a benefit

4	5

4. If the *Threat* is:

5. Key words (Qualities, Benefits) related to the "cause" will be:

DOMINANCE	Victory	Supremacy
	Success	Sovereignity
	Triumph	Mastery
	Superiority	Conquest
	Control	Dominion

DEATH & DESTRUCTION	Peace	Stability
	Safety	Tranquility
	Security	Calm

INVASION	Homeland	Native Country
	Fatherland	Birthright
	Community	Inheritance
	Neighborhood	Territory

RESTRICTION	Freedom	Self-determination
	Liberty	Liberation
	Choice	Emancipation
	Independence	Autonomy

INEQUALITY	Equality	Balance
	Justice	Retribution
	Right	Revenge
	Fairness	Vengeance

CHAOS	Order	Efficiency
	Prosperity	Honesty
	Progress	Ability
	Abundance	Integrity
	Plenty	Growth

Causes in Conflict

Direct conflicts. Sometimes conflicts are head-on confrontations, diametrically in opposition, in direct contradiction to each other, focused on the same issue, both sides claiming the same cause. In Palestine, for example, both Jews and Arabs claim the same land as their God-given ancestral homeland, both sides have suffered violence, seek justice and revenge, and both believe they have God on *their* side. In the case of two sides fighting over one property, it's possible to conceive of a simple conservative-progressive opposition: whoever currently possesses the land will seek to keep the "good" and the Have-Nots will seek to change the "bad." Thus, in current conditions, Israeli rhetoric urges peace and stability in the area, while the dispossessed Palestinian Arabs are fomenting instability.

However, very few conflicts are that dramatically direct. Most conflicts have great complexities both in kind and degree. For example, consider the political elections in the United States in which there is, superficially, a two-part dichotomy, a *two-party* system. Yet, the two parties are not in direct contradictory opposition to each other; there are so many sub-issues involved in any campaign, and so many different shades of Democrats and Republicans (including conservative democrats and liberal Republicans, and vice versa) that there are seldom clear-cut or sharply defined choices. So we end up voting for the greater-of-two goods or the lesser-of-two evils; such qualified choices are appropriate because we don't elect a person to solve a *single* issue; we elect a person for a timespan of many years in which a wide variety of issues have to be dealt with. On Election Day we seldom encounter candidates who can handle *all* possible situations better than their opponents.

Oblique conflicts. Most of the controversial issues we see are in oblique opposition, opposed to each other at angles, because the conflicting groups have different sets of threats feared and causes defended. In many respects, they are not even "speaking the same language," because they disagree so totally about values and priorities, about what's the *main issue* at stake. In the abortion controversy, for example, one side may see the main issue as "killing a person" ("Death & Destruction"); the other side may see the main issue as a woman's "right to choose" ("Restriction"). People often disagree on definitions and basic premises; such fundamental differences often get lost in the emotional charges and counter-charges made, in the name-calling and the "horror stories" told.

Dominance is often the unspoken issue, the "hidden agenda" in many conflicts between conservatives and progressives. Whether we're dealing with political issues between the Left and the Right, or any kind of social conflicts, there is a tendency for adherents on either side to support related groups. People look at the list of names of the Officers or the Board of Directors to see if they recognize "friends" from other affiliated groups. People often join, support, or endorse other groups within a movement simply so that "their side" will win, will dominate the opposition, no matter what the specific issue. Because "causes" tend to cluster, often overlapping each other, individual persons may sometimes feel confused or uncomfortable because they may support some related causes and not others. Some people in the "right to life" (anti-abortion) movement may declare themselves "pro-life," for example, and simultaneously support capital punishment and war efforts. Sometimes clusters are inconsistent and illogical because the "hidden agenda" is essentially *dominance* over the other side.

If all conflicts were simple and direct, then the use of the terms *conservative* and *progressive* would be clear, easily understood by all. But, because conflicts are oblique, and the participants have many differing goals (benefits) and threats (loss of benefits), these two terms often seem shifting or ambiguous. Furthermore, these terms describe a *relationship* which can change.

New relationships are created when change occurs. Roles reverse. For example, a group may use *progressive* rhetoric (change the "bad") to get elected, or to get a new law enacted; but once successful, once elected or the law passed, then the same group must use *conservative* rhetoric (keep the "good") to defend itself. The revolutionary, once successful, becomes the new Establishment, but then usually damns the opposition for being "counter-revolutionary" and discourages further change. This is often confusing; once the revolution is over, people like Thomas Paine are out of a job, and can't understand why their ideas are no longer popular. So too the dilemma of "conservatives" who find themselves attacking the Supreme Court (the very essence of law and order) whenever the Court rulings disagree with their opinions. They expect the Court to keep the existing "good," and, when there's any change in interpretation, such ultra-conservatives seek to change the Court: to "restore" to what it "really" should be.

SUGGESTIONS —
how to analyze . . .

Analyzing "cause" rhetoric is difficult, tough for anyone trying to be cool, calm, deliberate, and rational with words and images which are often deliberately designed to incite, inflame, stir up the emotions, make people angry or afraid.

- Only bits and fragments of political messages are most commonly seen: a slogan, a picket sign, a brief TV shot, rumor, an invective, a quote.
- The *sequence* (in which the parts are first noticed) varies; often the final response is the first thing noticed by outside observers. Re-sort, re-arrange, re-organize using the appropriate structural framework of "the pitch" or the "pep talk."
- Emotional intensity and group bonding are two prominent features of a "pep talk," but not all political rhetoric calls for *committed collective action*. Sometimes, as on many TV spot ads before an election, we get the simple "pitch": stressing *attention-getting* (especially name recognition), *confidence-building;* asking for a one-shot response, "vote."
- Surface variations, different ways of saying or suggesting the same basic concepts, are to be expected. In election attacks, for example, countless jokes, remarks, and nonverbal gestures can suggest that opponents are incompetent or untrustworthy.
- Inconsistency is common. People use different phrasings, definitions, often change focus or shift premises. Observers need to be alert, flexible, seek dominant impressions, and avoid pigeonholing.
- The association technique links (1) the idea, person, or policy, with (2) something *already* loved/desired by (3) the intended audience. In attacks: with something *already* hated/feared. Such associations are often very effective *(whether true or not, logical or not)* in persuading the audience. Thus, persuaders seek to know (by means of polls, surveys, studies, analyses) the desires and fears of their target audience.
- Relationships change, roles reverse, when real change occurs. A group may use *progressive rhetoric* (change the "bad") to get elected, or a new law enacted; but, once in power, then the same group uses *conservative rhetoric* (keep the "good") to defend it. Reformers and outsiders, once elected, become the Establishment.
- Analysis of patterns has limited value: it doesn't tell us which side is "right," what charges are true, what supporting evidence is reliable, or what to do. But such analysis does help us sort out some very complex emotional arguments, to identify the examples, and to define the key issues. Our understanding of predictable patterns may help us defend ourselves from being deceived or exploited by others, from being self-righteous or narrowminded ourselves. From our understanding of how others also see their roles, we may gain tolerance, perhaps compassion.

To analyze "Cause" Rhetoric —
Sort out the parts, using the basic pattern of the "pep talk":

THREAT What is the threat? The "bad" that is feared or provokes anger?

Can it be abstracted and categorized as: *death & destruction, dominance, invasion, restriction, inequality, chaos.*

Who is doing the "bad"? the agents of the actions? What names are being used to describe the foe?

Are these foes certain *kinds* of people? (rich, hawks, commies, hippies)

— an identifiable *group?* (blacks, women)

— represented, symbolized by a specific *person, a leader.*

Is the foe evil? Or misguided? A pawn?

What examples, what "horror stories" and "atrocity pictures" are presented to show the evil deeds of foe? What they did, or will do?

BONDING Who are the defenders? The "good guys" being asked to join together?

Who is the target audience?

Are there bonding appeals stressing *unity, loyalty,* and *quality?*

Any specific bonding action sought? Join, support, give, help, subscribe?

Any group activities? cheering, singing, marching, picketing, uniforms.

CAUSE Are there any "duty" words? (duty, job, task, mission; should, must, ought)

What is the "main issue"? The "good" sought? Can it be abstracted — described in terms of: victory, success, peace, safety, life, freedom, liberty, choice, equality, justice, order, prosperity, growth, honesty, integrity, etc.

RESPONSE What specific action is sought? After the group is bonded, what will it *do?*

Can the action be abstracted: as primarily *conservative rhetoric,* protection and prevention (to keep the "good" and to avoid the "bad") or *progressive rhetoric,* acquisition and relief (to get the "good" and get rid of the "bad")?

NUCLEAR POWER PLANTS

THREAT? Death (pollution)

VICTIMS? People, unborn generations, earth

FOE? Greedy exploiters, careless corporations

HORRORS? Pollution spills, leaks, meltdowns, flaws

THREAT? Loss(jobs), restriction
VICTIMS? workers, economy
FOE? Ignorant, naive do-gooders, hippies; bureaucrats
HORRORS? Unemployment, energy crisis, shortages

ERA

THREAT? Inequality, dominance

VICTIMS? Women

FOE? Male chauvinists, sexists; priviledged women

HORRORS? Low pay, low status, legal discrimination

THREAT? Chaos (breakdown of systems, values, hierarchy)
VICTIMS? Family, children women
FOE? Singles-lesbians, divorcees
HORRORS? Loss of perceived protections, advantages

GUN CONTROL

THREAT? Restriction
VICTIMS? Law-abiding citizens, gun-owners
FOE? Naive bleeding-hearts, criminals, commies
HORRORS? Home-invaders, crime, govt. controls

THREAT? Death & destruction
VICTIMS? Innocent bystanders, family members
FOE? Authoritarians, gun-lobby, NRA
HORRORS? Accidents, crazies, angry outbursts

ABORTION

THREAT? Restriction, dominance

VICTIMS? Poor women

FOE? Religious sects imposing beliefs

HORRORS? Amateur abortions; unwanted kids

THREAT? Death
VICTIMS? Babies
FOE? Selfish women, immoral
HORRORS? Dead babies

Benefits to the Individual: Self-Image & Role

Groups obviously benefit from successful "pep talks." Both the group organized and the group aided can benefit from the committed collective action of the individuals involved. But what of the individuals involved? Leaders, of course, are likely to receive benefits: at the least, power and prestige within the group. But what benefits do followers receive?

Individuals can benefit from being bonded together in a group to do something. Participation in a "cause" can change a person's life or outlook: instead of a meaningless life in a confusing, chaotic world, some people will gain a sense of meaning and purpose, a direction and a goal to achieve. For some, it's a way to gain a sense of self-worth, value, dignity, and importance. For some, it's an opportunity to "do something worthwhile," or to get involved in a struggle of "good" against "evil." For some, it's a way of *belonging,* getting a sense of community; often, in established groups, a feeling enhanced by a whole set of creeds to believe, codes to follow, and rituals to perform. For some, it's a way to transform an "ordinary" life into an extraordinary one.

Getting involved in a conflict, battling evil for a good cause, certainly adds drama, adventure and excitement to life. Radicals in the '60s who joked about "revolution for the hell of it," suggesting that action was a good way to get rid of boredom, weren't too far wrong. But most people are apt to be more solemn and serious in justifying their involvement: "doing one's duty . . . fulfilling one's destiny . . . bearing witness . . . showing support . . . demonstrating solidarity."

People are usually not conscious of their need to function within a role, nor would they likely describe themselves as *role-players,* a phrasing which has overtones of superficiality or artificiality, trivial play-acting. If asked why they participate in a group, people are apt to respond: "I feel I ought to be here . . . it's my duty . . . we have an obligation to help out . . . show our support . . . stand up for what's right."

Not only is there a genuine human need to belong, but also there's a deep desire people have that the world make sense, that there's some coherence and meaning in life. Belonging to a group, and working for a cause, gives that kind of feeling. Repetition has a cumulative effect on such belief. The more often people hear these same beliefs, repeat them, and reinforce each other, the more convinced they become.

A role exists within a wider context. To function well in a role implies a *belief* (a basic worldview), a *purpose* (goal, direction) and a *plan* (a process, a script, steps to be taken, a way) to get there with certain *behaviors* (specific acts; jobs, tasks, duties) to be done, and certain *rules* (a code of conduct, a list of "shoulds") to be followed. Within roles, there's some leeway and optional behaviors; people aren't clones doing everything exactly the same. Change and movement within roles can be accomplished easier than a complete abandonment or loss of the roles.

When roles are criticized by outsiders, this threatens a person's whole worldview. Thus, people defend their own roles, their own actions as "doing the right thing" for the right purpose, as an affirmation of "natural order," of how things should be. (It's easier for outsiders to recognize this in others; it's difficult for us to see *our own* functioning in roles and in the possibility of living life in other ways.) When roles are threatened, challenged, or when people are displaced from their roles, there's often an intense emotional response: fear of possible loss; grief, self-hatred, or anger at actual loss.

Roles can be imposed by others, or chosen by self. Some people who have "poor" roles (as subordinates, unimportant, etc.) assigned to them in their everyday jobs often compensate by choosing leadership roles in volunteer organizations (scouting, volunteer firefighters, sheriff's deputies, "cause" groups, etc.) in which they can "become important" and do "meaningful" things.

Role models are those ideal types, those people who set the standards of behavior for others to imitate or follow. Most people have a variety of role models for the many different roles we lead. Many of our domestic behaviors are modeled after our own parents, admired relatives, friends, and neighbors. Heroes and heroines in books, movies, TV programs, and even 30-second-spots constantly function as role models of expected behavior. Viewer involvement is often very intense; audiences can have great empathy with well-drawn characters. Millions of American men, for example, have secretly spent time in front of their mirrors practicing the gestures of John Wayne, Humphrey Bogart, James Dean, Marlon Brando, Alan Alda, and countless other male movie stars. Yet, such modeling behavior is not limited to such superficialities; the whole spectrum of social and political behaviors is learned by imitation.

"Pep talks" are not only *delivered* by people functioning in certain roles (prophet, liberator, reformer), but also are *received* by other people functioning in certain roles (defenders, crusaders, builders). Related to these "good causes" discussed here, there are many characters from both secular and religious literature on which we can base our self-images and role models.

Today, through books and movies we have access to so many competing myths and diverse stories that the specific images in our role models may be a bit confused, or at least curious and colorful. We're apt to have some elements of the *medieval romance* (crusaders or knights in armor, doing their duty for a good cause, with apt reward and recognition, allegiance and a hierarchy, etc.); of the *cowboy movies* (with their ever-present themes of injustice being righted, of land disputes and invasions, of social orders being created and destroyed); of *biblical* figures (David, Samson, Moses, Abraham, Christ; of *national* heroes (Paul Revere, Nathan Hale, Washington, Lincoln); as well as a lode of imagery from *Greek and Roman mythology* and *European history*. So the specific images and the mix may vary widely, but the underlying patterns are likely to be the same.

Common roles and self-images related to "pep talks":

	Warning-Giver	**ROLE & SELF-IMAGE** PROPHET SENTRY MESSENGER

Threats	**Causes**	
DOMINANCE	VICTORY	CHAMPION LEADER
DEATH & DESTRUCTION	PEACE	CREATOR BUILDER LIFE-GIVER
INVASION	POSSESSION	GUARDIAN PROTECTOR
RESTRICTION	FREEDOM	LIBERATOR DELIVERER
INEQUALITY	JUSTICE	JUDGE ENFORCER AVENGER
CHAOS	PROGRESS	PATRIOT REFORMER

Some people are probably more prone to be attracted to a "pep talk" than other people. Writers such as Eric Hofer, in *The True Believer,* have speculated as to the reasons why some people join "causes." Zealots and enthusiasts are not confined to any particular political ideology; the patterns presented here are likely to be used both for conservative and progressive "causes." But, perhaps the common tendency is the need for absolute certitude, for "being right," which contributes to a polarized kind of thinking, a "good guys/bad guys" mentality. One observable result is the pattern of descriptive language used not only to attack opponents, but also to proclaim one's own virtues.

Moral superiority. Nothing so pleases one's own advocates nor so infuriates the opposition as the claim to moral superiority. Because joining in a "cause" so favorably affects the self-image, advocates often feel very noble and self-righteous, not only about their "cause," but also about themselves. Sometimes this is expressed very explicitly, as when we hear people using military-religious metaphors: Onward Christian Soldiers, soldiers of the lord, defenders of the faith, and so on.

More frequently, the God-on-our-side attitude is an *implicit, unspoken assumption.* If we were specifically to claim such righteousness, such an explicit statement would often provoke skepticism and counterclaims by putting it so bluntly. But our *assumptions* are seldom investigated or scrutinized; many of our feelings and beliefs are not subjected to rational "proofs." Nevertheless they are very powerful influences on our behavior because we act out certain roles and follow certain role models, consciously or unconsciously, to a greater or lesser degree.

When people intensify their own "good," they tend to see themselves as being competent, informed, "possessing the Truth," and acting with "good intentions." Sometimes people see their opponents as intentionally evil: if so, the most common evils objected to are greed, selfishness, and disloyalty to a group. However, more commonly, many people see their opponents as ignorant, misguided, unintentional dupes of a more powerful "hidden enemy." Variations and synonyms are common, but the advocate's attitude can be expressed in one basic sentence: **"We are informed and good; they are ignorant and evil."**

Test this. What are some of the "causes" with which you disagree? How would you describe the advocates of those "causes"? What kind of people are they? What motivates them? (Are they malicious? Or misguided?) Another way to test this is to listen, for example in TV interviews, to "cause" advocates describe their opponents.

Many people in Left-wing movements view their opponents as "pawns" or "tools" of the rich (big business, capitalists, the Military-Industrial Complex, oil interests, Swiss bankers, Texas oil millionaires, cartels, corporations, conglomerates, organized religion, the Establishment, etc.) Right-wingers see their opponents as pawns of, or agents of communism (creeping socialism, the international communist conspiracy, etc.) or agents of the devil. Right-wing causes tend to use the God-on-our-side approach; the Left tends to be secular humanists fighting for the People. (Vox populi, vox dei?)

Common patterns in attacks:

The advocate's attitude: "We are informed and good; they are ignorant and evil."

Unintentional	Intentional
Ignorance	Evil
uninformed	greedy
unaware	profiteers
ignorant	hirelings
misled	mercenaries
misguided	stooges
misdirected	goons
naive	scabs
dupes of	parasites
tools of	lackey
used by	flunkey
pawns of	toady
victims of	running dogs
irrational	stool pigeons
crazy	fellow travelers
crackpot	hatchet man
screwball	fink
lunatics	traitor
extremists	treason
hard-core	disloyal
hysterical	Uncle Tom
fanatics	Judas
brainwashed	diabolical
gulled	malice

So far this book has emphasized "pep talks" consciously created by, or delivered by, *external* agents, often stressing the planned attempts by professional persuaders who are deliberately trying to manipulate a group. However, "pep talks" can also be *internalized* by individuals, rather unconsciously and haphazardly. People growing up in environments rich with propagandas are apt to create their own internal dramas of conflicts stimulated by external campaigns, but not under tight control. Individuals, for example, in their own memory and imagination may dwell on some rather strange combinations of "horror stories" and "atrocity pictures."

Occasionally, a crackpot or a crazy will try to assassinate a president or a pope, offering the rationale that they were only "doing their duty" or "doing God's will," bringing about justice for some earlier atrocity. More commonly, we'll see Letters to the Editor, or hear soapbox speakers, with a bizarre assortment of incoherent ramblings, a tirade of name-calling and invectives, and a disjointed collection of "horror stories," buzzwords, and jargon. Psychiatrists can offer a more extended analysis of the complex reasons why some individuals may do such things; but, even a layman can point out that we can reasonably expect a certain number of people today to be so influenced by the massive doses of "horror stories" and "atrocity pictures" that we all witness, often as part of unintended "spillover" audiences for "pep talks" aimed at others.

To recap: A "cause" involves a sense of duty to defend someone from a threat and gain a benefit. Causes often conflict, sometimes directly, more often indirectly. Opponents often disagree on what is the main issue. Dominance is sometimes the "hidden agenda" because related "causes" cluster and group-bonding attempts overlap. When change does occur, roles reverse: progressives, who had sought the change, now must use conservative rhetoric to defend it; vice versa. The pattern of the "pep talk" is a useful structural framework to identify and sort out parts of complex, emotional controversies. Advice for such analysis is given; illustrated by examples from some current "causes" in conflict (abortion, women's rights, nuclear freeze, pollution control, etc.) Individual participants often benefit from "pep talks" as their self-image is enhanced, playing meaningful roles in dramatic conflicts. Diverse roles exist (prophet, liberator, avenger) related to common themes; role-models from various sources often mix together. "True believers" in "causes" are likely to imply claims of moral superiority, epitomized in the advocate's attitude: *"We are informed and good; they are ignorant and evil."* But, opponents are more likely to be charged with unintentional flaws ("misguided, dupes") than with evil. Finally, individual people, as random receivers of the diverse "pep talks" within society, may internalize a strange mix of messages.

10

THE RESPONSE

The "pep talk" is a process, a movement toward an action. The intent of the "pep talk" is to gather together the collective energy of a group and direct it to take a specific action. This gathering process, the building up, or escalation, or "adding fuel to the fire," may go on in many different ways, but it commonly involves a continued and increasing series of "horror stories." These intensify the fears, increase the tensions, accumulate the forces, to the point where it is necessary to have a release, an explosion, a discharge, an overflow. In flight-or-fight terms of human behavior, the "pep talk" is part of a *fight* response: it is the verbal prelude to action, the threat returned.

The final part of the "pep talk" is the response, which involves the *triggering* of this release, and the *directing* of it.

Triggering the release is a matter of pacing and timing. The audience has to be sufficiently aroused and emotionally engaged in order for the spark to ignite the fire. Most of our language to describe triggering emphasizes degree and extremity: "last straw," "final insult," "crossed the line," "reached our limit," "breaking point," "had enough," "had too much," "more than we could bear," and so on. Our language suggests that the emotional intensity surpasses our rational powers of restraint: the adrenalin is flowing, we are out of control, we can't hold back, we've reached the breaking point. If a threat is removed, or when a danger passes, we are relieved: we "breathe a sigh of relief" and the tensions are relaxed.

Specific triggering devices include urgency words ("Now!" "Today") and the skilled use of questions ("Are you going to let them get away with that?") geared to elicit expected answers ("NO!"). This tactic can fail if the questions are poorly worded, poorly timed, or if the audience isn't sufficiently bonded or aroused; but, in favorable conditions, this is a very common triggering device. Most people have had some kind of personal experience listening to the build-up and triggering in the traditional "pep talks" given by athletic coaches.

Such experiences are examples in miniature of what the political persuader can do on a grand scale in a more sophisticated version. Hitler's propaganda machinery, a half century ago, for example, was very effective; it has provided us with horrible examples of what can happen when a skilled political persuader manipulates people. The Nazis, for example, originally seized control by using *provocateurs* and faked incidents (setting fire to the Reichstag) to create "horror stories" against the Communists. A few years later, Hitler started a systematic propaganda campaign against the Jews. At first, it was low-key, exploiting long-existing anti-Semitism. Little by little, the attacks kept escalating, until the climactic outburst of Kristalnacht, the night when "spontaneous" mobs throughout Germany broke the windows of stores and homes owned by Jews.

Direction. Ideally, an effective "pep talk" focuses the energy of the group on a specific course of action. A "pep talk" shouldn't end with a vague generality ("let's do *something*"), a qualification (". . . maybe . . . perhaps . . . if . . ."), or with an undirected hand-wringing, shoulder-shrugging "what *can* we do" letdown. The effective "pep talk" ends with the call for a *specific* action.

Sometimes this can be a simple call for *starting* motion ("Let's get going . . . go . . . fight . . . start . . . forward . . . onward") in contrast to passivity, rest, stasis, inaction. Calling for a "fight" or "struggle" is very common, almost an all-purpose call. Although this seems simple, it's very effective and frequently used. Robert Sam Anson, for example, in describing the political consultant David Garth (the media campaign manager on whom the movie *The Candidate* was based) wrote: "The rhetoric used by Garth and his aides reflects his obsession with combat. A campaign is a 15-rounder. Negative media is counterpunching. Coming from behind is getting off the deck. Winning, naturally, is a knockout. The imagery trails into the slogans Garth devises for many of his candidates: Fighting for the People of Illinois; Strong Enough to Speak His Mind, Tough Enough to Get Results; Give Yourself a Fighting Chance; Tough Young Men for Tough Hard Jobs; You Need a Fighter in Your Corner."

Sometimes the call can be for *endurance* ("Keep on . . . hold on . . . standfast . . . stick to it"); endurance words and slogans are very common because often efforts need to be sustained for long periods,

Words which *intensify*
Endurance

continue
do or die
don't give up, give in, give out
determined, determination
endure, endurance
forward
get going
go on
grit, true grit
guts
hang on
hold, hold on
keep, keep it up, keep on
keep going
move
never say die
never stop
never surrender
on, onward
outlast
outlive
persist, persistance
press
push
resist, resistance
resolve, resolution
stamina
stand, standfast, stand up for
stay the course
steady
stick, stick to it
stick to your guns
surmount
survive, survivor
take a stand
upward
withstand
work, work harder

"Attack words" intensify the opposite, undesirable qualities: coward, quitter, weakling, shirker, sissy, passive, apathetic, listless, etc.

against odds. Endurance often involves desperate situations in which the opponent is stronger. Common metaphors used in crisis situations include: "the chips are down," "back to the wall," "last ditch stand," "forced into a corner," "come from behind," "over my dead body"; closely akin to these are metaphors in defiance of danger: "come hell or high water," "through thick or thin," "to the gates of Hell." Historical allusions and quotations are often used to instill *esprit de corps* and to sustain morale: "Don't give up the ship," "Hold at all costs," "Fight to the last man," "Hold the fort," "Damn the torpedoes, full speed ahead," "Die with their boots on," "Winners never quit, quitters never win," "When the going gets tough, the tough get going," "Win one for the Gipper," the Spartans at Themopylae ("They shall not pass"), 3rd Division in WW1 ("the Rock of the Marne"), the Alamo.

Sometimes the call is to *re-direct* energies (to transform, change, channel, convert) away from "misdirected" or "misguided" efforts into other specific actions. Sometimes the call is to "join," "support," or "donate" (treated earlier): actions bonding the individual to the group, for the later ultimate purpose of taking some other action.

Often the response is specifically in contradition to the threat. Thus, if the *threat* is dominance by another, the *"cause"* is victory, and the *response* words and slogans will reflect this. In the following charts, the basic pattern of threat/cause/response is illustrated by some examples of slogans from recent political history.

The wording and meaning of slogans vary with the context. "Peace with honor," for example, may mean *keep fighting;* "Peace at any price" may mean *stop fighting.* "Damn the torpedoes, full speed ahead" simply exhorts continued effort and endurance through danger. "No Irish Need Apply" may sound quaint and unfamiliar today, but this phrase, discriminating against the Irish immigrants, was so common in the nineteenth century, it was simply abbreviated as NINA. In political struggles, opponents can turn a slogan ("Better Red than Dead"—"Better Dead than Red") and humorists can create a gallows humor in the midst of serious controversies: "Draft Beer, Not Students," "Kill a Commie for Christ."

Emotional connotations of these slogans depend much on the receivers' ideology; the same "victory" slogans might repel some audiences if they heard them being used by the communists ("Hasta La Victoria Siempre"—Cuba) or the fascists ("Sieg um Jeden Preis"—Nazi: "Victory at any price"), but might please the same audiences if they heard their local football coach say that "Winning isn't *everything, it's the only* thing!"

Clusters of related causes will always appear. This book divides and categorizes in order to clarify patterns, but in reality these artificial divisions imposed here seldom exist in any pure form. Any "invasion" or "restriction," for example, usually involves force, and implies domination. Thus, brief slogans and catchphrases can often cram many related concepts into a few words: "Peace, Prosperity, Progress" (Northern Ireland, Liberal Party); "Unity, Prosperity, Progress" (India, Congress

Party); "Sicher Arbeitsplatze, Stabile Wirtschaft"—"Guaranteed Employment, Stable Economy"—Germany Social Democrats).

Focusing the direction of response seeks to get a specific *kind* of action, the "right" kind. However, the *degree* of action must also be appropriate, neither "too much" nor "too little." The response sought must, in the context of the situation, appear to be *reasonable* and *appropriate*.

The appropriateness of the response is an important ethical issue. The threats may be real, but the responses suggested may be inappropriate. The problems may be real, but the solutions offered may be the wrong kind ("misguided") or the wrong degree (too weak, or too strong). For example, the severity of a resonse may be totally out of proportion to the threat: consider the world's condemnation of the Soviets for shooting down a Korean civilian airliner which strayed into Russian airspace. Generally, people have common standards of appropriateness so that there is not a major penalty for a minor transgression, nor a severe sharp response for a mild or vague threat.

Ethical decisions about appropriate responses are usually made after considering the whole context: of causes and effects, of the relation of part to whole, of the various options available, of the priorities of the person and the group. For example, a "save-the-animals" cause letter may be true and accurate in its re-telling of the "horror stories," but if the response sought is "Kill the hunters," this is blatantly unreasonable and inappropriate. So also, a Jewish "holocaust" atrocity picture may be a *true* and *accurate* record of Nazi crimes, *useful* and *effective* to bond a Jewish group; but if the ultimate response sought is to destroy an Arab town, then such new factors create serious ethical problems.

Or consider a closer example: football coaches often incite their teams with "pep talks," bonding the group together for concerted team effort. In most circumstances, such a "pep talk" with a closing exhortation of "giving one's all" is reasonable and appropriate. But what about the coach who urges a disabled star to keep playing with a knee injury? This might result in a short-term benefit to the group, but a long-term harm to the individual. Should an individual athlete be encouraged to take this kind of risk, or make this kind of sacrifice for game, for a temporary elation, for friends' sake, or perhaps even for a coach's career? What about dying for a "good cause"? Which one? Who?

People have the right to join a cause, to support a group, and to take action. But, they also have the right to refrain, to be skeptical, and to withhold action. There are times when a group must bond and perhaps must fight or take other action. But, there are also times when a group need not. The "pep talk" leads to action. But, action often leads to *others'* reaction. One action can start a sequence, a chain reaction, often producing unanticipated and unwanted results. The "pep talk" is not always appropriate, prudent, or wise; instead of stimulating response, action, or aggression, it might be more appropriate to have a "peace talk": words used to calm, to negotiate settlements, to reduce tensions, to reach compromises and mutual understandings.

KEY CONCEPTS		SLOGAN EXAMPLES

DOMINANCE
UP	Power to the People
GO	We're Number One
CONTINUE	All the Way with LBJ
WIN	Venceremos
GAIN	We Shall Overcome
FIGHT	Sieg Heil

DEATH & DESTRUCTION
VIVA	Viva La Papa!
BUILD	Long Live the King
CREATE	Peace and Prosperity
WORK	Peaceful Co-existance
MAKE	Negotiate Now
	Make Love, Not War

INVASION
WELCOME	The Yanks Are Coming!
COME IN	I Shall Return
GO IN	
RETURN	

RESTRICTION
FREE	Freedom Now
LIBERATE	Let My People Go
RELEASE	Free the Chicago Seven
DELIVER	Liberty or Death!
RESCUE	Break the Bonds

INEQUALITY
MORE	EQUALIZE	We Want Our Fair Share
INCREASE	BALANCE	Equal Pay for Equal Work
RAISE	RECTIFY	It's Our Turn
ADD	RETALIATE	Remember Pearl Harbor
EXPAND	REGAIN	Never again!
ENLARGE	RECOVER	59¢

CHAOS
KEEP	Keep America Safe
PRESERVE	You've Never Had It So Good
CONSERVE	Don't Let Them Take It Away
CONTINUE	Keep Cool with Coolidge
RE-ELECT	Let Us Continue

KEY CONCEPTS	SLOGAN EXAMPLES

DOMINANCE

DOWN	Down with Nixon (1972)
STOP	Dump the Hump (1968)
QUIT	Stop the War
CEASE	No Nukes!
END	Hell No. We Won't Go
	Strike! Boycott!

DEATH & DESTRUCTION

DEATH	Death to the Shah (1979)
DESTROY	Kill the King
KILL	Burn, Baby, Burn (1968)

INVASION

GET OUT	DISMISS	Yankee Go Home
KEEP OUT	REMOVE	Get Out of Vietnam
EVICT	REJECT	Love It or Leave It
OUST	REPEL	No Irish Need Apply
EJECT	RESIST	Pigs Off Campus

RESTRICTION

BAN	Ban Guns, Save Lives
SEIZE	Ban Commies, Not Guns
PROHIBIT	Close the Porn Shops
OUTLAW	Curb Speeders

INEQUALITY

LESS	Unfair to Organized Labor!
DECREASE	Better Working Conditions Now!
REDUCE	No Substandard Housing
LOWER	A Day's Wage for A Day's Work
SUBTRACT	Equal Rights for All
	Civil Rights Now

CHAOS

REFORM	Throw the Rascals Out
CORRECT	Time For a Change (1952)
CHANGE	Leaders, For A Change (1976)
AMEND	Let's Get America Moving Again
RENEW	Beat the Bosses
REVISE	*New* Deal, *New* Frontier

To recap: The ultimate goal of a "pep talk" is the response: the target audience is moved to action. The final part of the process involves *triggering,* often by means of loaded questions and urgency words; and *directing* the gathered energy toward a specific action: e.g., starting, continuing, redirecting, supporting a struggle against the threat. Examples from recent political history illustrate how various slogans express key concepts related to common threats and causes. The actual kind and degree of actions reasonable and appropriate to the situation are important ethical considerations.

11

IMAGES & ISSUES:
THE CONTENT OF ELECTION
RHETORIC

Political rhetoric in a modern democracy has some inherent complexities: the sheer number of speakers, quantity of information, diversity of viewpoints, variety of candidates and issues clamoring for our attention, the impact of the electronic age, and the growing sophistication of modern persuasion techniques. In an election year thousands of claims and charges, promises and threats, made by politicians and professional persuaders, advocates and amateurs, are broadcast to millions of people.

One result has been that many people, overwhelmed by the chaos of this blitz, drop out completely, justifying their position with universal attacks: "it's all lies . . . all phony promises anyway." Another common response is that people take sides too early (often inheriting the parents' beliefs), ignoring or discounting everything which doesn't fit into their preconceived notions. Other people get disgusted because "politicians are always arguing" or because reformers are "always complaining about something." Such an attitude doesn't recognize that conflict is essential in a democracy in which people with different interests, different values, and different viewpoints are free to disagree.

To analyze political rhetoric, the first step is to focus very closely on the **content** and **form,** to identify *what is being said* and *how it is being said.* While this may seem obvious and self-evident, it's all too seldom done. Most political discussions are characterized by their randomness and lack of coherence as people switch from one topic to another and soon lose any continuity or direction. In addition, such discussions often generate intense emotional involvement, not at all conducive to a rational discussion or systematic analysis.

To clarify complex issues, it helps to impose some kind of pattern or structure to identify and sort out the various messages. Such patterning also gives a greater sense of detachment and perspective. Various approaches are possible. Earlier, the "Intensify/Downplay" schema was used to analyze how we can *intensify* some elements of communication by means of repetition, association, and composition, and *downplay* other aspects, by means of omission, diversion, and confusion. Applicable to any kind of persuasion including commercial advertising and political persuasion that pattern concentrates on techniques on **form.**

To analyze **content,** here is one sentence which epitomizes or sums up the basic content of domestic political rhetoric: **"I am competent and trustworthy; from me, you'll get more (good) and less (bad)."**

The claims about the intellectual and moral virtues of the speaker and the promises about the benefits to the listener can be made positively or negatively, stated directly or suggested indirectly, made in broad generalizations or specific instances. In political attacks, for example, this sentence is reversed, stated negatively in the charges: "My opponents are incompetent and untrustworthy; from them you'll get more (bad) and less (good)."

Claims and Charges

This statement has three claims about the virtues of the speaker. The two obvious ones are "competent" and "trustworthy" corresponding to the traditional division of the *intellectual* and *moral* virtues. The hidden claim here is that of being a *benefit-giver:* "from me, you'll get . . ." Thus, these three correspond to Aristotle's concept of the *ethos,* the desirable projected image of the speaker as being *expert, sincere,* and *benevolent,* or, as some translators put it, as having *good sense, good moral character,* and *good will.*

Competency is the ability or potency to do the job. As an *intellectual* virtue, this would include knowledge, logical reasoning, and practical wisdom. Knowledge of information is basic, to be informed rather than ignorant. But, knowledge alone is not sufficient. The intellect must also be able to process this information in an organized systematic logical method. Finally, there is that quality which, in traditional philosophy, was called "prudence," the virtue of "practical wisdom" appropriate to the situation. In addition to these intellectual qualities, competency, as used here, would also include *physical ability* (adequate health, vigor, stamina, and endurance) and the element of *will, willpower*. Such qualities prepare someone for dealing with any future circumstances or crises. In popular slogans, the claim is "ready, willing, and able." The most common way to claim competency is to emphasize experience in similar situations, past achievements or accomplishments: "look at the record . . . proven ability. . . ." Presidential candidates, for example, stress parallel experiences; former state governors and corporation presidents will emphasize executive duties in organizing and managing; ex-legislators, ex-military leaders, and ex-diplomats all stress their particular *insider* status ("know-how," "knowing the ropes," "inner workings," etc.).

People have commonly distinguished competency apart from moral virtues. A competent person, for example, may be morally corrupt and totally untrustworthy. As Cardinal Newman expressed it: "Knowledge is one thing, virtue is another . . ."

The third major claim made is that of benevolence, here meaning that the person is a *benefit giver* or a *benefit promiser*: *"from me, you'll get. . . ."* This claim is the active link between speaker and audience, the key relationship of a transaction. This is not merely the passive description of a hero, but an active claim related to the desired effect: "I (my party, my plans, etc.) am (will be) the cause of these future good effects." Politicians (and advertisers) are benefit-promisers. We, their audiences, are benefit-seekers. It's not a one-sided affair; it's a mutual relationship in which both roles have their own goals. As we sort out the various claims of persuaders, we should remain aware of this two-way transaction; these persuaders are not only seeking something from us, we are also seeking something from them. Again, the actual expressions used to claim benevolence will vary. At present, the fashionable words are "concerned," "interested," "caring." Most "plain folks" appeals ("peoples' choice," "common man," "one of us") have this element of the persuader as being *one with* the audience.

If the common claims relate to these three major categories of the virtues of being competent, trustworthy, and benevolent, then the common *charges* in political attacks refer to their contradictories, the qualities of being incompetent, untrustworthy, and not benevolent.

Frequently, such charges are called *ad hominem** attacks. Be aware, however, that the phrase *"ad hominem* attack" is seldom used as a neutral describer; it is usually used as an attack phrase to criticize others. Those who make personal attacks justify these charges as being necessary to show that the opponent is incompetent or untrustworthy. Those who

*Ad hominem attacks in recent elections: *Incompetent:* 1964. Goldwater as extremist ("bomb"); 1968, Humphrey as vacillating. ("wishy washy"): 1972 McGovern as naive ($1,000 bill): 1976, Ford as clumsy bumbler: Carter as "hick"; 1980, Reagan as actor. *Untrustworthy:* 1964, Johnson as "wheeler dealer"; 1968, 1972, "Tricky Dicky" Nixon; 1976, Ford, a "fix" (Nixon's pardon).

are attacked respond that such charges (in addition to being untrue) are not relevant, that is, diversions away from the "real" issues. In practice, both sides usually attack and counterattack while simultaneously calling for the other to "stick to the issues."

Many personal attacks are untrue and unrelated. Nevertheless some *ad hominem* attacks can be true and can be *relevant* to the issues. There's no easy solution here, but an observer starts by first sorting out and recognizing what message is sent before examining the truth and relevancy.

The truth about some charges relating to factual matters sometimes can be proved or disproved. But, false charges about motives or intentions cannot. Thus the most intense personal attacks often focus on motives; even good deeds may be attacked for having ulterior motives, for being done for "the wrong reason," especially that of opportunism (personal ambition) and favoritism ("partisan politics"). Attackers can raise suspicions, cast doubts, or create misgivings in nearly any situation simply by attacking or questioning motives. The rhetorical question becomes a powerful weapon: "What's the *real* reason he did that?" "Did she *really* mean that?" It's a tough attack to fend off. No wonder politicians spend so much effort affirming and reaffirming their own virtues: "I am competent and trustworthy; from me you'll get. . . ."

Direct and Indirect

Claims and charges may be stated directly or suggested indirectly. Explicit statements are fairly easy to recognize, but people do not usually speak in precise terminology, nor reason in tidy syllogisms. We are more apt to encounter fragments of arguments, expressed in informal language and gestures or facial expressions. Nevertheless, these can be translated and ordered into patterns.

To say that a man is "incompetent" is a direct explicit statement; to say "he can't chew gum and tie his shoes at the same time" is an indirect suggestion which implies the same message. But the audience has to infer it, that is, to co-create with the sender, to receive an oblique fragment of a message and "translate" it.

In the 1980 primaries, for example, *flaky* was used to attack Jerry Brown's competency, and humorists spoke in quivering voices and imitated doddering-old-men to attack Ronald Reagan's fitness.

On the *surface,* the variations of different words and images, and the variations in emphasis, proportion, arrangement, frequency, duration, and speakers can be endless. Such claims and charges can be brief or extended, single or clustered, prominent or obscure. For example, a long extended series of biographical sketches about a candidate's business background or previous political experience might all repeat the same basic theme, and could be aptly summarized in one word as one claim, competency. On the other hand, multiple charges can be clustered and crammed into one sentence: ''Would you vote for a man who's a failure and a fanatic, a drunken sot, disloyal to his wife, his party and his country?''

Other speakers usually make positive claims and charges on the behalf of a candidate. It would be considered vain, egotistical, immodest, unseemly for the candidate to say so. Yet this praise must be made. Thus, various associates (advisors, advocates, presenters, endorsers, press agents, campaign managers, masters of ceremonies, radio and TV announcers, hired hands, etc.) function as speakers calling attention to these virtues. So also, in attack propaganda, it's usually considered poor form for the main candidate to engage in such attacks. Thus, the ''dirty work'' is done by a ''hatchet man'' who points out that the opponent is incompetent or untrustworthy.

Underneath the surface variations, there are basic patterns and limited options, as expressed here in the statement: ''I am competent and trustworthy; from me, you'll get more (good) and less (bad).'' We may never see or hear any candidate making a direct explicit statement in these exact words, but that sentence provides a useful structure for observers to perceive patterns and recognize relationships as we translate the indirect messages implied or suggested by metaphoric language, allusions, and nonverbal communication.

In everyday situations, most of our communication is in indirect metaphoric speech and nonverbals. If we don't like someone, we seldom use terms like *unpleasing* or *obsequious* because we have a rich vocabulary of metaphoric descriptors: turkey, creep, jerk, nerd, and all the *vulgar* expressions. In analyzing political language, we can look for the same sort of metaphoric speech. Instead of hearing the word *fortitude* we're more apt to hear candidates praised for their *backbone* or *guts*.

References (direct) and allusions (indirect) are ways of linking one thing with another person, place, or event. Every political party has its litany of heroes: for Democrats, a speech wouldn't be complete without references to Jefferson, FDR, and JFK; for Republicans, Lincoln has to be mentioned a few times; in communist countries, Marx and Lenin. Every political party and nationality also has its storehouse of nonverbal allusions—symbols, flags, patriotic music, all intended to create favorable associations.

The audience must share a common background to understand these references and allusions. Such references can relate to the historical past (the Alamo, Gettysburg, Pearl Harbor), to widely known current events (Watergate, the Bay of Pigs), or to any number of known customs or conventions within a society (April 15, CIA, Superbowl). Some cultural conventions can be more subtle. We are accustomed to seeing, for example, pictures of male political candidates, posed with the wife, four kids, and a dog. The message sent by this paternalistic *family man* image is clear: responsible, stable, protector, straight, trustworthy. Another mandatory campaign picture shows the candidate out on the farm or in the factory with rolled-up shirt sleeves. The message implied—hardworking, one-of-us, plain folks. Thus, such references and allusions can function as a shorthand (a condensation symbol) in which a word or a picture can suggest a whole cluster of associated ideas.

Wouldn't it be nice to know what are the qualities already loved or desired by an audience? Politicians think so, and advertisers too; that is the purpose of the billions spent for opinion polls, audience and market research.

But in general, we can already predict the things already loved by or desired by people: in the candidates, to be *competent, trustworthy,* and *benevolent;* in the issues, the basic benefits desired from domestic politics—*peace and prosperity.*

Promises and Threats

When we speak of *issues* in a political campaign, we're concerned basically with the "goods" (the benefits, the advantages) that people want, and the "bads" (the harms, the disadvantages) that people seek to avoid.

What are these good and bad things? They could be anything. (What's good for one may be bad for another) and they could be expressed in a variety of ways. Thus, in our simple formula, parentheses are used to suggest that any different kind of good or bad might be inserted into the statement "from me, you'll get more (good) and less (bad)."

For example, politicians might promise "more jobs," "greater opportunities," "safer streets," "increased Social Security benefits," "stronger military capability," "better government," "greater efficiency," "faster bus service," "greater prosperity," or "more responsive government."

Or, switching tactics slightly, the promises may be relief from the disadvantages: "lower taxes," "reduced inflation," "less wasteful," "lower crime rate," "fewer restrictions," "no more war," "lower unemployment," or "no nukes."

Furthermore, any of these promises can be suggested or indirectly phrased, but still related to the same basic message. To call for a "balanced budget" or to "tighten the purse strings," for example, basically says "less spending," i.e., less (bad).

In a typical campaign, there may be many specific issues and even more ways of referring to them. To get some kind of handle on this complexity, we need both to translate some of this material into more explicit statements and to impose some kind of sorting system somewhere between the highest levels of abstraction and the specific concrete instances.

At the highest level of abstraction, we can use the terms *good* and *bad*. A few words may represent this broad category: benefits and harms; advantages and disadvantages; opportunities and problems.

At some lower level of abstraction, yet still very abstract, are qualities and states such as happiness, virtue, peace, prosperity, liberty, security, and justice.

At a lower level are those more concrete, specific issues ("more jobs," "higher wages," "less crime," etc.) which are the constituent sub-categories, *the causes or conditions leading to the higher categories*, e.g., we fear inflation because it means loss of our money.

Observers are likely to disagree on how to categorize and sub-categorize many abstract terms which have multiple meanings freely and loosely used by people shifting meanings to fit their purposes. But we always are involved in such categorization, whether we do it formally or informally, systematically or not. Here are some categories commonly seen: in domestic political rhetoric, the basic benefits promises are *peace* and *prosperity;* in war rhetoric, *dominance;* in reform and revolutionary rhetoric, *justice* and *freedom;* in religious rhetoric, *salvation.*

These are not mutually exclusive categories. In practice, they are often clustered. American national political issues, for example, are a deeply interwoven mesh of international cold war issues *(dominance)*, of internal civil rights issues *(justice, freedom)*, and, often, fervent religious fundamentalism. Perhaps local city and state elections would be a better example of purely domestic politics. Seldom do politicians at that level have to get involved in war rhetoric or religious rhetoric. They can concentrate on promises that the system will run efficiently and honestly for the greatest possible benefit.

People usually agree in *general* and disagree about *specifics;* agree about *ends,* disagree about *means.* The higher the level of abstraction (the wider the generalization), the more agreement there is. At the highest level of abstraction, for example, all people seek "the good." Thus, the basic formula that the persuader promises "more (good) and less (bad)."

People usually agree at a slightly-lower level of abstraction when speaking about *qualities* or *states of being* as goals: For example, most people agree that "peace" and "prosperity" are desirable *goals.* (When "war" is praised, it's usually as a *means* to an ultimate "peace"; when material poverty is praised, it is usually as a *means* to another, spiritual, goal.) Thus, all politicians may be in favor of "prosperity" and against "inflation," yet disagree about the specifics of how to attain the good or avoid the bad.

"Honest disagreement" usually means a disagreement about specifics, the *means,* but it could refer to a different *goal* (a "mid" goal, not the ultimate "good"); or, relating to multiple goals, the wrong *degree* (proportion: which things get more money, time, etc.) or the wrong *priorities* (sequence: which things get done first). Even when focused on "the issues," such arguments about the "right way" usually imply claims of comparative competency: speakers have a better plan because they "know better."

People shift emphasis in different situations. In party primaries, for example, rival factions emphasize their *specific differences;* once a nominee is chosen, parties seek to emphasize their *general similarities* with "unity" and "loyalty" pleas, usually expressed in domestic metaphors (family spat, fence-mending, healing wounds, ironing out differences).

Politicians are often criticized or satirized for speaking in generalities about "Truth" and "Justice" and "the American Way of Life," but they know that such abstractions allow audiences to insert or to visualize *their own specifics.* When politicians do *get down to specifics,* they often lose the support of those who disagree.

It may be in the persuaders' interest to speak in general terms to please the widest audiences, but it is in the audiences' interest to keep seeking specifics. One function of journalists, as a voice of the people, is to keep asking politicians for specifics. An election campaign, for example, not only allows the candidates to perform (in their paid ads, intensifying their own "good" and attacking their opponents' "bad"), but it also allows voters to witness and assess how well candidates can handle multiple goals and multiple audiences in the give-and-take of interviews, debates, and unrestricted questioning.

When we attempt to analyze the numerous issues possible in a campaign, we usually have to do several things at once depending on the explicitness of the message and the level of abstraction. Frequently we have to translate indirect messages into more explicit statements, while simultaneously shifting levels of abstraction: for example, attacks against "red tape" translate to "unnecessary or wasteful procedures or paperwork" to "less waste" to "less (bad)."

Normally, we do such things spontaneously, a complex mental process of picking up cues and hints to understand the gist of the message. But if we wish to do it more systematically, we must methodically sort things into categories, noting the levels of abstraction within such categories. We may note the distinction, for example, whether a promise is a general one ("reduce government spending") or a specific one ("no MX missile," "no FTC") without claiming that one level is *better than the other*.

Perhaps the best result of our focusing on these promises of benefits is our own increased awareness that politics is a two-way transaction; not only are the persuaders *benefit-promisers,* but we are *benefit-seekers.* We are deeply involved. Too often we scapegoat politicians or "vested interests" without recognizing that we, too, are looking out for our own interests.

If we see such self-interest as a reasonable survival behavior, then politics, instead of being something dirty in which only nasty people get involved, can be seen as a clever human adaptation of conflict, a less violent way of handling conflicting interests without brute force. "I was told repeatedly not to enter politics," said the late Governor Nelson Rockefeller, "that politics is a 'dirty business'. . . . However, politics is the lifeblood of democracy. To call politics 'dirty' is to call democracy 'dirty.' "

Classroom Exercises

1. Tape-record a spontaneous political discussion (e.g., "What do you think of the recent campaign?") *prior* to any instruction in these patterns. Re-play later. Analyze.

2. Videotape TV campaign ads, news reports. Re-play. Analyze. Note wording, camera angles, backgrounds, editing techniques, time.

3. Clip ads, news reports: underline or circle quotes, key words and images, post on bulletin board.

4. Collect editorial cartoons (newspapers, magazines) and campaign jokes (hearsay, word-of-mouth). Look for these categories of being incompetent (bumbler, fool, unfit, inept, too old, etc.), untrustworthy (dishonest, extreme, etc.), not "on our side" (self-seeking, tool of others, etc.). Discuss caricatures, stereotyping, satire.

5. Create an *allusion* list of names, places, events (Lebanon, Central America) often mentioned during the campaign, intended for some emotional effect.

6. Write political slogans or TV scripts for candidates (fact or fiction) using the content here in various forms: balanced sentences in antithesis, parallel paragraphs, etc.

7. Generate a list of one hundred ways to suggest indirectly that someone is untrustworthy: "Would you . . .?" snake-in-the-grass . . . Judas . . . Iago . . . backstabber . . . watch your wallet (or, as Emerson put it: "The more he talked of his honor, the faster we counted the spoons"). Afterward: sort into major categories, such as rhetorical questions, allusions, irony, metaphors, etc. Sub-sort metaphors by content (nature, body, war, sports, etc.).

8. Create "translation" exercises, getting the gist of a message indirectly suggested. For example: Father says, "No car tonight!" Son says, "Seig Heil!" What's the gist of the son's message?

IMAGES

Checklist: Sorting out the content of Election Rhetoric

1. IDENTIFY ANY CLAIMS	2. IDENTIFY ANY CHARGES

"I AM COMPETENT . . .   (INCOMPETENT)

Competency is the result of being informed, reasonable, wise, healthy, active, experienced in the past, determined for the future.

____ informed, knowledgable, aware

____ reasonable, coherent, rational

____ wise, prudent, practical, adroit

____ healthy, fit

____ active, hardworking

____ experienced, proven, prepared

____ strong, determined, decisive

____ ignorant, uninformed, unaware

____ unreasonable, incoherent, irrational

____ foolish, imprudent, impractical, clumsy

____ unhealthy, unfit

____ passive, lazy

____ inexperienced, untried, unprepared

____ weak, vacillating, indecisive

AND TRUSTWORTHY . . .   (UNTRUSTWORTHY)

Being trustworthy results from being honest, fair, courageous, temperate, dependable, and loyal.

____ honest, truthful, sincere

____ just, fair, impartial

____ courageous, brave, bold

____ moderate, temperate, controlled

____ dependable, reliable, predictable

____ loyal, faithful

____ dishonest, deceitful, untruthful

____ unjust, unfair, biased

____ cowardly, afraid, fearful

____ intemperate, extreme, uncontrolled

____ undependable, unreliable, unpredictable

____ disloyal, unfaithful

FROM ME, YOU'LL GET . . .

Benefactor; benefit-promising; being "on your side."

____ friendly, concerned, interested

____ kind, generous, sharing

____ "on our side," "one of us"

____ unfriendly, unconcerned, uncaring

____ selfish, ambitious, opportunist

____ working for others, favoritism

& ISSUES

3. IDENTIFY THE PROMISES AND WARNINGS

. . . MORE (GOOD) AND LESS (BAD)

Consider the level of abstraction: *People usually agree in general (goals, ends), disagree about specifics (means).*

Highest level of abstraction; broadest generalization	benefits advantages opportunities	harm disadvantages problems
Very high level of abstractions; (qualities, states of being) — very broad generalizations	peace, tranquility prosperity, abundance, freedom, liberty, justice, equality, dominance success, efficiency, integrity	war, conflict loss, poverty restriction, slavery injustice, inequality humiliation, failure waste, corruption
More specific, more concrete; (*causes or conditions* of the higher-level *abstractions*)	more jobs higher wages better roads increased services	less taxes less crime fewer unemployed reduced inflation

To recap: To help analyze the content of election rhetoric, one sentence can usefully summarize the basic claims and promises: "I am competent and trustworthy; from me, you'll get more (good) and less (bad)." In attacks, the core content of the charges and warnings is the reverse: "My opponents are incompetent and untrustworthy; from them you'll get more (bad) and less (good)." The "surface variations" and indirect ways of saying or suggesting these things are endless, but this sentence provides a useful frame, or memory device, to focus on and to sort out a candidate's key claims (expert, sincere, benevolent: Aristotle's *ethos*) and to emphasize the transaction that political benefit-promising is linked with our own benefit-seeking.

"To doubt everything or to believe everything are two equally convenient
solutions: both dispense with the necessity of reflection."

—Poincare

12

LIES & DECEPTIONS: PROBLEMS OF TRUTH AND ACCURACY

Any discussion of the language of advertising and of politics eventually has to deal with lying and deception. Do advertisers lie? Are politicians deceptive? Although some people may answer these questions very quickly, there are complex concepts involved which deserve some thought: "truth," "opinion," "bias," "puffery," "illusions," "delusions," "errors," "lies," "deceptions," "evasions," "suggestions," "imitations," "white lies," and so on.

This book primarily focuses on language techniques, on how people can use words and images. But this chapter introduces a new element: the *intent* to deceive. Neither the motivation nor the morality of deception can be given full attention; these complex matters can be best treated more fully by psychologists and philosophers. But these matters are introduced here to suggest some of the wider issues and contexts in which the techniques of language operate. (This chapter is strongly indebted to Sissela Bok's *Lying: Moral Choice in Public and Private Life,* Pantheon, 1978, an excellent survey of the philosophic backgrounds and moral issues.)

Sorting out what is *not* deceptive often helps to clarify some issues and to focus on the problem areas. If we can reach agreement on what isn't deceptive, we need not waste time and effort arguing about the wrong issues. Many of the current debates about deceptive advertising and political lying can be simplified by a systematic sorting out process.

Some Basic Sorting

To clarify, it helps to use a simple branching diagram to show some of the options: the information conveyed could be *true* or *not-true;* if the information is *not-true,* the speaker may *not-know* (an error) or may *know;* if the speaker *knows* the information is *not-true,* there may be *no intent* to deceive (a fiction) or an *intent* to deceive (a deception); a deception can be made *explicitly* in a statement (a lie), or *implicitly,* by some kind of suggestion or evasion.

The diagram below represents these four options, and the shaded areas represent the "gray areas" or "borderlines" in which nearly all the problems and difficulties occur. Not diagrammed here, but discussed later in the chapter, are such issues as the effectiveness of deception, the purposes and results, good intentions, white lies, paternalism, and the credibility gap. First, the basic diagram:

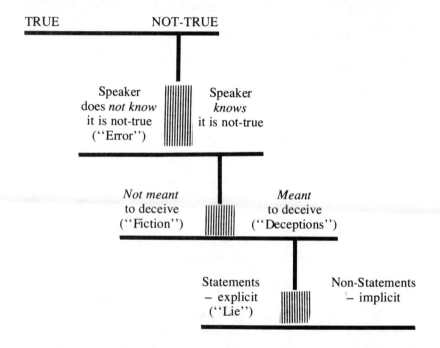

A "lie," for example, is usually defined as "a statement or assertion of something known or believed by the speaker to be untrue with intent to deceive." This diagram helps clarify by distinguishing lies from errors, fictions, and implied deceptions.

In everyday usage, a common cause of confusion is a shifting definition of the word *lying*. Sometimes this word is used very broadly, as a
synonym for *deception*. Usually we do this when other people are
vaguely deceptive or are evading a direct answer, and we call them
"liars"—a strong attack word. But, when we are evading a direct
answer, we often use the more restricted definition of lying, limiting
lying to explicit verbal statements. We are prompt to assert our innocence: "I didn't *say* that . . . I never *said* that."

When the word *lie* is used here, it will be very restricted and precise,
limited to explicit verbal statements. *Deception* is the wider category
which includes all kinds of nonverbal messages and implications.

Before we leave this branching diagram, note how it can be applied
to common excuses. If a person is caught in a lie, the standard defense is
to plead the lesser offense, to shift across the border to safer areas. Note
how each of the common excuses illustrated below shifts away from the
more serious charge of lying.

Truth/Non-Truth
"It seemed to me . . ."   (Affirming truth, opinion)

Known/Not-Known
"I was mistaken . . ."   (Affirming unintentional error)

Fiction/Deception
"I was just kidding . . ."   (Affirming non-intent to deceive)

Statement/Non-Statement
"I didn't *say* that . . ."   (denying one is a *liar*)

Good Intent/Bad Intent
"I only meant to help . . ."   (Affirming good intentions)
"I didn't mean any harm . . ."   (Denying bad intentions)

Good Result/Bad Result
"It was for your own good . . ."   (Affirming good result)
"It didn't hurt you . . ."   (Denying bad result)

Some Basic Assumptions

Any statement can be a lie.
Any behavior can be deceptive.
Any person can deceive, or be deceived.

Any statement can be a lie. There's no way to tell, from the words used, if a statement is true or false, or if it has the intent to deceive. If someone were to say "that's my car," or "I flew in from Chicago last night," there's no clue in the words to indicate any falsity or any deception. There may be nonverbal clues or situation clues, but nothing in words themselves to indicate lying. Lying is not identifiable by the words used.

Any behavior can be deceptive, can have the intent to deceive. The ability to deceive another about intentions is seen here as a survival behavior for the individual: *successful or effective deception gives the deceiver an advantage,* both in defense and attack situations. However, because people are social animals, society counter-balances this advantage by placing strong injunctions (laws, penalties, guilt) against deception. Very strong injunctions are placed by both church and state against aggressive deception; lesser penalties apply and more loopholes are available when deception is used in self-defense.

If we choose the advantage of deception, society counter-balances, and we run the risk of other penalties. One of these penalties, for most people, is the sense of guilt, shame, embarrassment, or uneasiness when they tell a lie or are deceptive. Frequently, the guilt and anxiety are shown in certain behaviors such as blushing, sweating, stammering, averting the eyes, which *some time* accompany lies and deception by *some* people. So, in one way, there are some cues which tip-off a lie.

However, not all people react this way. Psychopathic liars with little social concern are less likely to show such behaviors than people who have been raised with a strong social and rigid religious upbringing. Lie detectors and voice-stress analyzers and other devices which claim to measure truthfulness have limited effectiveness. Although some popular books about nonverbal communication have claimed that we can learn to "read" the nonverbal cues and *know* when people are lying, the serious scholars in this research do not make such unqualified claims. The cluster of cues we normally associate with lying and deception can also have other causes, and some people can deceive without any external tipoffs.

Any person can deceive, or be deceived. Everyone is able to lie and to deceive. But some people are "better" liars than others, that is, some people are more effective in deceiving others, in having their lies accepted by others. On the receiving end, some people are more gullible, more naive than others; some people are more likely to be deceived than others. The effectiveness of deception depends both on the senders *and* receivers. In actual practice, few people are extremely deceptive or extremely gullible. Degree is important here. In different situations, we're apt to have greater or lesser degrees of gullibility or deception.

The *potential* for deception is greater today than in the past, simply because of the mass media which allows instant access to millions of people and which takes away some of the natural defenses against deception, some of those nonverbal cues or "leakage" which would tip off some deception. A commercial or political advertisement can simply edit out, in a videotaped presentation, any unwanted or unfavorable images.

Political leaders and business leaders often bemoan the "credibility gap" today, the fact that people are becoming more skeptical of information sent to them by these leaders. But, such growing distrust of the professional persuaders may well be a very reasonable response: reducing the degree of blind-faith acceptance of incoming messages may well be a survival behavior countering the increased potential for deception.

Lies and deceptions, generally speaking, are not illegal. Most of the lies told in this world are among family and friends and acquaintances, and there are only a relatively few situations in which laws prohibit deceptions. Usually such laws are concerned with social interactions where money is involved (fraudulent misrepresentation in business transactions) or a public trust (official documents, legal witnesses). Such situations are so rare that the occasions are usually marked by a visible social gesture: a public oath with raised hand, a signed certificate, a notarized statement affirming the truth.

Under oath we swear to tell "the truth, the whole truth, and nothing but the truth." The spirit of the law can be followed; the literal letter cannot: there is no way to convey the "whole truth." This poetic phrasing is an encouragement to full disclosure, not a statement of an attainable reality.

For centuries, common law tradition has focused on the intent to deceive as an important element in determining fraudulent misrepresentation. In contrast to this, the Federal Trade Commission (FTC), which has been empowered to stop "deceptive advertising," does not have to prove *intent,* but the *ability* or capacity to deceive. Such a distinction made it easier to define or identify a "deceptive" ad simply by the opinion or judgment of the Commissioners, but the FTC was severely limited in enforcement and penalties.

Basically, there was a trade-off. The FTC got some reasonable flexibility in defining deception, but didn't get the power to send someone to jail or to levy fines. The basic FTC penalty was a "cease and desist" order which prohibited the ad from appearing, without charging the violators with illegal acts. In practice, an ad campaign could run its course before the necessary legal action could get it stopped. In some cases, legal appeals delayed the process for ten or fifteen years, while the deceptive ads kept appearing.

Misunderstanding the limitations of the FTC can cause people to have a false illusion of security. Because most people are vaguely aware of the general intention of the laws to prohibit deceptive advertising, some people assume that the government protects them from all deception: "It must be true, or else the government wouldn't allow it on TV!"

This is not so. <u>No matter what laws are on the books, it's almost impossible to stop fraud and deception.</u> Consider the history of the Postal Service which has been trying to enforce the laws against hard-core mail frauds: con games, swindles, chain letters, Ponzi schemes, etc. Despite their efforts of surveillance and enforcement, every year Americans will lose more than $50 million dollars to the same old hard-core frauds. Laws alone do not protect.

Instead of trying to catch crooks, after the fact, today the general trend of the FTC is toward preventative measures. During the 1970s, consumerist reforms were reflected in new experiments by the FTC designed to reduce deceptive advertising: requirements to substantiate claims, encouragement of comparative advertising, and use of "corrective" ads. Perhaps the most influential reforms are going on unnoticed by the general public: the setting up of "industry guidelines" suggesting, in advance, what the FTC would consider deceptive if it were to be used. Such suggestions do not have the force of law, but they do keep many advertisers away from the borderlines. Such voluntary restraint and self-regulation will not deter someone who is bent on deception. But these guidelines have shown their usefulness already in helping to clarify some complex problems about the legality of some deceptions and lies.

Religious precepts cover much broader ground and define many more lies as "sins." Moralists are often concerned with the degrees of seriousness of lying, ranging from "venial sins" for lesser offenses (fibs) to "mortal sins" for serious lies and deceptions. Secular social sanctions, too, are very strong against lying and deception. We condemn duplicity and mendacious behavior; there are strong feelings against someone who is two-faced or a double-dealer.

If any statement can be a lie, intended to deceive, consider some of the ways this can be expressed using the four-part pattern of aggressive behaviors:

People can lie *to intensify their own "good."*

Call this a *"false claim." Advertisers, for example, can make false claims* about products.

People can lie *to intensify others' "bad."*

Call this a *"false charge,"* or a *"false witness,"* or a *"calumny."*

Such aggressive lying has the strongest social and religious prohibitions against it, probably because of the potential harm done to others. To malign someone is against the law (*slander* and *libel*), and has strong religious injunctions against it: "Thou shall not bear false witness against thy neighbor."

People can lie *to downplay their own "bad."*

People can *explicitly deny* something (different from passive omission, evasions, or other implicit deceptions).

People can lie *to downplay others' "good."*

People can *explicitly deny* the "good" of others (different from passive neglect).

Most people would agree that we can *intensify* either with or without
an intent to deceive: truths, lies, deceptions, or errors can be repeated;
things can be associated together truthfully, deceptively, or erroneously;
truths or lies can be well-composed. There's no necessary relation between the techniques used and the intent.

However, some difficult questions occur with *downplaying.* Some
people may believe that downplaying is deceptive in itself, or that evasions are intrinsically deceptive. Although it is true that the intent to
deceive may be more common and probable, it is not intrinsic or necessarily related to the techniques of downplaying.

While some *omissions* may be intended to deceive, we do recognize
that omissions can also occur without the intent to deceive—through
accidental error or because of our subjective focusing on some things,
omitting others. So also, *confusion* can be an unintentional error. *Diversion* is difficult to explain as an accident or error, because it seems that
when one diverts attention away from a main issue, there exists intentional choice. Nevertheless, it is a common situation to hear two people,
in sincere disagreement, tell each other "you're not listening to what I'm
saying . . . you missed the whole point." Neither one intends to deceive,
yet one person's main issue may be a side-issue to the other; each one
unintentionally diverts the incoming main issue, treating it as a side-
issue, "missing the point."

Opinions

Opinions are our personal beliefs, our subjective feelings, our judgments in favor or against something. Opinions are conclusions, based on
some observed facts. Often opinions are formed very fast, very ran-
domly, but they are conclusions based on a mass of incoming data that
we see, hear, or otherwise sense. We quickly convert the conclusions into
premises on which new reasoning takes place. Once we form a strong
opinion, then new incoming information gets flavored by it. Often, to
defend opinions we now hold as "true," we adjust by filtering out new
information which doesn't correspond to our held opinions.

Opinions are treated here as the disputed borderline between those
things which are generally agreed upon to be true and those which are
generally agreed upon to be not true; most people will agree on the
extremes.

The observer's interests and background influence not only the focus (the basic selection/omission process) but also the evaluation.

FOCUS:
Selection/Omission process
Observer's interest

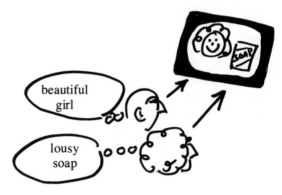

Yet, even if we agree on focus, we can differ in judgments.

OPINION:
Observer's evaluation

Puffery is the term commonly used today to describe what used to be called "seller's talk." In defending puffery, advertisers frequently like to downplay any bad connotations by adding modifiers: "*mere* puffery" or "*harmless* puffery." In *The Great American Blow-Up*, (1975), Ivan Preston, summarizing the legal history of puffery, states, "The law holds that people who act reasonably will automatically distrust puffery, will neither believe it or rely upon it, and therefore cannot be deceived by it." (Preston himself dissents, argues that puffery is deception, and seeks changes in the laws: "Puffery deceives, and the regulations which have made it legal are thoroughly unjustified.")

"By legal definition," Preston writes, "puffery is advertising or other sales representations which praise the item to be sold with subjective opinions, superlatives, or exaggerations, vaguely and generally, stating no specific facts." Universal generalizations about feelings, such as "*everyone loves*," or assertions that "you'll love . . . you'll feel . . . just what you've always wanted" are usually permitted by law.

True claims about specific facts and measurable items present no problem. Some products and services *are* superior, the best in their category; sellers and workers certainly have justifiable pride in making truthful claims of such excellence. Even in cases where there might be an argument about excellence, sometimes, an honest enthusiasm, a kind of "esprit de corporation" might lead sellers to believe their own press releases. Extravagant claims may exist without the intent to deceive.

False claims are both illegal and immoral. There are some practical problems of *detecting* false claims. Until the late 1970s, the FTC efforts at checking claims were random and sporadic: advertisers frequently made unsubstantiated claims, withdrawing them only if their ads happened to be threatened with a "cease and desist" order. After the FTC started its systematic program to require advertisers to substantiate claims, it was swamped with masses of paperwork, the details and statistics needed to back up the claim. There is no simple solution to the practical problems of enforcing the law, but there's no disagreement that false claims are both illegal and immoral.

Most borderline problems of puffery occur with *parity products* (those with little or no differences) or with products, such as autos, in which the unmeasurable qualities of personal satisfactions are very important. Puffery can be seen both as an opinion and as an "expected" fiction or hyperbole.

Puffery: "... subjective opinions, superlatives, or exaggerations, vaguely and generally, stating no specific facts."

TRUE CLAIM	**PUFFERY**	**FALSE CLAIM**
Legal & Moral	"Borderline" problem area	Illegal & Immoral

"one owner . . . two seats . . . three ashtrays . . . four tires . . . five passengers . . . six cylinders . . . seven . . ."	"Beautiful . . . fantastic value . . . good looking . . . useful . . . fast . . . rare . . . classic . . . elegant . . . a real joy . . . ideal"	"Goes 150 miles an hour . . . gets 85 miles per gallon . . . driven less than 2,000 miles . . ."
Many true claims possible: problems may occur with *priorities* —which are most important.		Many false claims possible: problems may occur with *detection* of false claims or *enforcement* of laws.

Illusions

An illusion is a misinterpretation of something really existing (in contrast to a delusion—in which there's nothing really "out there"); the common usage of the term suggests falseness, but is ambiguous whether we have been mistaken or have been deceived.

Often, to be *disillusioned* is simply a recognition that our previously-held beliefs were simply our opinions, and not the "truth." When we speak of someone whose illusions were shattered or destroyed, we're usually describing a situation in which the person had totally intensified the "good" and downplayed the "bad" of one's own position: a kind of self-deception, not realizing that there may be other ways at looking at the same reality.

The most likely things we are apt to have illusions about are those things which have been highly praised, intensified, idealized. Consider, for example, that many of our religious and patriotic ideals are taught by sincere adults to young children and are accepted, uncritically. A child often accepts opinions as "truth," and ideals as realities. Later, when the person finds out that religious and political leaders have feet of clay, or that corruption exists, or that reasonable people disagree, some believers become disillusioned. A common reaction is overreaction: going to the other extreme, cynicism, an attack position which intensifies the "bad," denies the "good" of that which had previously been idealized.

Commercial advertising is also likely to cause disillusionment because ads intensify the "good," downplay the "bad." People who are most strongly antagonistic toward advertising are probably those who were once believers. Considering the way television toy commercials have hyped children in the past generation, there may be millions of people so affected: still cynical about advertising because of those broken promises from their childhood.

Errors

Errors are not lies. An error is *unintentional;* the human brain is capable of making mistakes. Incoming messages, for example, can be misunderstood due to noise, interruptions, ambiguity in the words or the signals; or the receivers might be impaired physically, slightly blind or deaf, mentally retarded, fatigued, limited in the language, or in their vocabulary. Even if none of these factors are present, people still make mistakes because of some inner "short circuits" in the brain. Such unintentional behavior is most dramatically seen as a result of drugs or chemical imbalance, but everyone experiences errors daily.

While some errors may be "Freudian slips," revealing some repressed secret, most errors can be described almost in mechanical terms of standard sequences of actions. In some errors, we omit a step in a sequence ("slipped my mind," "forgot it"), or select an inappropriate step from another sequence (pick up a ringing phone and say "Come in''). We can be focused or pre-occupied with one thing and block out other things; or we can lose focus, get distracted and forget what we were doing. At times we can be overloaded, disorganized, scatterbrained, with many sequences out of order. When we speak, we can be tongue-tied or have mental blocks or transpose words (Spoonerisms, for example); we can have errors in hand-eye coordination (type the wrong letter), be awkward, clumsy, stumble, "trip over one's own feet," and so on. All are evidences of little errors, wrong connections in our mental wiring. All of these things may affect the preception or transmission of the "truth" of a message, yet such unintentional errors are not considered lies.

If people are caught telling a lie, they often claim it was an error, that is, they downplay their own "bad" because it is commonly less serious to be guilty of an error than a lie. Because there is difficulty in proving intent, we do have common phrases which are used to emphasize the innocence of the speaker's intention when an error has been committed, or to accuse another of a bad intention.

Common phrases used to emphasize intent:

ERROR	*LIE*
(usually defensive, intensifying own "good")	*(usually accusations, attack, intensifying others' "bad")*
"an honest error"	*"that's a deliberate lie"*
"an honest mistake"	*"a bold-faced lie"*
"purely accidental"	*"a brazen lie"*
"just an accident"	
"I didn't mean it"	

When an "error" works out to the advantage of the person who makes the error, others often suspect that the intent may have been deliberate. "Accidentally, on purpose" is an old phrase (made into a song title in the 1940s) used to express skepticism in such cases. Many "underestimated bids" or "cost overruns" are highly suspect when the "error" is made in favor of the bidder.

Individuals are more likely to make errors than groups working together. In public persuasion, for example, the editorial process and the committee work involved in preparing advertisements or political propaganda usually discovers the errors made by individuals within the group. In most cases, such errors are corrected, deleted or revised before the work is made public. Occasionally, there will be a misprint or a typo, a minor error here and there. But we do expect a level of competency, and if any major error of substance occurs, it is reasonable for observers to infer the possibility of deception.

Delusion, as used here, is restricted to mean that kind of error which is caused by a disorder in the nervous system, an abnormal psychotic condition of the mind. In contrast to "illusion," in which something "out there" is misinterpreted, with a delusion (or hallucination) there is nothing out there. A delusion has no basis in reality; the stimulus comes from within (e.g., the sensory hallucinations produced by LSD). However, psychoanalytical jargon ("delusions of grandeur," etc.) has been used so loosely in common speech that we're likely to hear the word used to describe *any* kind of fantasies, daydreams, illusions, or wishes about the future.

Fictions

Fictions are not lies. Fictions are stories and tales, plays and dramas, "made-up" products created by the human imagination. Fictions are not "true," but they have no intent to deceive.

The traditional theory of literature sees storytelling as a kind of imitation of life *(mimesis),* a representation or recreation of the experience of life in words. Fiction often claims a kind of universal truth, that such a thing could have happened, or that something similar has happened, or might happen under certain circumstances. Audiences recognize such "truth" in works well written, and often through literature, can gain new insights into their own lives.

Within the realm of storytelling, we can recognize extremes: at one end, we have fantasy stories of exotic, strange, improbable or impossible things which are obviously unreal; at the other end, we have realistic stories, with a sense of verisimilitude—the appearance of truth or reality. In addition to stories, "fiction" here will include certain non-literal uses of words—hyperbole, metaphor, and irony—as ways we use language, not literally true, but without intent to deceive.

Literature has certain conventions, certain customs which are mutually recognized by writers and audiences. Conventions can involve the words used, or certain styles of writing appropriate to certain topics. In the drama, conventions involve all kinds of mutually-accepted stagecraft devices such as costumes, masks, scenery, stage whispers, asides, gestures, soliloquies, and so on. Deception is not involved because of the audience's awareness, consent and approval. As Coleridge phrased it, we have a "willing suspension of disbelief" which allows us to have a literature of the imagination.

A minority opinion holds that fictions are lies. The Puritans, for example, in 1640 closed the English theaters as being the "devil's workshop" because they believed acting was lying. A small percentage of people, even today, consider all fairy tales and fictions (such as Santa Claus) as lies—shameful and sinful. A somewhat large number of people are literalists in language: while they may not object to stories (or give up watching movies and TV), they do insist on a literal interpretation of words (often involving the King James Version of the Bible) and have a hard time with hyperbole, metaphors, and irony.

However, even if the majority opinion is accepted, that we do have standard conventions, problems still arise because writers are notoriously clever and inventive, coming up with new ideas, breaking old conventions, and always making new borderline cases between fact and fiction, creating new areas which are not covered by such mutual awareness, consent, and approval. Are these borderline areas deceptive?

Borderline cases in literary works commonly cause trouble for critics. Anytime there is not a clear-cut distinction between fact and fiction, there is apt to be some kind of controversy about the borderline. The French term *roman à clef* is used, for example, to describe a novel closely based on real characters and incidents, often described as a thinly-disguised fictionalized version with minor changes in names and places. Whenever a *roman à clef* is published, there's usually an argument over the key or the identifications. While some frame devices (such as the "outside narrator" telling a story-within-a-story, or purported "editors" who "found the manuscript") are commonly recognized and accepted as fictions, other literary techniques generate arguments about "reality." When Truman Capote, for example, used the term "non-fiction fiction" to describe his book *In Cold Blood,* based on an actual murder case, critics recalled that Theodore Dreiser had used pages of verbatim courtroom transcripts worked into *An American Tragedy* a half-century earlier. The blending of real and fictional characters and events (such as Doctorov's *Ragtime,* or Dos Passos' *U.S.A.* trilogy, or any number of historical romances) creates such borderline problems, leaving the reader unsure of what is "made up" and what is not.

The New Journalism (Tom Wolfe, and others) which blends observed facts together with the reporter's inferences, also creates borderline problems. So too, in any book based closely on psychoanalytical case-histories or case-studies, the clear-cut distinctions are gone.

In the movies and on television, "docu-dramas" present a fictionalized history which can seem very authentic because of the skillful use of camera techniques (grainy film, hand-held camera, etc.); in some cases, film footage and clips of the "real" thing are edited together with the dramatized portions so that it is almost impossible to separate illusion from reality. In 1970, a newspaper survey indicated that some Americans did not believe that the moon landing had actually happened; they felt it had been faked by movie and television techniques, a political hoax to deceive the public. In 1978, a popular movie *(Capricorn One)* used this as a basis for a story about NASA faking a Mars landing in order to keep their program (and budget) alive. In the future, borderline problems in fiction will probably become more complicated as technical ways to reproduce and imitate become more sophisticated.

Disclaimers are often required by law to identify works of fiction. In movies, for example, the printed disclaimer appears in the opening credits—a long complex phrase in fine print that goes by so quickly it is hardly noticed—which tells us that the work is fiction and "any similarity" to real people or real names is "purely coincidental."

Borderline cases in advertising occur in all of the media. Some television commercials, for example, appear to be program material: they *look like* news programs, interviews, or documentaries. Because of this blurring of the borderline between program and non-program material, the FCC has required some labeling of commercials ("Demonstration," "Dramatization"), but borderlines constantly change and disclosure regulations are not easy to formulate. In print media, the borderline cases are those advertisements which *look like* news stories or editorial content in newspapers and magazines. These ads will use the same style, typeface, headlines, and photos with captions, in an apparent effort to deceive the reader into believing that an outsider was writing about the product. By law, these ads must carry a "slug line" notice ("Advertisement"), but this law is not very rigorously enforced.

Jokes are fictions, not meant to deceive. Americans are most accustomed to exaggeration: the tall tale, the stretcher, the whopper; British humor tends to understate. In both extremes, "truth" or "reality" is intensified or downplayed for humorous intent. We laugh at the incongruities, because we know things aren't really that way. The greater the exaggerated difference, the easier it is to recognize the humor.

A borderline case in humor is the "put-on"—in which the message and intent are ambiguous. The audience is never quite sure whether it's a joke or "for real": "are you putting me on?" In most kinds of kidding, the fun is in letting the victim *know* a trick has been played; the victim of a put-on never has certainty.

In informal conversation, a borderline case occurs with slightly exaggerated storytelling, not the deliberate, obvious exaggerations of a tall tale. Some people tend to exaggerate, inflate, embellish: intensify their own "good" and others' "bad." War stories told by veterans, adventures told by travelers, sporting events recalled by fans are apt to select those details which intensify their "good" (their courage, skill, wit, endurance, etc.) or the opposing "bad" (the dangers, difficulties, etc.) Even everyday "adventures" are hyped up, to make them more exciting or more interesting (to the audience? to the storyteller?); such a tendency to make one's own stories (and life) more interesting is rather common. Historians soon learn to take eye-witness reports with a grain of salt.

Metaphors are not lies. Metaphors are fictional conventions. When we metaphorically say that something *is* something else ("He's a tiger" or "He's a chicken") we are not making a literal statement, but we are implying that one has certain qualities of the other.

Many products use metaphoric names, associating the product with something favorable. The names of automobiles, for example, are often selected for their connotations of speed, power, sleekness, freedom, vitality: Mustang, Maverick, Pinto, Cougar, Falcon, Skyhawk. (It's unlikely

that Ford will ever feature a Sloth, Pig, Chicken or Turkey.) Such metaphors are not deceiving. When people go to a Ford dealer to buy a
Mustang, they do not expect it, literally, to have hooves, eat hay, and
neigh.

On the other hand, if people purchase something with the name or
label "Natural Wool," "Genuine Leather," or a "Virginia ham," they
do expect it to be a certain type and quality of product, and not a
metaphoric use of the words. Such use would be deceptive: *"literally
misdescriptive names."* Laws concerning deceptive product names and
labeling are often much stricter and more specific than laws about deceptive advertising in general, Names may not be literally misdescriptive; a
substitute or synthetic may not be given a misleading name. Many strict
regulations exist, for example, regarding names of wines, liquors, foods:
"Virginia ham" must be ham raised and processed in Virginia; the term
"cognac" is restricted to brandy distilled in the Cognac region of France;
"Roquefort" to that high-quality cheese made in the village of Roquefort. In actual practice, many restaurants violate these laws by listing
"Roquefort dressing" on their menu when they are really serving a
less-expensive blue cheese. Some cities have tried to write Truth-in-Menu
ordinances to prohibit this kind of fraud, passing off frozen vegetables as
"fresh," microwave meals as "home cooking," etc.

Hyperboles are not lies. Hyperboles are fictional conventions, figures of speech usually defined in terms of "extravagant exaggerations."
If we say that we have a "million things to do today," or if a seller offers
"mile-high" ice-cream cones or a pocketknife with "thousands of uses,"
we recognize these overstatements as hyperboles. The law generally rules
that hyperboles are not deceptive; in fact, sellers are on safer legal
grounds with such great exaggerations than with little overstatements
closer to the borderline of deception: to claim that a 4-blade pocketknife
had 6 blades would be false and deceptive; to claim that it had "thousands of uses" would not be deceptive. McDonald's got in trouble with
the FTC once about the exact weight claims for its "Quarter-Pounder"
hamburger, whereas Burger King is not likely to have any problem using
the vague claim implied in a "Whopper."

Irony is not a lie. Irony is a fictional convention, a figure of speech:
to say one thing and mean another, usually the exact opposite of the
literal meaning. Irony involves a double-message in which the nonverbal
elements (tone of voice, inappropriate context, use of quotation marks)
overshadow the verbal. Irony depends on an aware audience. Ironic remarks can go over the head of an unaware audience: for example, children, speakers of a foreign language, readers of obscure satiric literature.
Irony can be missed, can be misinterpreted; receivers can be uncertain if
the message is ironic or straight ("Are you putting me on?"). However,
the usual intent of irony is to emphasize, to be witty, to criticize, to
express displeasure—but not to deceive.

Imitations

Imitation repeats the composition pattern of something else. We can imitate, reproduce, mimic, mock, feign, simulate, copy anything else — including actions. Although the word "imitation" (in contrast to "real," "original," "genuine," "authentic") has negative overtones of something "inferior" or "deceptive," people have always done a great deal of imitating and copying, most of which has value and is not deceptive.

Imitation can be deceptive. Anything can be imitated; anything of value is often imitated with intent to deceive. It's not the act of imitating, but the intent and attempt to pass it off as original which constitutes deception. Obvious examples of imitation with intent to deceive would be such frauds as counterfeit money (or stocks, bonds, documents, stamps, licenses, admission tickets, etc.); forgery (of signatures on checks, documents); art forgeries, fake antiques, or "paste" diamonds being sold as authentic; plagiarism. Most fraud laws are concerned with theft by deception or misrepresentation. Because the *intent* to deceive is often hard to prove, some laws state that the mere possession of certain imitations (e.g., counterfeit money) is sufficient evidence to establish guilty intent.

In contrast to these rather clear-cut examples of imitations with intent to deceive, there's a complex and difficult borderline area involving problems of imitation and copying. The whole area of laws concerning copyrights and patents is very complicated. The 1978 Copyright Law, for example, was nearly a decade in preparation (and it appears it will be more decades in the courts) trying to define the rights of individuals and society in the copying of information.

Suggestions

Most communication is implicit, suggested, not specifically stated. In person-to-person speech — and in its electronic extension, television — we imply most of our meanings. Most of these suggestions are probably nonverbal: the facial expressions (smiles, frowns), body gestures (shrugs, waving, pointing), the pauses and pacing of our speech, the dress and ornaments worn, the possessions displayed (cars, homes), the location and context of our messages.

Even most of our verbal transactions are made up of fragments of sentences, brief words ("you know . . . you know . . .") which, together with eye-contact or the situation, send messages which the person "completes" as they are being received.

Such implicit communication leads our audience to make the final step, to "jump to a conclusion." We set up a common or expected *sequence* of thought, but do not totally complete the sequence. Or we set a common or expected *pattern* or context, leaving the audience to fill in the blanks, or put the pieces in the puzzle.

We speak in such shorthand very commonly, implying more than we actually say explicitly, and most of our implications are not deceptive.

But, just as any explicit statement can be a lie by intent, so also any implicit communication can be intended to deceive.

In terms of persuasion, the association technique is frequently used as a way of suggesting. The persuader need not explicitly state a relationship: simply by placing the product (or person, etc.) together with something already desired by or loved by the intended audience (or hated or feared, if "attack" propaganda), the associative link is made. Such suggestions can be truthful, or deceptive.

Just as words can have multiple meanings, so also implied messages such as nonverbal gestures can have multiple meanings. Although most people do learn to "read" and "understand" such implicit messages, we don't have the same degree of clarity in defining them as we do with words. Although there is a growing interest in the topic, "dictionaries" of nonverbal gestures are still in their infancy.

□ □ □ □ □ □ □ □ □ □ □ □ □ □ □ □ □ □ □ □
□ □ □ □ □ □ □ □ □ □ □ □ □ □   □ □ □ □ □

IMPLICATION

The sender IMPLIES

sends:
an indirect message,
an unexpressed message,
an incomplete mesage

to suggest, to hint, to imply.

INFERENCE

The receiver INFERS

brings in, links up,
deduces, derives,
concludes, puts together,
surmises, guesses at:

the expected pattern
or logical sequence

Most implied language requires cooperation, an action by the receiver, who *infers,* makes an *inference,* completing the logical sequence
or pattern which had been implied, suggested. Because we normally
spend our lives doing such routine completing of sequences, it's very
common to "jump to conclusions." Implicit messages can be either
truthful or deceptive, but we normally don't consider jumping to conclusions a problem—except when we are deceived.

Evasions

Most implications, suggestions, hints are *leading toward* a conclusion; but evasions are *leading away from* a completion of a sequence.
One reason why we dislike evasive language (used by others) is the
frustration we have at this lack of closure. Evasions prevent or delay the
receivers from completing a sequence.

SUGGESTIONS   EVASIONS

Evasions are used to defend against a possible harm, a danger perceived. In physical terms, evasion may mean to run, flee, get away,
dodge, hide, disguise; the phrase "evasive action" may give mental
pictures of zig-zagging, or unpredictable irregular motions away from
"closure" by the pursuer.

Because evasions are *defensive,* in reaction to a threat, they are more
likely to occur in the give-and-take situations of private life or, in public
language, in social or political arguments. There are fewer evasions in
advertising simply because advertisers purchase the time or the space to
present one view, to intensify their own "good". In this purchased time,
ads are free from attack, have no need to take evasive action. So it's
more likely that we'll speak about a politician being evasive in response
to reporters' questions.

In language usage today, most of what we call "evasion" has bad
connotations; to be evasive is to be "slippery as an eel," "hard to pin
down," or someone who uses "weasel words."

Most evasions can be described here as *omissions* (silence, half-
truths) or *diversions* ("changing the subject," jargon, ambiguous words
or phrasing, vague abstractions, double messages, etc.). In addition,
there are certain *qualifiers,* words which stress uncertainty: maybe, perhaps, possibly, sometimes, may, might, guess, estimate, in some cases.

DID YOU TAKE THE CAR LAST NIGHT?

Consider the spontaneous evasions, unpremeditated, which might occur if an angry father were to ask his teen-age son, "Did you take the car last night?" In this example, "no" would be a lie.

External Response	Comment
Silence. No response.	"Stonewalling" it. Legally, silence does not convict. Socially, most people would *infer* guilt: "silence means consent."
Silence. Horizontal Head-Nod (Internal response: "I didn't *say* no.")	Nonverbal message *implies* no; deception, but not a lie.
No. (Internal response: "I *borrowed* it" or "It was early this morning.")	Lie, but mental reservation. Quibbling. Overprecision, nitpicking.
No. (fingers crossed)	Superstition.
What did you say? Would you repeat the question? I didn't hear what you said. Would you repeat the question? Why do you ask? Why? Did something happen? How could I?	Stalling for time, often while mentally processing options, degree of threat, risks, and consequences (of a "caught lie," straight truth).
Why are you always picking on me? You're always accusing me. Do you think I would?	Diversions. *Ad hominem* attacks against father, trying to divert attention from main issue.
I don't remember. I can't recall.	To plead uncertainty about a recent past event usually requires additional reasons ("I was too drunk") often more of a problem.
Yes. Don't make such a fuss. Certainly. It's only . . . Sure. Why not?	Truthful admission. Quick diversion, downplaying importance or intensifying another issue.
Yes. (sobbing) I'm sorry. Yes. I didn't mean any harm. Yes. I didn't know I shouldn't have.	Truthful admission can be quickly followed by a plea for mercy, a claim of ignorance, of error, of good intentions—intensifying own "good."

This example of a son, threatened, evading the question of an angry father simply suggests some of the quick answers, unpremeditated spontaneous replies that might occur. Don't underestimate the potential complexity of evasion. If so many evasive answers about a simple situation can come so quickly from an unprepared amateur, consider also that sophisticated professionals, involved in complex situations, with prior knowledge, preparation, and planning, can produce some very complicated evasions—which are sometimes deceptive.

People can deceive with evasions. In courtrooms, for example, witnesses under oath and afraid of lying (which would be *perjury*) might use deceptive evasions, claiming loss of memory ("I can't recall") or stressing vague memory ("As I recollect now . . . to the best of my memory") or non-responsibility or non-awareness ("I was too drunk") or any excuse to conceal *intent* to deceive. In political situations, people have used evasive tactics to deceive; in recent years, presidents and others have used "executive privilege" and have invoked secrecy, National Security, Higher Authority ("I'm not at liberty to tell you . . . I can't release that information") as deceptive excuses to evade questioning.

Evasion is not necessarily deceptive. People do evade direct responses for reasons other than deception, reasons they would call *prudence, caution, discretion, flexibility*—"keeping your options open."

Evasion can often be an appropriate response. One of the "counter-propaganda axioms," for example, recommends "when they intensify, downplay." An evasive answer is a form of downplaying, frequently an appropriate response when pressured by a seller who seeks to close a sale. The seller seeks closure, a "straight" yes or no answer; but we often evade: "I'll have to ask my wife . . . I'll have to see my husband about it." Evasion? Yes. Deception? Depends on the intent.

When evasion *is* used to deceive, it's often not effective. Some people, for example, if they receive an evasive answer will infer (correctly or incorrectly) that the evasion is deceptive.

Politicians and diplomats are frequently criticized for their evasive answers. But many evasions are very appropriate in order to avoid simplistic thinking or dangerous consequences. Many news reporters use "leading questions," for example, to try to lead politicians into a yes/no response to a complex question. If a reporter were to ask a presidential candidate during an election campaign "Would you ever use the H-Bomb?", a simple yes or no answer would lead to headlines: JONES WOULD USE BOMB or JONES WILL NEVER USE BOMB. Most experienced politicans would reply with *qualifications* ("Under certain circumstances . . .") or *hypotheticals* ("If the situation were . . ."), appropriate evasions in response to questions which omit qualifications, oversimplify complex issues. The use of vague abstractions also allows flexibility. In a threat situation, for example, it's often better for a diplomat to threaten a vague "appropriate action" than to specify a specific response ("We'll bomb Moscow"). This vagueness gives both sides some leeway to compromise without losing face or being forced to go ahead with the threat. Intrusive questions into the private lives of some public figures would be another example of a reasonable use of evasive answers ("no comments") as a way of protecting a right of privacy.

Everyone agrees that there are times when a specific, direct statement is necessary. But fewer people recognize that there are times when a vague or evasive answer is also appropriate. Some readers might prefer a blanket condemnation of evasion. But evasion is a human behavior, sometimes appropriate to a situation, sometimes effective, sometimes with no intent to deceive, sometimes deceptive for a "good" purpose.

Evasions *in time* are common: stalling for time, delaying tactics, preventing closure. Many legal manuevers are designed to stall; sometimes this can be draining on an opponent who does not have the money or endurance. Lawyers who "have the meter running" may not care how long it takes to settle a case. Yet, all time delays need not be evil, wasteful, or deceptive; certainly there are situations in which it is reasonable and proper to "take a break," "let things cool down," or "let the dust settle."

Promises And Threats

Promises and threats about the future can be deceptive or not; again, it is the intent which is important. The common problems involved in such future promises are usually related to *not fulfilling* a promise, or *contradicting* it. Both of these could be intentionally deceptive. However, there could be other factors involved: *inability* (impotency, weakness, people sometimes promise more than they can deliver); *circumstances* (accidents do happen, times change, this is not a static world); *errors* (mistakes in judgment, planning, execution, etc.).

Deceptive intent may be difficult to prove. But reasonable people can make other judgments about promises or threats involving the future. We judge such things on our estimate of their reasonableness, on the ability to be fulfilled under normal conditions. Desire alone ("wishful thinking") does not guarantee a future event. If someone does not have the means to an end, the power and the opportunity, then we dismiss such foolish promises and idle threats.

Borderline problems concerning errors usually are about issues of responsibility and culpable ignorance. Responsibility involves a duty, obligation, or legal liability because of (1) the job, role, or function of someone; (2) their training, experience, or expertise; (3) their receipt of benefits, usually money. Responsibility can be established in many different ways (law, custom, prior agreement, contract, consent), but basically the key questions are: Was it your job? Did you know how to do it? Were you getting paid to do it? The most common excuses to defend an error are usually: "It wasn't my job" (denying responsibility) or "I didn't know" (ignorance). "You *should have* known," is the common response: if you function in the job, and receive the benefits, you have the obligation to know, otherwise it is *culpable ignorance*.

Good Intentions . . . Bad Results

Opinions, errors, and fictions have been treated here in terms of their non-intent to deceive; the essence of lies and other deceptions is in the intent to deceive. Digging deeper into human motives we can ask: "Why do people intend to deceive others?"

The assumption here is that people seek to gain a benefit, either as a defensive measure or as offensive attack. Deception, which is successful or effective, *does* give the deceiver an advantage both in defense and offense.

What is an advantage to one person, may not be to another. What is an advantage to an individual, may be a disadvantage to the society. Thus, societies have strong codes against deception to protect the common good. There would be many more frauds, tricks, lies, and deceptions if there were not laws and penalties established to deter individuals from taking advantage of others. It's easy to see the bad intentions involved in such aggressive exploitation as deliberately deceptive advertising, or frauds, or con games. But, if we exclude these extreme cases, we find that most lies are told with good intentions. Good intentions, however, may have bad results.

Certain situations increase the potential for deception. In defensive situations, the greater the threat, the more likely people are to use lies and deceptions in their defense. To reduce deception, reduce the threat. In everyday situations, it's common to hear people who are seeking the truth to guarantee safety to other persons: "I promise I won't hit you . . . won't be mad at you . . . if you tell me the truth." In criminal law, it's common practice to grant immunity to certain key witnesses to gain their truthful testimony by reducing a threat.

In attack situations, the reverse tactics are useful. Aggression is more likely to occur in situations in which it will be most successful, that is, where a gain can be made without danger to the aggressor. Therefore, to reduce aggressive deception, increase the threat or penalty, make it more risky for the deceiver. Society, through governments, can create strong deterrents against aggressive deception by strong individuals or groups: fraud laws and the regulations against deceptive advertising are good examples. A great deal of progress has been made in the recent past and such appropriate efforts should continue. Less has been done, however, to reduce the aggressive deceptions by governments abusing power. Although the stakes may be higher, we have relatively fewer controls. While some progress has been made recently in terms of disclosure laws (Freedom of Information Act, reforms of classified secrets, etc.), we don't have adequate laws or penalties to cope with the aggressive lies which can be told by politicians and bureaucrats.

White Lies

"White lies" suggest lies about trivial matters, or harmless lies told for good purposes: benevolent lies, for the benefit of others, and paternalistic lies. Benevolent lies are often related to civility, the care and consideration for the feelings of others. Examples of such lies, which promote a general social bonding, include: *polite social formulas* ("nice to see you"); *polite false excuses* ("I *can't* go tomorrow," instead of "I don't *want* to"); *flattery* ("you look so nice today"); *polite false gratitude* ("just what I always wanted"); *placebos* (given by doctors); *inflated grades* (given by teachers, as the norm goes up); and *pro forma* letters of recommendation ("outstanding work"). Paternalistic lies are those told to protect, to shield, to comfort, to encourage, to stroke, to nurture, to defend young children from harsh truths and realities with which they're not yet able to cope.

Other lies with good intentions include lying for self-defense, to protect one's own right of privacy, to ward off unwarranted requests and illegitimate questions. Bok speaks of mutual deceits, of a "quite common, often poignant human arrangement," in which people, by mutual understanding, knowingly continue a serious game of deceit: "Most friendships and families rely upon some such reciprocity to sustain illusions, suppresses some memory too painful to confront, and give support where it is needed." All of these examples of well-intentioned lies are quite common in everyday life. We need not think of extreme situations (lying to a murderer seeking information, lying to save a life, etc.) to demonstrate what Aquinas termed "helpful" lies.

Assume that every lie can be defended, by the liar, as having good intentions. Benevolence and justice are the two major defenses that most people will use to explain their reasons for lying and deception. These two reasons apply not only to the common excuses offered for everyday "white lies," but also to the elaborate rationales concocted by business and political leaders explaining their reasons for wholesale deception.

Benevolence, here, means that the liar's intention is to do good or avoid evil. Self-defense, survival, preservation are often claimed as the basis for a lie: "if I didn't say that, then harm would have come to me." However, usually such an excuse is accompanied by an emphasis on altruistic motives: the "self" has been extended to include a wider group—family, friends, kin, group, nation. When people lie, they usually claim that they are selflessly doing good for the benefit of the wider group. Political lies, for example, are often defended, by the liars, in terms of "national security," "national defense," "national unity," "party unity," and so on. Commercial lies (or "occupational lies") such as deceptive advertising, are often rationalized in terms of "keeping the system going," of "just doing one's job . . . doing what I'm told." The on-the-job liar also seeks to avoid evil—losing a job, perhaps. The greater good of the whole is used by many people within corporations or organizations, a kind of plea to a higher law justifying that any lies they tell will basically or eventually be doing good for the organization, or the wider society.

Justice is the other basic defense of the liar. Everyone is in favor of justice. Everyone defends their own positions as being fair, and, in conflict situations, defends their own actions as seeking an equality which is just. But each claims that the other side violates justice. The "Haves" seek to maintain balance, to preserve the *status quo,* the way things "should be." To them, others are unjustly seeing to upset justice, to destroy, to usurp, to take away that which they have earned, worked for and deserve, their "just rewards." The "Have-Nots" seek for a justice which they feel has been denied to them; the "Have-Nots" want fairness, justice, and their "just rewards," too. In this situation, everyone can defend their lies by claiming that the deception was done in the ultimate service of justice. Retribution ("an eye for an eye") also implies the element of justice: we punish people, seek retribution, give our enemies "what they deserve," all in the name of justice.

Political lies often involve additional factors, such as a sense of duty, frequently a sense of crisis, and, concerning lies from the leaders, a sense of superiority. The sense of duty that people have when working for a country or a "cause" is much more intense than the mere occupational task of doing a job. People involved in a "cause" (political, religious, racial) with great emotional meaning to them are apt to justify deceptions almost as a solemn duty or obligation. In many political situations, the sense of crisis or urgency also is used to defend lying: "If we had more time, we'd be able to give out the real information . . . the time isn't right now . . . the situation is too delicate . . . history will confirm the wisdom of our decisions . . ."

The sense of superiority is frequently found in the justifications given by political leaders to defend their lies. While this might be expected from a dictator or a tyrant, it's especially inappropriate and ironical coming from the elected leaders of democratic countries. Yet, recent American presidents have given ample evidence of this elitist feeling of superiority, a smug paternalism, that the leaders are justified in lying to the people because the leaders have greater understanding, insight, knowledge, and judgment. The common people are seen as unsophisticated, unable to cope with bad news, unable to understand or respond appropriately, too emotional, too ignorant to see the big picture. Thus, our leaders lie to us, with good intentions.

In *The Politics of Lying,* (1973) David Wise claims that the major political development in recent years has been the growth of systematic deception of the American people by its own leaders and government. From the U2 affair in Eisenhower's administration to the early days of Nixon's Watergate affair, the book focuses on the growth of deceptive practices and the changing relationships of the government and the people. Wise points out the danger of this tendency: "The consent of the governed is basic to American democracy. If the governed are misled, if they are not told the truth, or if through official secrecy and deception they lack information on which to base intelligent decisions, the system may go on—but not as a democracy. After nearly two hundred years, this may be the price America pays for the politics of lying.''

President Lyndon Johnson's lies about his strategy in Vietnam certainly contributed to his election victory in 1964; Barry Goldwater had been labeled the war candidate, while Johnson made promises of peace, in lies which were not exposed until the famous Pentagon Papers were released years later. In *Lying,* Bok uses the example of LBJ as a crucial moral and political problem: ''President Johnson thus denied the electorate any chance to give or to refuse consent to the escalation of the war in Vietnam. Believing they had voted for the candidate of peace, American citizens were, within months, deeply embroiled in one of the cruelest wars in their history. Deception of this kind strikes at the very essence of democratic government. It allows those in power to override or nullify the right vested in the people to cast an informed vote in critical elections. Deceiving the people for the sake of the people is a self-contradictory notion in a democracy. . . .''

Every recent political and governmental deception has been defended, by the liars, in terms of good intentions: doing good, avoiding evil, seeking justice and fairness, doing one's duty in a crisis, knowing—better than others—what's really best for the country. The deceived public, however, has not expressed a reciprocal gratitude for being lied to and deceived. When the lies are exposed, most people are outraged that the leaders have betrayed the public trust. From the outside, the liar's ''good intentions'' are seen to be self-serving rationalizations to retain power, to cover up errors, embarrassments, vindictiveness, corruption, minor vices and major abuses.

Two common reactions to political lies are vague indignation and cynical resignation. Cynical resignation leads some people to shrug their shoulders, and say that ''nothing can be done . . . all politicians lie anyway.'' Vague indignation leads some people to quick anger that ''something ought to be done,'' which often turns to frustration when complex problems do not yield quick and easy solutions.

Both extremes can be avoided. In a democracy, we can make progress, or at least move toward an equilibrium to counterweight the problems of political deception. We can reward genuine honesty and candor of political leaders who admit to doubt and difficulties. We can support legislation which encourages openness in government and that which penalizes deception. We can value a free press and the essential role of the investigative journalist, the reformer, and the gadfly. We can teach young citizens the realities of human rationalizations. The more citizens, for example, who know the patterns and probabilities that ''national security'' and ''good intentions'' will be dragged out to support every lie, the less likely the excuse will be effective.

Deception, like violence, has always been a part of the human condition. To recognize this does not endorse deception nor justify inaction.

We do take actions to control violence, to reduce the degree, to limit the kinds, to reduce the causes and ameliorate the effects. Although violence exists, and "everybody does it," we do not simply shrug our shoulders and say "nothing can be done about it." So also we can take actions to reduce deception within our society.

If a democratic society is to remain free, citizens should not be encouraged to be docile, trusting, and naive. If any statement can be a lie, any behavior deceptive, and all lies and deceptions defended for their good intentions, we're not likely to find simple solutions. Our best defense may be in our ability to analyze language, to make critical judgments, to transform vague trust or distrust into specific acceptance or rejection. We can do this better if we are more aware of the borderlines, more conscious to distinguish lies and deception from errors, opinions, and fictions; if we recognize the common situations in which deceptions are more probable, and the common excuses and justifications offered by the deceivers.

To recap: any statement can be a lie, any behavior deceptive; such lies and deceptions can be used to attack or defend, to intensify one's own "good" or the others' "bad," to downplay one's own "bad" or the others' "good." Lies and deceptions involve intent, not technique. To focus on the real problem areas, it may help to sort out what is *not* deceptive, to clarify common controversies. People have differing *opinions,* sometimes *illusions* and *delusions,* and can make *errors.* Furthermore, *fictions* (including metaphors and hyperboles) and *imitations* need not be deceptive, nor are implied messages (including *suggestions* and *evasions)* involving omitted elements. *Promises* and *threats* about the future also involve elements of ability and changing conditions. "Good intentions" motivate most deceptions, including *white lies* in everyday situations and *political lies* told by leaders; if discovered, liars usually claim lies were told for "your own benefit." However, people deceived seldom appreciate such "good intentions" and often see them as self-serving rationalizations. Issues of governmental lying and deception are very crucial in a democratic society and need more attention.

Appendix

Several simple teaching aids, designed to be photocopied by teachers, are included here. Permission is granted for classroom use.

- **The 30-Second-Spot Quiz** (pp. 205–208) Photocopy, cut, reassemble as a one-page, two-sided, folded pamphlet, with p. 205 as front, p. 209 as rear.
- **Not-So-Great-Expectations** (pp. 210–211)
- **Images & Issues** (pp. 174–175)
- **The Intensify-Downplay Schema** (pp. 50–51)

the 30-Second-Spot quiz

Based on *The Pitch* (c) 1982 by Hugh Rank

How to Analyze Ads:
Use this 1-2-3-4-5 sequence of questions, (see next page) to focus on the *"skeleton"* underneath the *"surface variations"* of radio and TV commercials, newspaper and magazine ads.

Recognize that a 30-second-spot TV ad is a **synthesis**, the end product of a complex process in which scores of people (writers, researchers, psychologists, artists, actors, camera crews, etc.) may have spent months putting together the details. TV commercials are often the best *compositions* of our age, skillful combinations of purposeful words and images. Be patient and systematic: **analysis** takes time to sort out all of the things going on at once. **We perceive** these things *simultaneously*, but we must discuss them *sequentially.* Use this 1-2-3-4-5 pattern of "the pitch" as a sequence to start your analysis.

Recognize "surface variations": in 30 seconds, a TV spot may have 40 quick-cut scenes of "good times" (happy people, sports fun, drinking cola); or 1 slow "tracking" scene of an old-fashioned sleighride through the woods, ending at "home" with "Season's Greetings" from an aerospace corporation; or a three-scene drama: a problem suffered by some "friend," a product/solution recommended by a trusted "authority," and a final grateful smile from the relieved sufferer. But, the structure underneath is basically the same.

Recognize our own involvement in a mutual transaction. Persuaders are *benefit-promisers,* but we are *benefit-seekers.* Most ads relate to simple "trade-offs" of mutual benefits: consumers get a pleasure, producers get a profit. However, investigate issues relating to any non-consumer ad; these are paid presentations of only one side of an issue, often involving more than a simple purchase transaction.

Understand that advertising is basically persuasion, not information nor education, *And not coercion!* Many important moral and ethical issues (concerning intent and consequences, priorities, individual and social effects, truth and deception, legal and regulatory problems) are related. The more we know about the basic techniques of persuasion, the better able we are not only to cope with the multiple persuaders in our society, but also to consider these ethical issues.

What ATTENTION-GETTING techniques are used?

Anything unusual? Unexpected? Noticeable? Interesting? Related to:
- [ ] **senses:** motions, colors, lights, sounds, music, visuals (e.g., computer graphics, slow-motion)
- [ ] **emotions:** any associations *(see list below):* sex, scenery, exciting action, fun, family, pets.
- [ ] **thought:** news, lists, displays, claims, advice, questions, stories, demonstrations, contest.
  (*Popular TV* **programs** *function as* attention-getters *to "deliver the audience" to advertisers.)*

What CONFIDENCE-BUILDING techniques are used?

- [ ] Do you *recognize, know* (from earlier repetition) the **brand name? company? symbol? package?**
- [ ] Do you *already know, like,* and *trust* the **"presenters":** the endorsers, actors, models?
- [ ] Are these "presenters" **AUTHORITY FIGURES** (expert, wise, protective, caring,)? Or, are they **FRIEND FIGURES** (someone you like, like to be, "on your side"; incl. "cute" cartoons) ?
- [ ] What key **words** are used? (*Trust, sincere,* etc.) **Nonverbals?** *(smiles, voice tones, sincere look)*
- [ ] In **mail** ads, are computer-written *"personalized"* touches used? On **telephone:** tapes? scripts?

What DESIRE-STIMULATING techniques are used?

(Main part of ad)

Consider (a) **"target audience"** as (b) **benefit-seeking;** and persuaders benefit-promising strategies as focused on (c) **product claims,** or, (d) **"added values"** associated with product.
- [ ] a. **Who is the "target audience"?** Are *you?* (If *not,* as part of an unintended audience, are you *uninterested* or *hostile* toward the ad?)
- [ ] b. **What's the primary motive of that audience's benefit-seeking?** Use chart at right. Most ads are simple acquisition *(lower left).* Often, such motives co-exist, but one may be dominant. Ads which intensify a **problem,** (that is, a "bad" already hated or feared; *the opposite, or the absence of,* "goods") and then offer the product as a **solution,** are here called **"scare-and-sell"** ads. *(right side).*

To keep a "good" *(protection)*	To get rid of a "bad" *(relief)*
To get a "good" *(acquisition)*	To avoid a "bad" *(prevention)*

☐ c. **What kinds of product claims are emphasized?** *(use these 12 categories)* what key words, images? Any *measurable* claims? Or are they *subjective opinions, generalized* praise words ("puffery")?

SUPERIORITY *("best")*
QUANTITY *("most")*
EFFICIENCY *("works")*
BEAUTY *("lovely")*
SCARCITY *("rare")*
NOVELTY *("new")*

STABILITY *("classic")*
RELIABILITY *("solid")*
SIMPLICITY *("easy")*
UTILITY *("practical")*
RAPIDITY *("fast")*
SAFETY *("safe")*

☐ d. **Are any "added values" implied or suggested?** Are there words or images which associate the product with some "good" already loved or desired by the intended audience? With such common human needs/wants/desires as in these 24 categories:

"basic" needs:
FOOD *("tasty)*
ACTIVITY *("exciting")*
SURROUNDINGS *("comfort")*
SEX *("alluring")*
HEALTH *("healthy")*
SECURITY *("protect")*
ECONOMY *("save")*

"certitude" needs:
RELIGION *("right")*
SCIENCE *("research")*
BEST PEOPLE *("elite")*
MOST PEOPLE *("popular")*
AVERAGE PEOPLE *("typical")*

"territory" needs:
NEIGHBORHOOD *("hometown")*
NATION *("country")*
NATURE *("earth")*

love & belonging needs:
INTIMACY *("lover")*
FAMILY *("Mom" "kids")*
GROUPS *("team")*

"growth" needs:
ESTEEM *("respected")*
PLAY *("fun")*
GENEROSITY *("gift")*
CREATIVITY *("creative")*
CURIOSITY *("discover")*
COMPLETION *("success")*

Are there URGENCY-STRESSING techniques used?

(Not all ads: but always check.)

☐ If an urgency appeal: What words? *(e.g. Hurry, Rush, Deadline, Sale Ends, Offer Expires, Now.)*
☐ If **no** urgency: is this **"soft sell"** part of a *repetitive, long-term ad campaign* for standard item?

What RESPONSE-SEEKING techniques are used?

Persuaders always seek some kind of response!)

☐ *Are there specific triggering* words used? (Buy, Get, Do, Call, Act, Join, Smoke, Drink, Taste, etc.)
☐ Is there a **specific response** sought? (Most ads: to buy something)
☐ If **not:** is it **conditioning** ("public relations" or "image building") to make us **"feel good"** about the company, to get favorable public opinion on *its* side (against any government regulations, taxes)?

Observe. Understand. Judge. (In *that* sequence!)Observe closely what is explicitly said and shown; consider carefully what may be implied, suggested either by verbal or nonverbal means.

Anticipate Incoming Information. Have some way to sort, some place to store. If you know common patterns, you can pick up cues from bits and fragments, recognize the situation, know the probable options, infer the rest, and even note the omissions. Some persuaders use these techniques (and some observers analyze them) consciously and systematically; others, intuitively and haphazardly.

Categorize, but don't "pigeonhole." Things may be in many categories at the same time. "Clusters" and "mixes" are common. Observers often disagree.

Seek "dominant impressions," but relate them to the whole. You can't analyze *everything*. Focus on what seems (*to you*) the most *noticeable, interesting,* or *significant* elements (e.g. an intense "urgency" appeal, a very strong "authority" figure). By relating these to the whole context of "the pitch," your analysis can be *systematic, yet flexible,* appropriate to the situation.

Translate "indirect" messages. Much communication is *indirect,* through metaphoric language, allusions, rhetorical questions, irony, nonverbals (gestures, facial expressions, tone of voice), etc. Millions of specific concrete ways of communicating something can be grouped in the general abstract categories listed here as "product claims" (3c) and "common needs" (3d). Visuals imply.

Train yourself by first analyzing those ads which explicitly use the full sequence of "the pitch," including "urgency-stressing" and a specific "response-seeking." Always check for this full sequence; when it does not appear, consider what may have been omitted: *assumed* or *implied.* "Soft sell" ads and corporate "image-building" ads are harder to analyze: *less is said, more is implied.*

Practice. Analysis is a skill which can be learned, but needs to be practiced. Take notes. Use print ads. Videotape, if possible; replay in slow motion. No one can "see" or "understand" everything during the actual 30 seconds while watching a TV spot. At best, we pick up a few impressions. Use the pattern of "the pitch" to organize your analysis and aid your memory. Such organization helps to avoid randomness and simple subjectivity.

Are ads worth all of this attention? Ads may not be, but *your mind is* . If we can better learn how to analyze things, to recognize patterns, to sort out incoming information, to see the parts, the processes, the structure, the relationships within things so common in our everyday environment, then it's worth the effort.

Professor Hugh Rank   Governors State University   Park Forest South, Illinois

Arnhart, Larry. *Aristotle on Political Reasoning*. DeKalb: Northern Illinois University Press, 1981.

Blumenthal, Sidney. *The Permanent Campaign*. Boston: Beacon Press, 1980.

Bok, Sissela. *Lying: Moral Choice in Public and Private Life*. New York: Pantheon Books, 1978.

Bowers, John Waite and Donovan J. Ochs. *The Rhetoric of Agitation and Control*. Reading, Mass.: Addison-Wesley, 1971.

Canetti, Elias. *Crowds and Power*. New York: The Viking Press, 1966.

Dieterich, Daniel. *Teaching About Doublespeak*. Urbana, Il.: NCTE, 1976.

Eck, Marcel. *Lies and Truth*. New York: The Macmillan Company, 1971.

Edelman, Murray. *The Symbolic Uses of Politics*. Urbana: University of Illinois Press, 1974.

Ellul, Jacques. *Propaganda*. New York: Vintage Books, 1973.

Geis, Michael L. *The Language of Television Advertising*. New York: Academic Press, 1982.

Graber, Doris A. *Mass Media and American Politics*. Washington, D.C.: Congressional Quarterly Press, 1980.

———. *Verbal Behavior and Politics*. Urbana: University of Illinois Press, 1976.

Hess, Robert D. and Judith V. Torney. *The Development of Political Attitudes in Children*. New York: Anchor Books, 1968.

Hoffer, Eric. *The True Believer*. New York: Harper & Brothers, 1951.

Huff, Darrell. *How to Lie with Statistics*. New York: W. W. Norton & Co., 1954.

Johannesen, Richard L. *Ethics in Human Communication*. Prospect Heights, Il.: Waveland Press, 1983.

Kaufman, Herbert. *Red Tape*. Washington, D.C.: The Brookings Institution, 1977.

Preston, Ivan. *The Great American Blow-Up*. Madison: University of Wisconsin, 1975.

Primeau, Ronald. *The Rhetoric of Television*. New York: Longman, 1979.

Rank, Hugh, ed. *Language and Public Policy*. Urbana, Il.: NCTE, 1974.

———. *The Pitch*. Park Forest, Il.: Counter-Propaganda Press, 1982.

Safire, William. *Safire's Political Dictionary*. New York: Random House, 1978.

Smelser, Neil J. *Theory of Collective Behavior*. New York: The Free Press, 1962.

Weissberg, Robert. *Political Learning, Political Choice, and Democratic Citizenship*. Englewood Cliffs, N.J.: Prentice-Hall, 1974.

Not-So-Great Expectations

Too many people get *disillusioned* by political language because they start with *illusions* about it — erroneous ideas and unrealistic expectations. It's better to start with realistic attitudes, practical information, and not-so-great expectations.

- Expect **conflict,** arguments, disagreements. If you believe in freedom, then expect dissent. Silence, lack of opposition, is often the sign of dictatorship imposed.

- Expect **compromises,** concessions, trade-offs, deals: *most* issues are negotiable, but some (dealing with principles or absolutes) may not be. Define the areas in which negotiations are possible.

- Expect very few clear-cut **choices** between "good" and "bad": most problems involve the *greater-of-two-goods* or the *lesser-of-two-evils;* most arguments are about *degree* (how much) or *priority* (what should be done first).

- Expect people to agree about **general goals** (We all seek the "good"), but to disagree about **specific means.** Expect politicians to use *generalities,* so that their audiences will imagine their own *specifics.*

- Expect most political language to be **persuasion** *(not coercion)* using words *(not weapons)* to get others to do something: to vote for, to support, to agree with, the politician, the party, or the policy.

- Expect persuasion to be a **mutual transaction** between benefit-seekers and benefit-promisers. Expect all people to be **benefit-seekers;** expect all persuaders to be **benefit-promisers:** Advertisers usually offer *individual* benefits ("you'll be happy, beautiful, beloved . . . if you buy XYZ") and politicians offer *social* benefits ("We'll have more peace, prosperity, lower taxes, fuller employment . . . if you support XYZ.")

- Expect politicians to make certain claims about themselves: basically, they seek to project the **image** of being *trustworthy, competent,* and *benevolent* ("on your side"); in attacks, they charge that opponents are *untrustworthy, incompetent, self-seeking.*

- Expect **self-righteousness** in conflicts. Advocates often claim *knowledge* and *virtue* for self, and charge opponents with *ignorance* (unintentional misguided, dupes) or *malice* (intentional, evil, plots, conspiracies).

- Expect **one-sided arguments.** When people advocate their own position (policy, party, candidate), they will intensify their own "good" and downplay their own "bad."

- Expect people to **downplay** their own "bad" by *omitting* unfavorable information, by using *"softer" language* (euphemisms), by *diverting* attention, or by *obscuring* it with jargon, confusing words, or complicated statistics.

- Expect persuasive messages starting with a **problem** (a threat feared) will end, offering a **solution.** (Do this . . . vote for X.) Expect **problems** to be intensified during election campaigns (and at budget time): *the greater the problem, the more the need for the solution.*

- Expect, from the **Haves,** a conservative rhetoric stressing *protection* (keep the "good") and *prevention* (avoid the "bad").

- Expect from the **Have-Nots,** a progressive rhetoric stressing *relief* (change the "bad") and *acquisition* (get the "good").

- Expect many political messages to be simple **repetition** of names, pictures, key words, symbols, slogans; such items often trigger a cluster of associated ideas.

- Expect common use of the **association** technique which links (1) the person, party, or policy with (2) something *already* loved or desired by (3) the intended audience. (In attacks: with something *already* hated or feared.) Thus, the importance of surveys, polls to find out what the target audience likes.

- Expect that ideals of accuracy and truth are not always reached: at times, people — including politicians — can make **errors,** be uninformed, or deliberately **deceive.**

- Expect no sure or simple test for "truth": **any** statement can be a lie; **any** behavior can be deceptive.; **any** person can deceive or be deceived.

- Expect people in power to publicize their own "good" usually by means of a large "public relations" department. From the press releases of the White House, the State House, and City Hall, expect the only news to be "good news."

- Expect **money** to play a major role in human activities, including persuasion and politics. "Follow the dollar" is good advice for investigators seeking to trace power, analyze budgets, expose corruption.

- Expect to see some slick, well-planned, conscious, purposeful persuasion from some sources, but also some random, strident, irrational, and crazy talk from others. Not all people are wired the same; some have a few loose screws!

- Expect **your own** attitudes to develop or change as you have more experience, know more, and understand more of history, sociology, and psychology.

- Expect it to be **difficult** (sometimes impossible) to sort things out, clarify isues, understand each other, set priorities, or resolve conflicts; yet, such constant efforts are vital to a free, democratic society.

Be disillusioned, but not discouraged:
Lose your illusions, but not your courage.

From *The Pep Talk* © 1984 by Hugh Rank. (Permission granted to photocopy for classroom use.) Published by the Counter-Propaganda Press   Box 365   Park Forest, Illinois 60466

This is my Watts Towers: weekend work
homemade, handhewn, hacked up
parts picked up here and there;
unsponsored, unendowed, even uninvited,
probably violating zoning laws,
yet now part of the landscape,
as those termite towers in Africa
are, bearing witness to an urge
inarticulate to build:
my heroes are Soleri and Veblen
and that mad Simon Rodia of Watts.

ABOUT THE AUTHOR

HUGH RANK is a Professor of English at Governors State University, Park Forest South, Illinois. Educated at the University of Notre Dame (B.A., M.A., Ph.D.), he has previously taught at Arizona State University, Sacred Heart University (Connecticut), Saint Joseph's College (Indiana), and as a Fullbright Professor (Copenhagen, Denmark). He has also served as a Public Information Officer in the U.S. Army (Germany).

In 1972, he became the first Chairman of the Committee on Public Doublespeak, of the National Council of Teachers of English (NCTE), a group with which he has worked now for over a decade. He has edited *Language and Public Policy* (NCTE, 1974), written *The Pitch* (1982) and *The Pep Talk* (1984) and has been a frequent contributor to the academic journals. In 1976, he released the "Intensify/Downplay Schema" (reprinted here) as a new way of teaching propaganda analysis; in that year his colleagues awarded him the George Orwell Award *"for distinguished contributions toward honesty and clarity in public language."*

INDEX